# Professional Rhythmic Skills
## 2nd Edition

## By Daniel Bukvich
### Edited by Brian Chin

common tone
press

Second Published Edition ©2014
First Published Edition ©2011
Compiled from original material ©1993

ISBN:  978-0-692-27822-2

Library of Congress Control Number:  2014948890

Cover design by: Chad McCullough


CommonTonePress.com
Seattle, WA

# Contents

# METRONOME

A method employing the human **pulse** to establish **tempo** in music was described by Lodovico Zacconi in 1596.

> *Pulse (puls) n.   1.   The regular beating in the arteries, caused by the contractions of the heart.*

> *Tempo (tem'po) n.   1.   The rate of speed at which a musical piece is played.*

In 1696 E'tienne Loulie invented the <u>chronométre</u>. It consisted of a perpendicular board with a right-angle projection at the top.  A pendulum was hung from this projection, its length (rate) of swing determining the tempo.

Pendulum-type devices and the human heart-beat served as the most important means for setting musical tempo until Johann Nepomunk <u>Maelzel</u> invented the mechanical **metronome** in 1812.

> *Met-ro-nome (met'r nom') n.  [  Gr. metron, measure + nomos, law]*
> *A device that beats time at a desired rate, as for music practice.*

<u>Tempo markings</u> at the beginning of a piece of printed music (MM120) refer to "Maelzel's Metronome" (MM) and indicate the number of "ticks" per minute (120).

> *A clock is a metronome that is permanently set to "tick" 60 times per minute (MM 60).*
>
> *A metronome is a clock that can be adjusted to "tick" at any rate from 35 to 250 times per minute (MM 35 to MM 250).*

<u>This book is meant to be used along with a metronome.</u>  Suggested metronome settings for exercises and etudes will be indicated in the following manner:

(120)           ( = MM120)

Exercises and etudes with no metronome setting will work from (35) to (70) .

# PULSE

**Pulse** in music is called the **beat** or **beats.**

| |
|---|
| *Pulse (puls)  n.  2.  Any regular beat.* |

| |
|---|
| *Beat (bet)  n.  5.  A unit of musical rhythm.* |

Beats:  (Read left to right)

Every culture in the world uses some type of vocalization (**vocalize**) to teach or keep track of pulse and rhythm.

*Vo' cal ize (vo' k'l iz') vt. To utter, speak, or sing.*

**Count** the following beats <u>out loud</u>, saying the correct number <u>at the same time</u> that the metronome "ticks":

*Count (kount) vi. 1. To name numbers or items in order.*

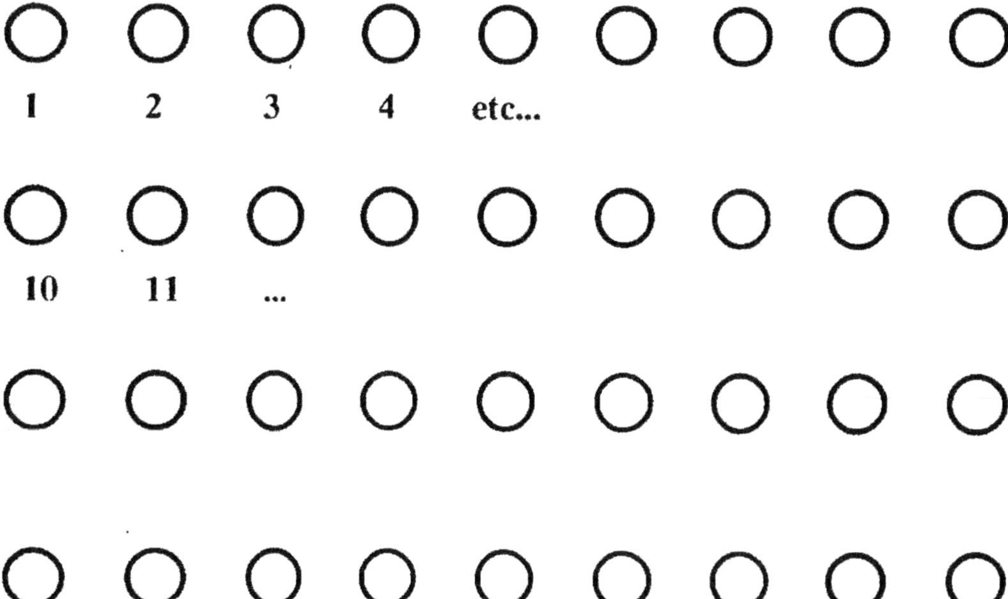

Rather than counting the total number of beats in a musical composition, we organize them into smaller, more manageable units. These units are of 1, 2, 3, or 4 beats; most commonly 2, 3, and 4.

Measure every 2 beats and draw a vertical line (called a <u>measure line</u> or <u>bar line</u>):

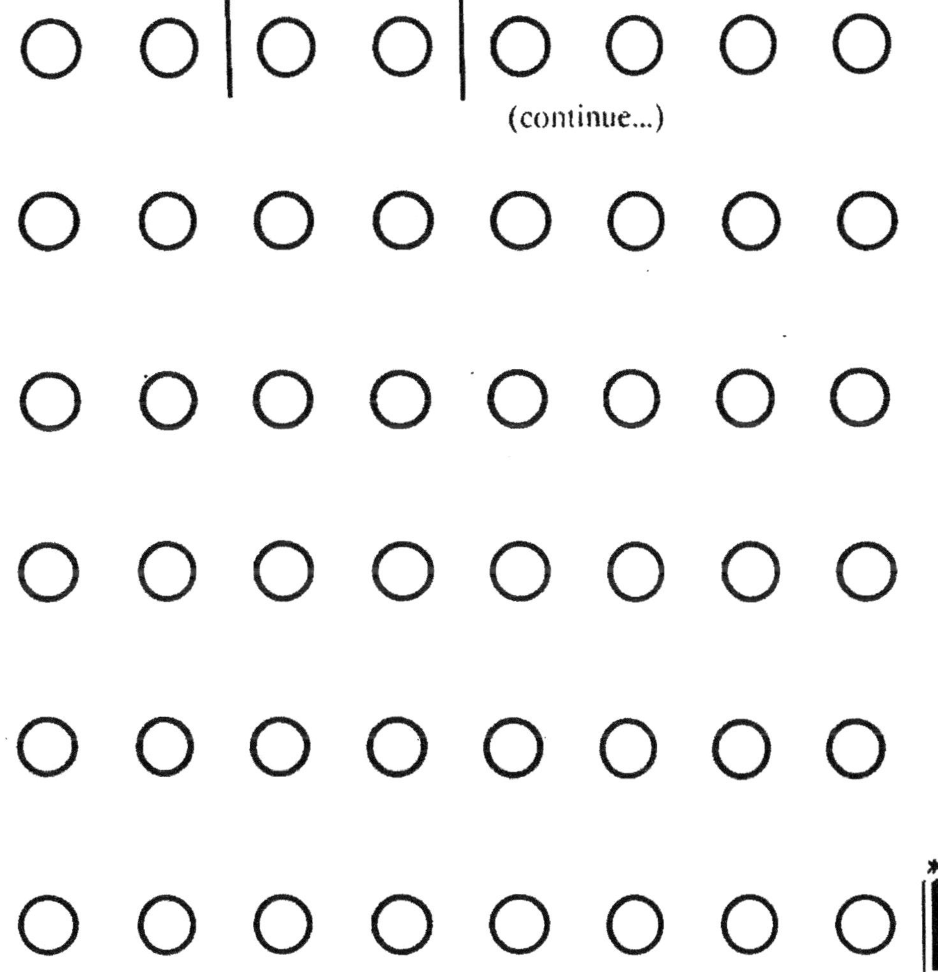



* A final double bar ( ▐▐ ) indicates the end of an exercise or piece of music.

Measure every 3 beats.  Remember to draw a <u>final double bar</u> at the end:

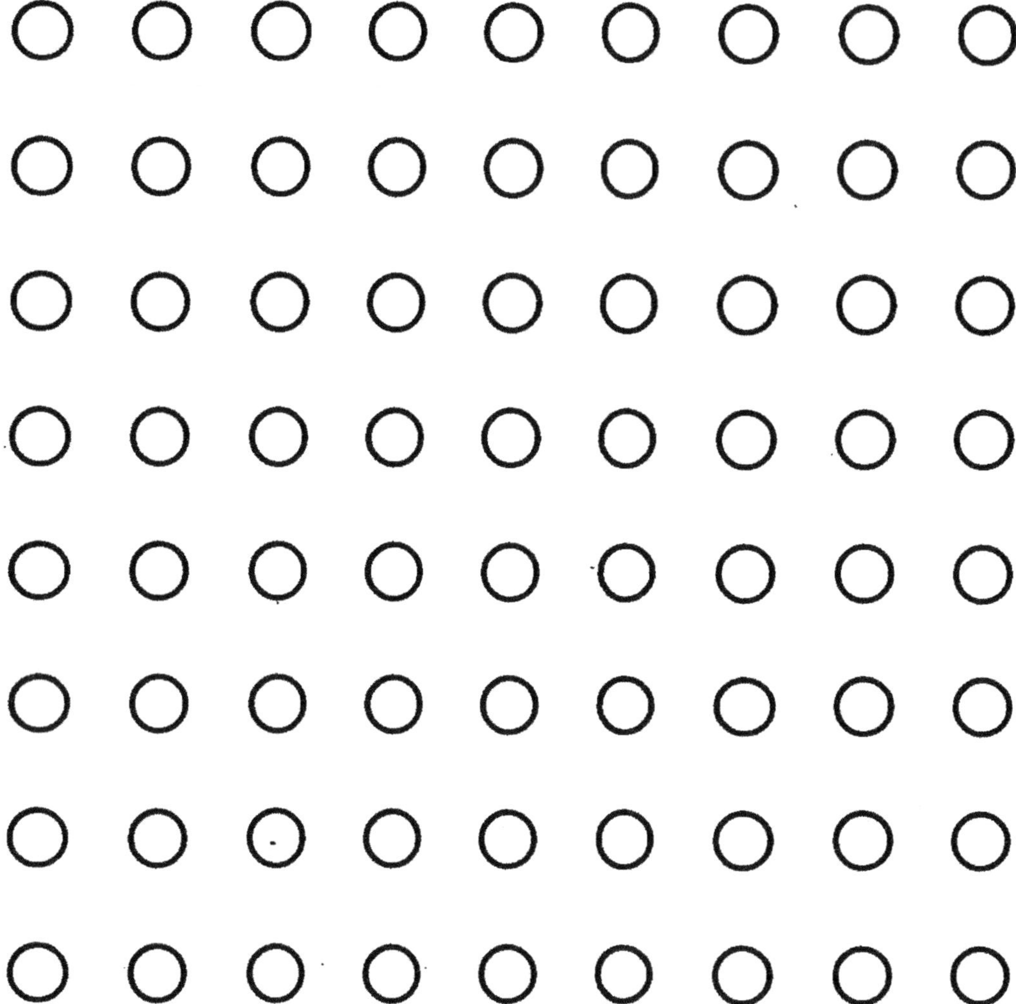

Measure every 4 beats:

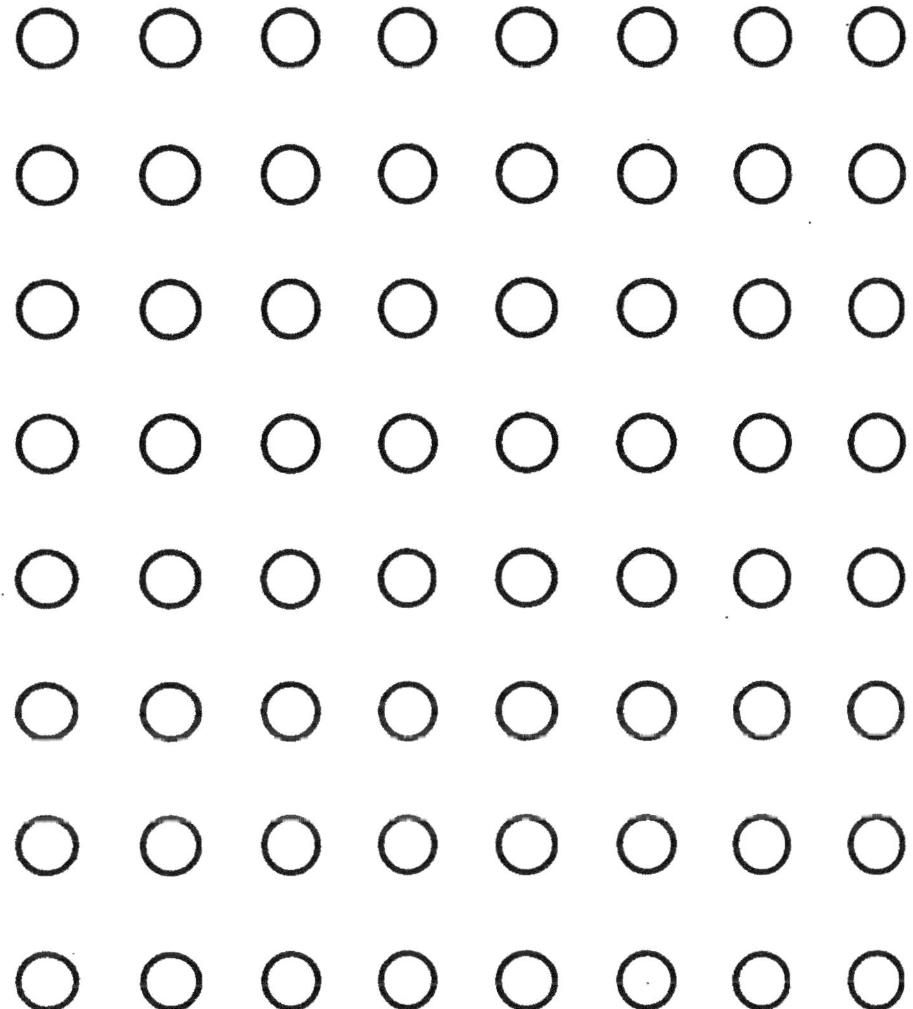

# METER

These units are called **measures** or **bars** and the number of beats in each determines musical **meter**.

---

*Meas ure (mezh' r) n. 3. a) A unit of measurement. 9. A rhythmical unit, the space between two bars (<u>measure</u> lines) in a piece of music.*

---

*Bar (bdr) n. 10. Music a) A vertical line dividing music into measures. b) A measure.*

---

*Meter (mŌt' r) n. 2. Rhythmic pattern in music.*

---

A measure of two beats is called <u>duple meter</u>:

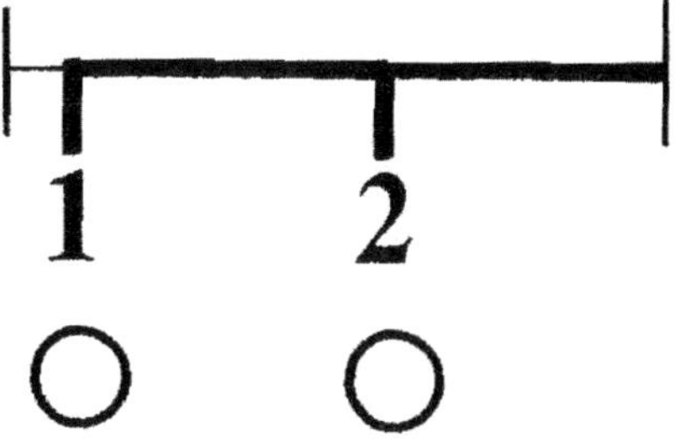

A measure of three beats is called <u>triple meter</u>:

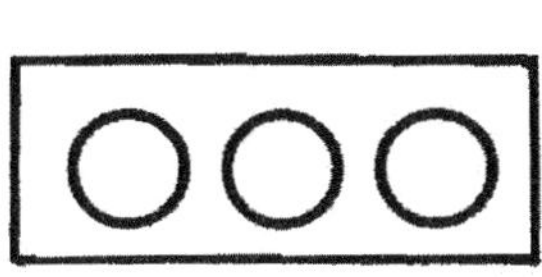 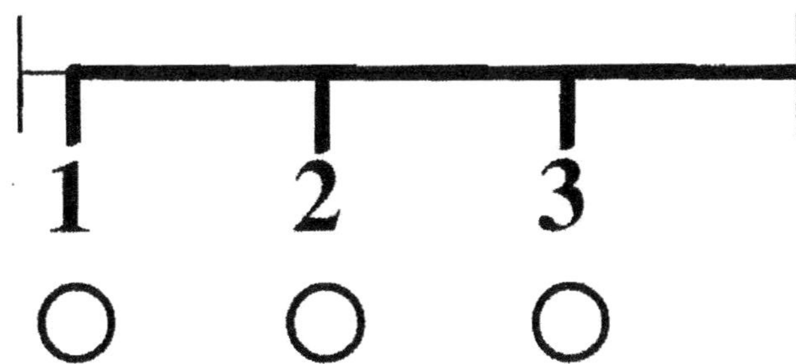

A measure of four beats is called <u>quadruple meter</u>:

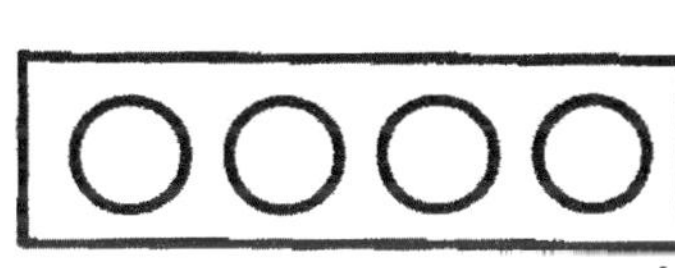 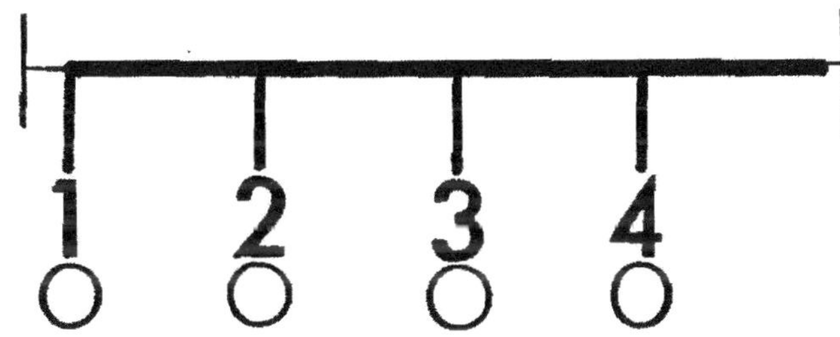

Rulers measure <u>visual distance</u> using feet, inches, one-half inches, one-quarter inches...

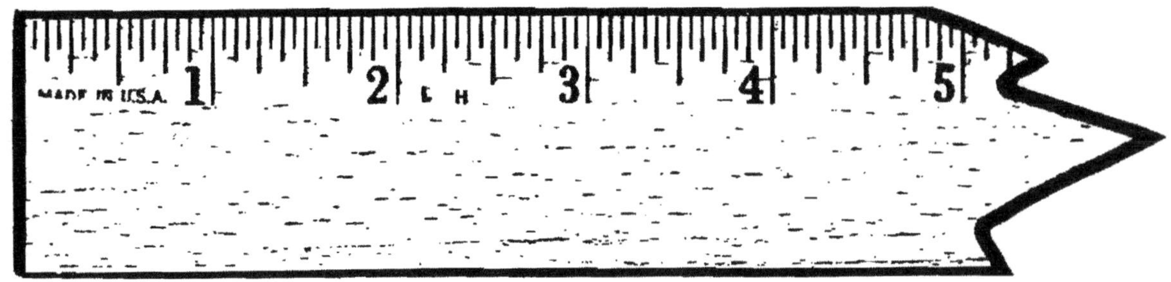

Rulers come in different lengths; 6 inches, 12 inches, 36 inches, etc.

<u>**Rhythm rulers**</u> represent <u>aural distance</u> by measuring <u>visual distance</u> using beats, division of beats, **and subdivision of beats:**

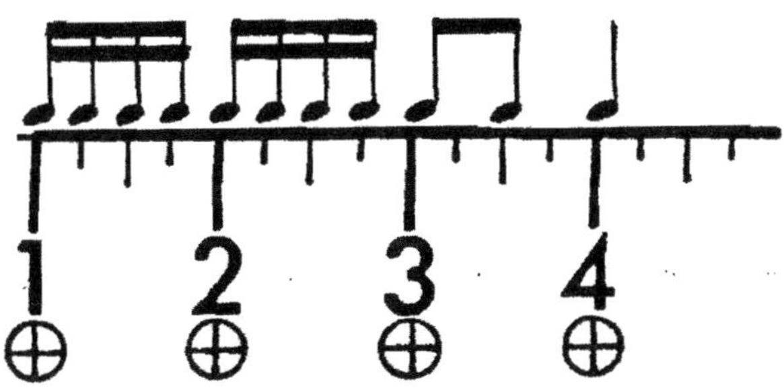

Rhythm rulers come in different lengths; 2 beats, 3 beats, 4 beats:

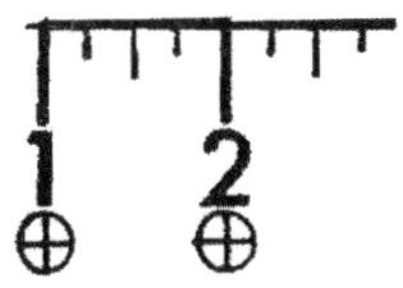 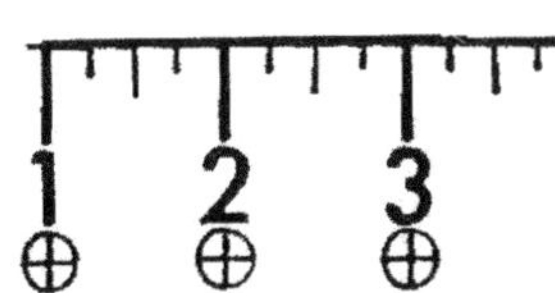 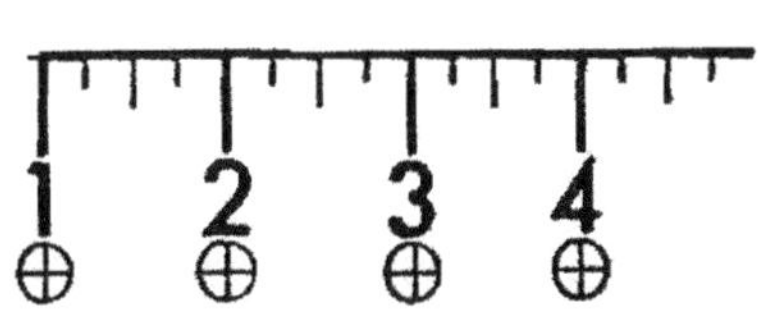

# SIMPLE DIVISION

Beats may be **divided** into smaller parts.

| *di-vide (də·vīd')  [   L. dividere]  1.  to separate into parts* |
| --- |

The simplest way to divide anything is **to cut** it in half:

When using rhythm rulers to measure beats, we divide by drawing a line half-way between beats:

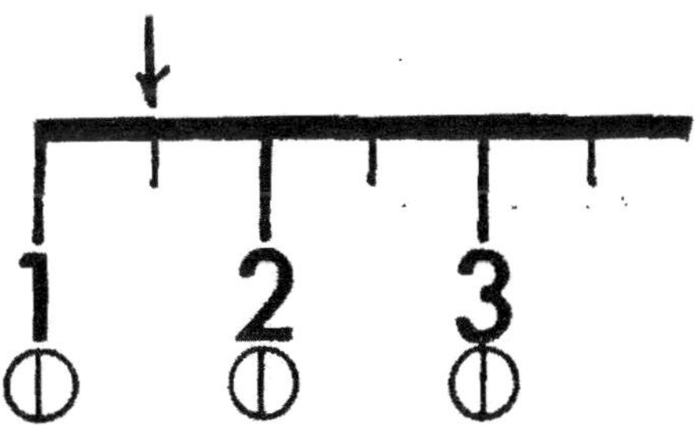


This gives us two equal sized parts for every beat and is called <u>simple division</u>.

The previous page gave a <u>visual</u> example of simple division of the beat by using a rhythm ruler. When combined with a rhythm ruler, the first line of the familiar nursery rhyme "Baa Baa Black Sheep" should give you an <u>aural</u> example of beat and simple division (notice the rhythm ruler indicates <u>duple meter</u>):

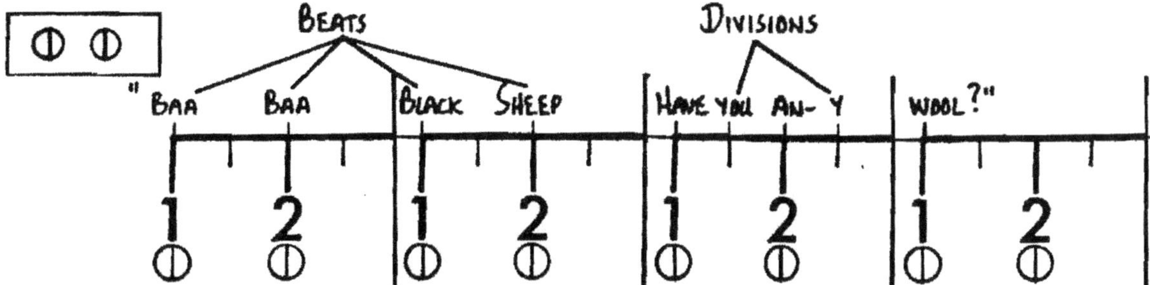


The <u>counting pattern</u> or <u>vocalization pattern</u> for "Baa Baa Black Sheep" is not the rhythm you ended up with when you recited the rhyme, but is <u>an aural version of the rhythm ruler</u> that appears beneath the words in the example above. In order to recite "Baa Baa Black Sheep" in rhythm with the metronome, you must first be able to "recite" (vocalize, count) this rhythm ruler.

(This exercise book, because of its use of the ruler analogy, uses the traditional "number counting" system...any and all systems work and utilize the same basic concepts of beat, division of beat, etc.)

You have already counted beats along with the metronome in duple, triple, and quadruple meter. Simple division adds the one syllable word "and" between beats:

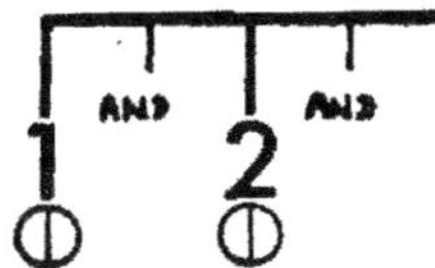


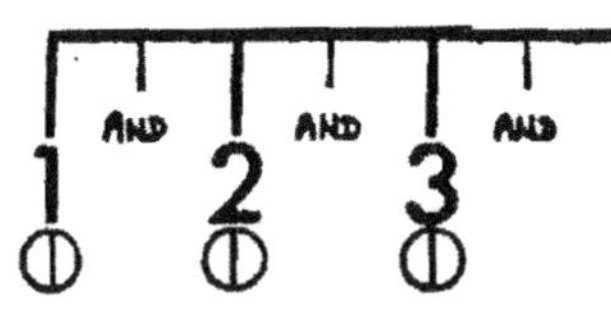


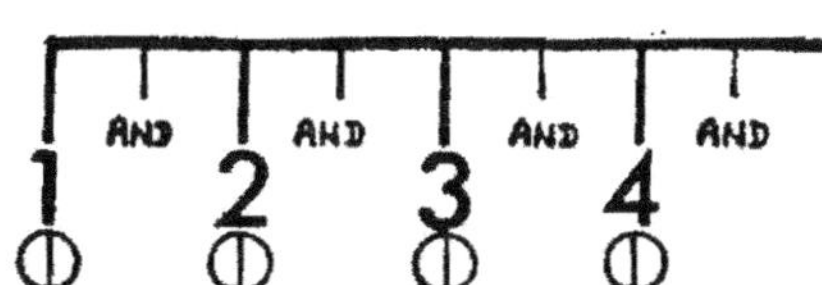


These rhythm rulers are represented by the following <u>meter boxes</u>. Meter boxes tell you what vocalization pattern you should use to create an aural rhythm ruler.

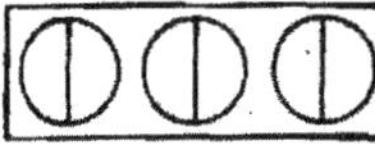

Recite once more the first line of "Baa Baa Black Sheep":

Now clap your hands in the same rhythm...(Clap "Baa baa black sheep have you an-y wool?"):

In "Measured Music" we represent the rhythm you just clapped in the following manner:

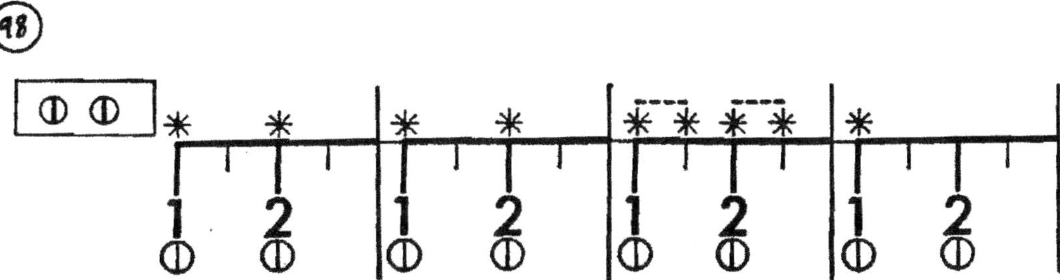

The asterisks represent hand claps (or drum beats, or accents within the vocalizing pattern, etc...) and the dotted lines above them connect asterisks that are in the same beat. The meter box tells you what your counting or vocalizing pattern should be (duple meter with simple division of the beat..."one-and-two-and...") and the rhythm ruler gives you a visual representation of the sound. Remember that the symbol ( 98 ) tells you what your metronome setting should be. Notice that this symbol uses a number (98) within a beat sign ( ) to indicate that the metronome is clicking on the beat.

Using your metronome, vocalize the correct meter box/rhythm ruler (beat and simple division) and clap the first line of "Baa Baa Black Sheep" at the same time:

# BEAT AND SIMPLE DIVISION

In the following exercises the single-beat example within the rectangle presents the rhythm that will be clapped, accented in the vocalization pattern, or played in each beat of duple, triple, or quadruple meter:

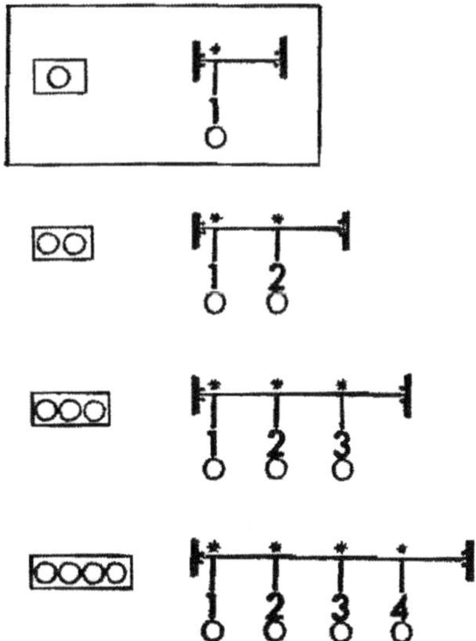

In traditional music notation double bar lines with dots ‖: :‖ enclose a single measure or group of measures that are to be repeated (played twice). Exercises in "Measured Music" that are within these <u>repeat signs</u> are to be played/counted as many times as necessary in order to feel comfortable with the rhythmic patterns.

Exercises and etudes with no metronome setting will work from (35) to (70) .

**1**

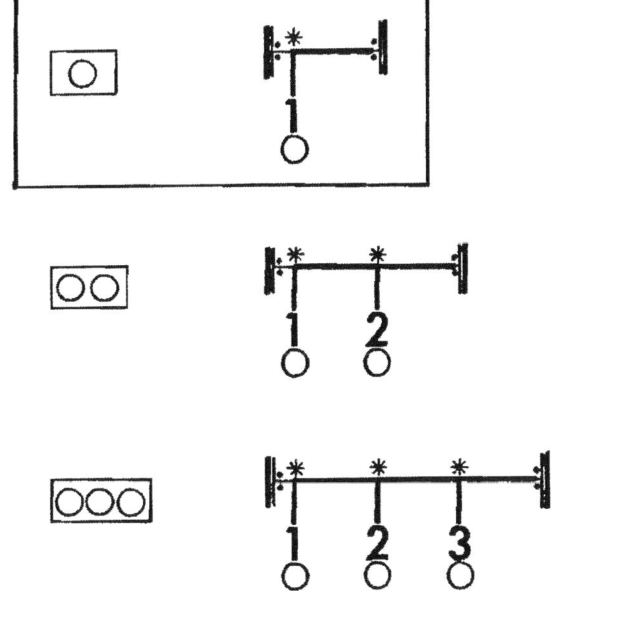

**2**

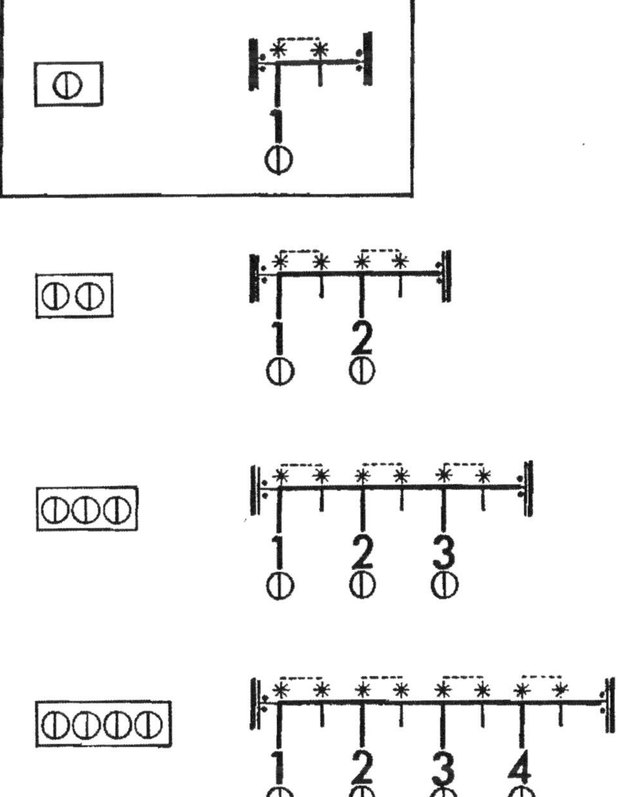

**3**

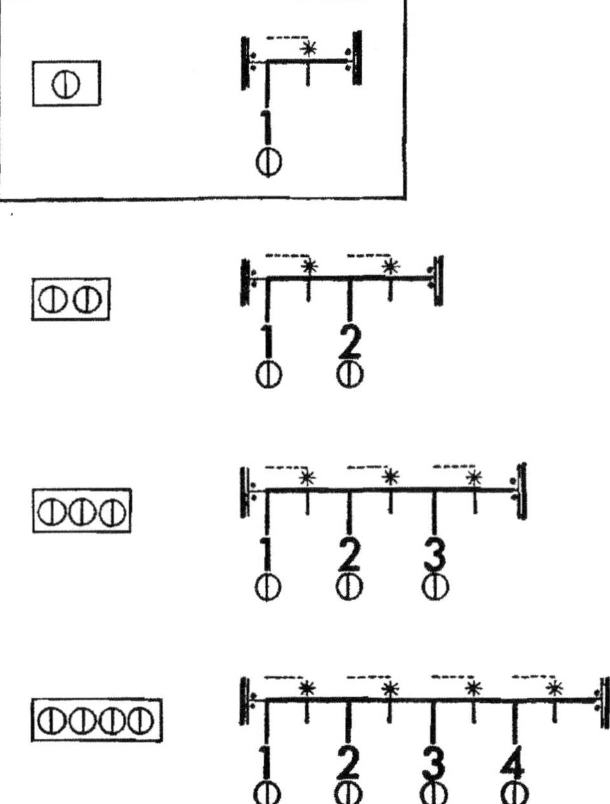

# SUBDIVISION

Just as the beat may be divided or cut in half, each of these halves may be divided again.
We call this **subdivision**.

*sub-di-vide (sǝb-dǝ-vīd) vb: to divide into several parts.*

Beat                     Simple Division                     Subdivision

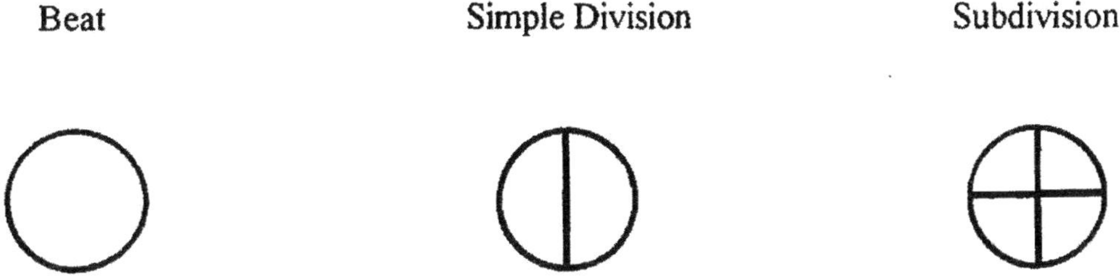

On a rhythm ruler <u>subdivision</u> looks like this:

To find out what subdivision sounds like, pretend you are counting seconds while
everyone else hides in a game of "hide-and-seek":

"One-one-thou-sand Two-one-thou-sand Three..."

You are <u>subdividing</u>.

**1**

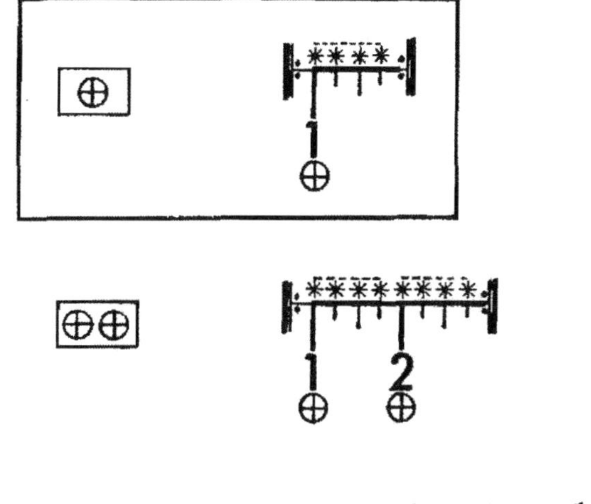

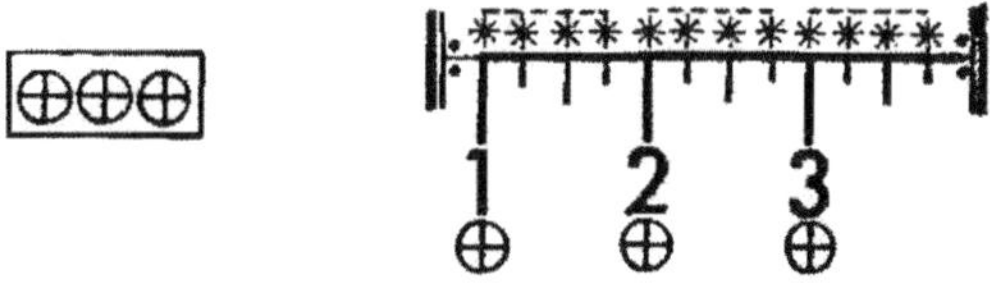

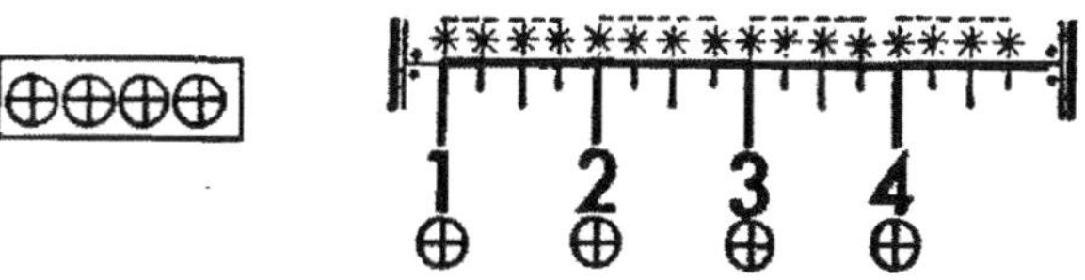

**2**

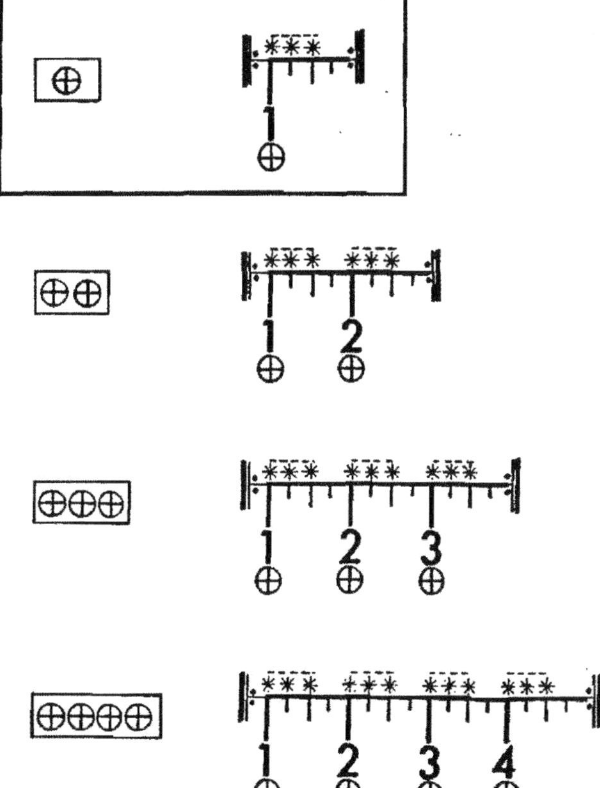

**3**

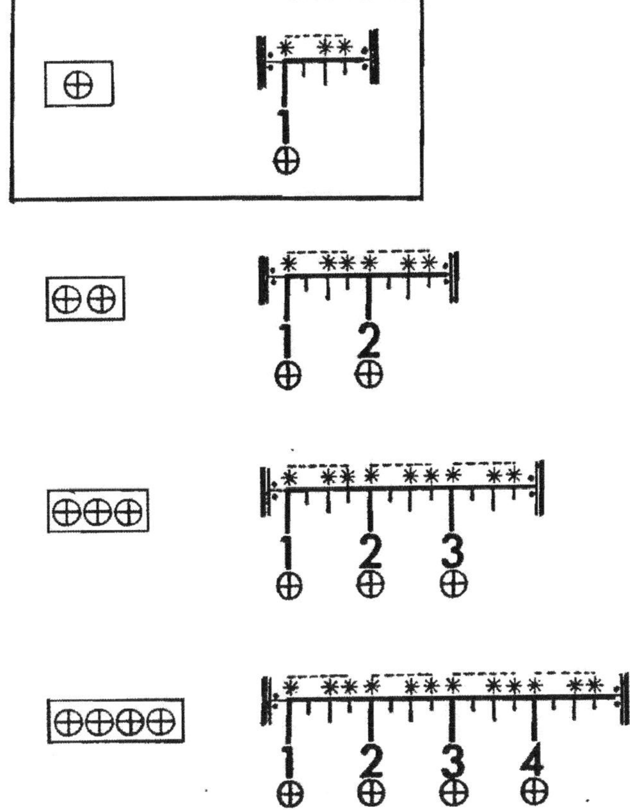

**4**

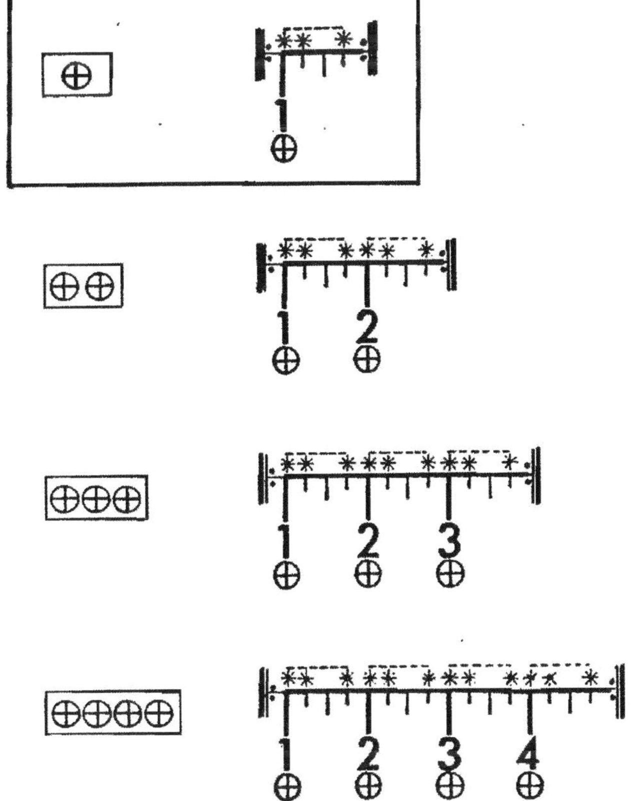

**5**

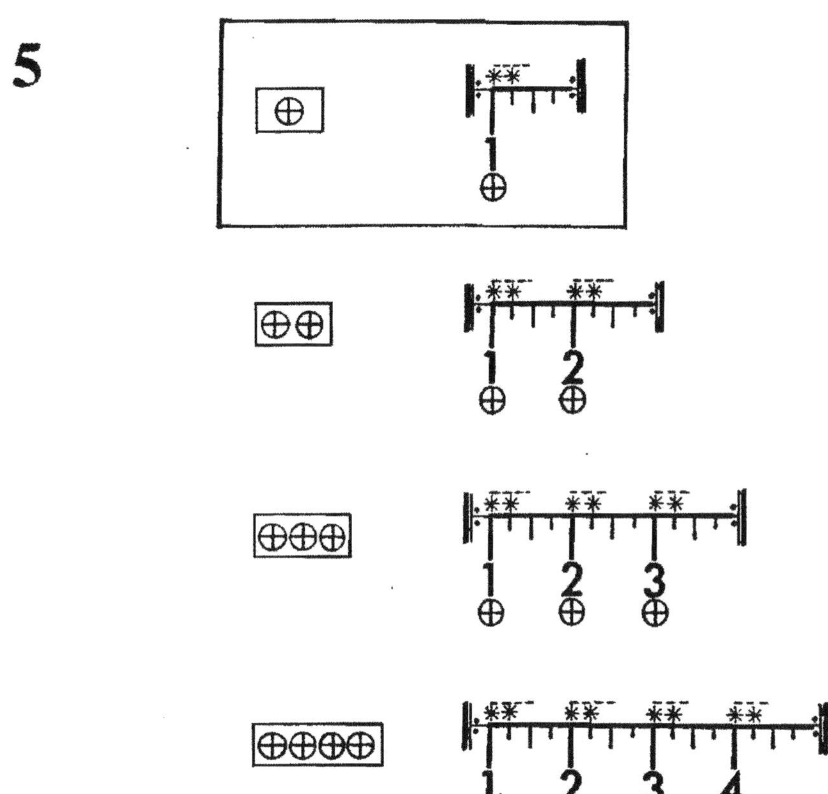

**6**

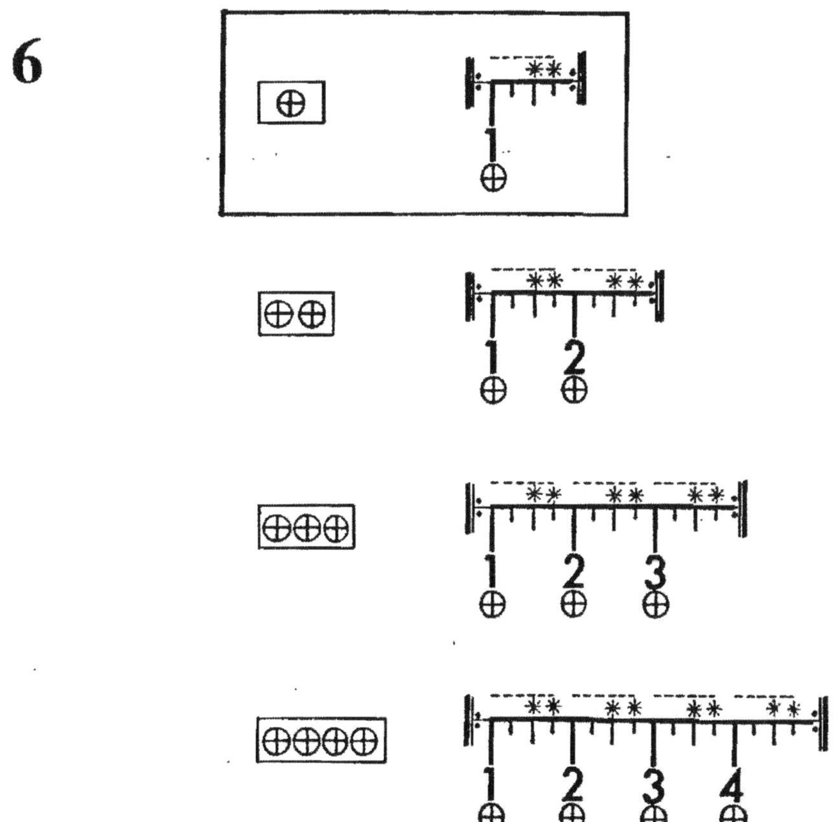

**7**

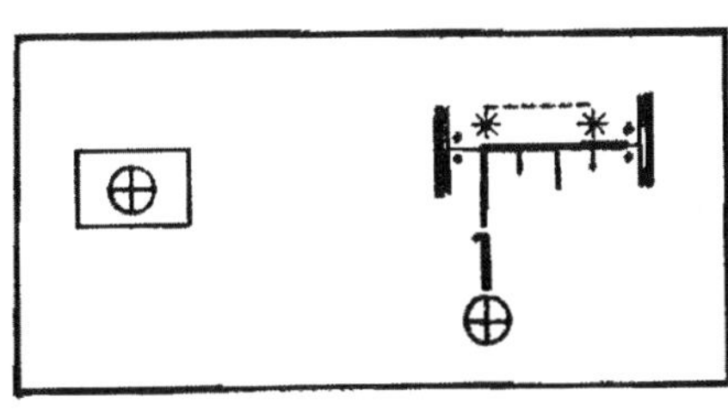

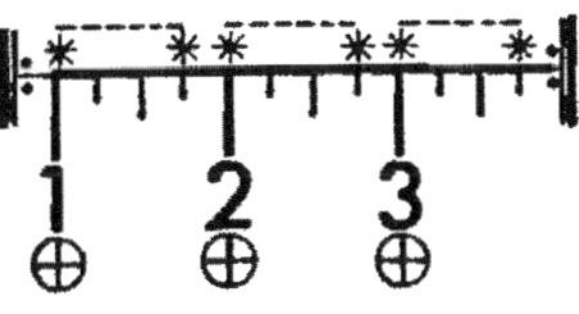

**8**

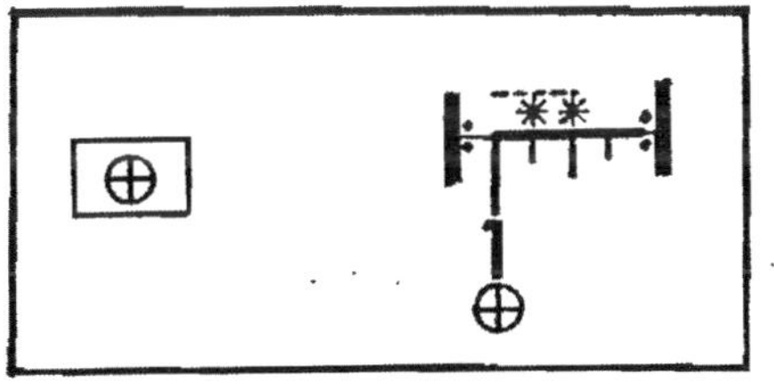

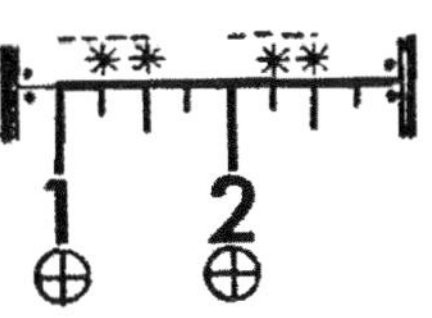

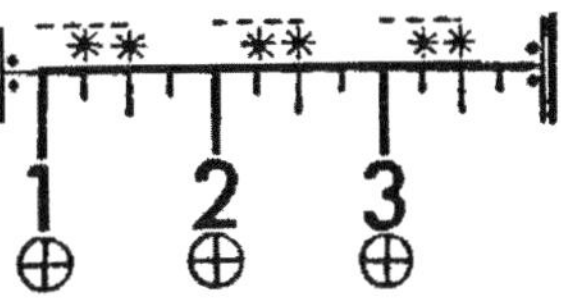

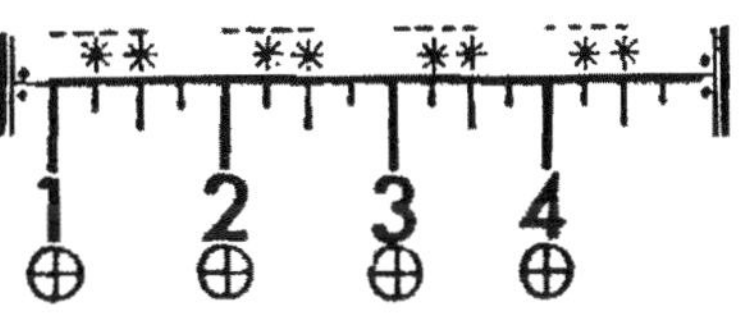

**9**

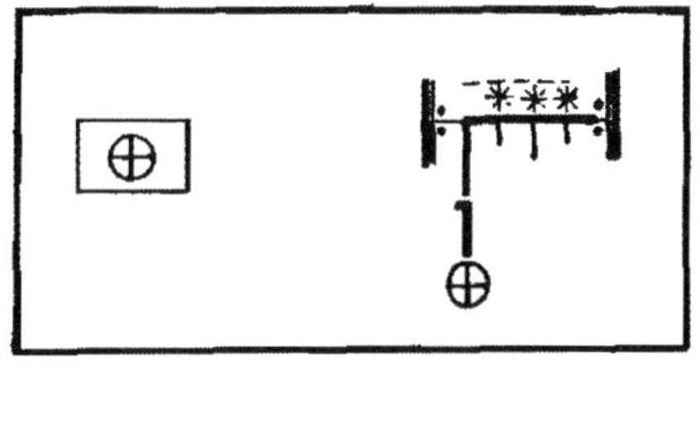

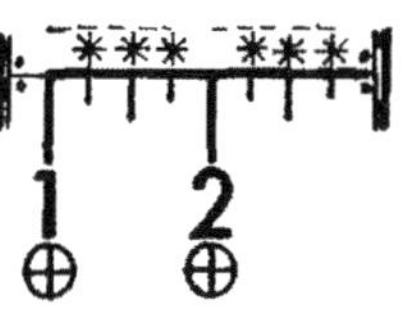

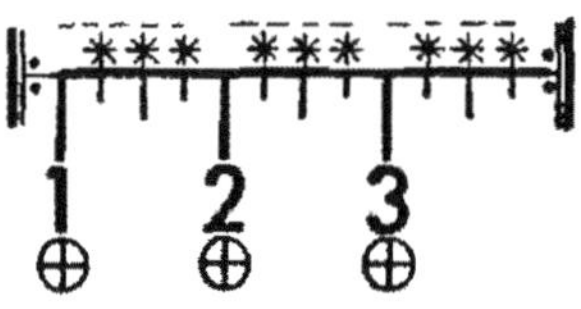

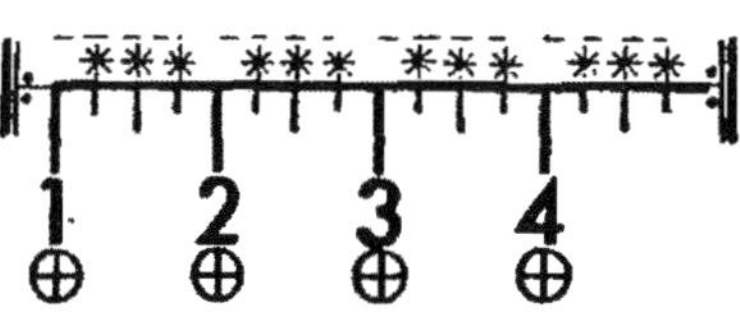

**10**

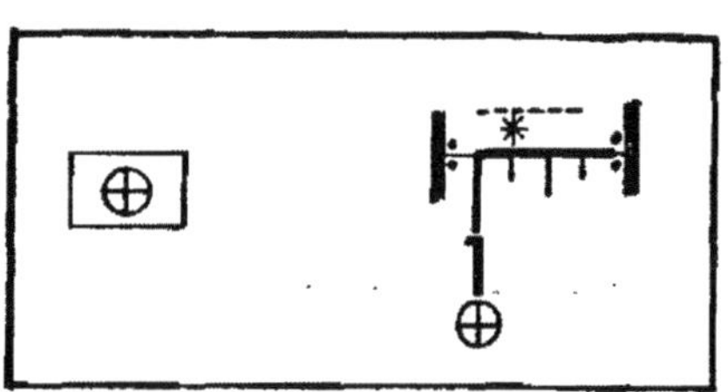

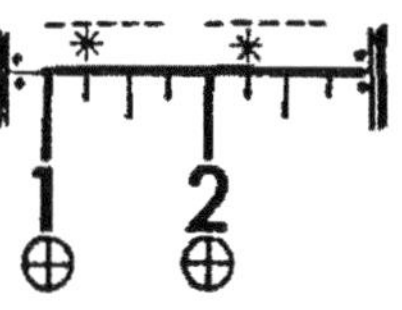

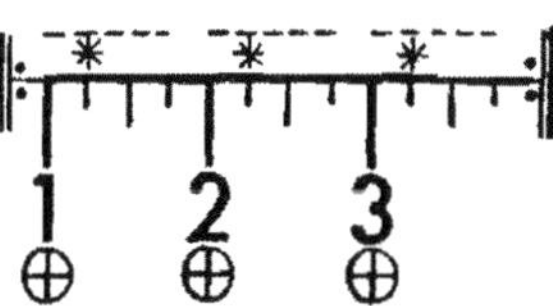

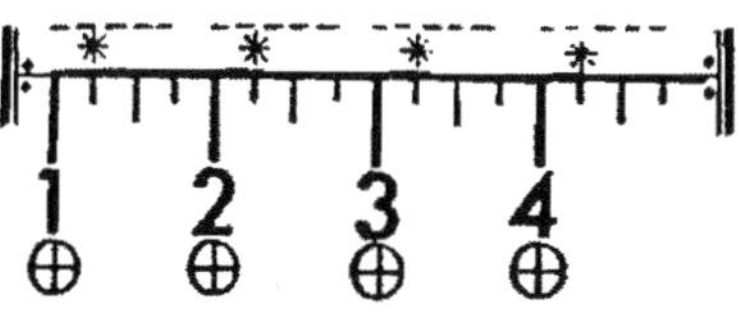

**11**

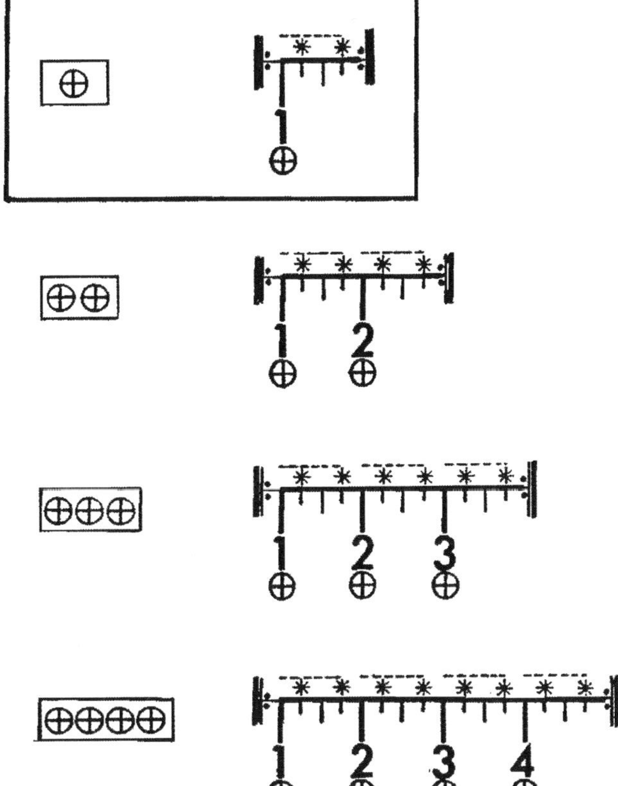

# COMPOUND DIVISION

Simple division divided each beat to two parts.  **Compound division** divides each beat to three parts:

compound division   1. division resulting in multiple parts.

The rhythm ruler used to measure compound division looks like this:

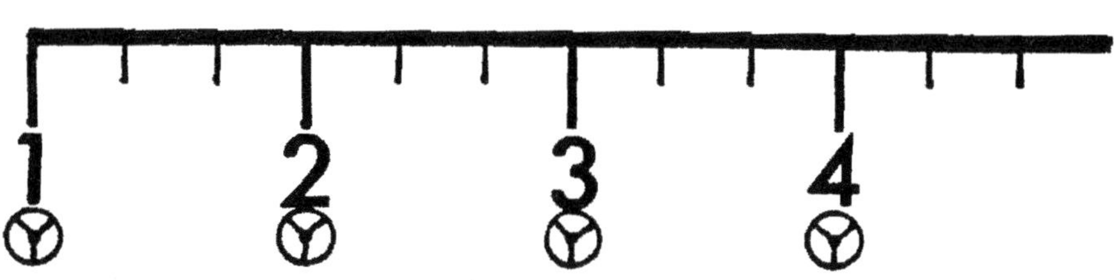

Since compound division divides each beat in three, we identify the symbol that represents the beat in compound division by placing a dot on its right side:

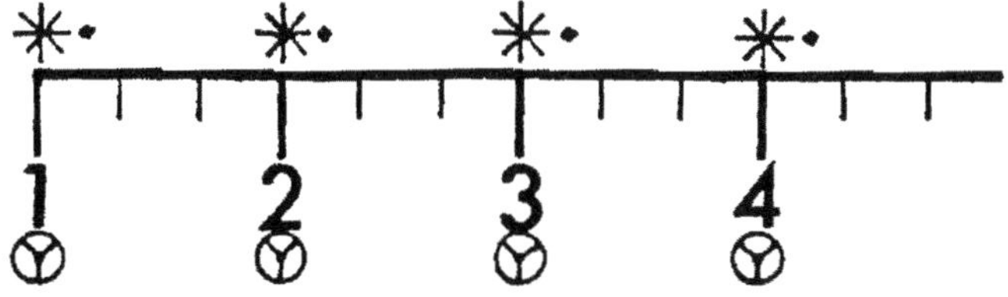

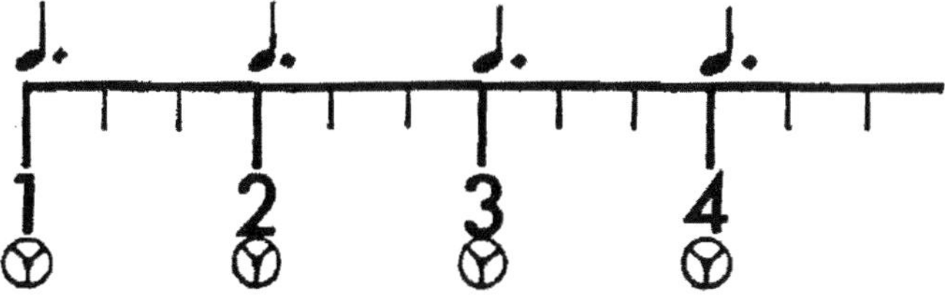

**1**

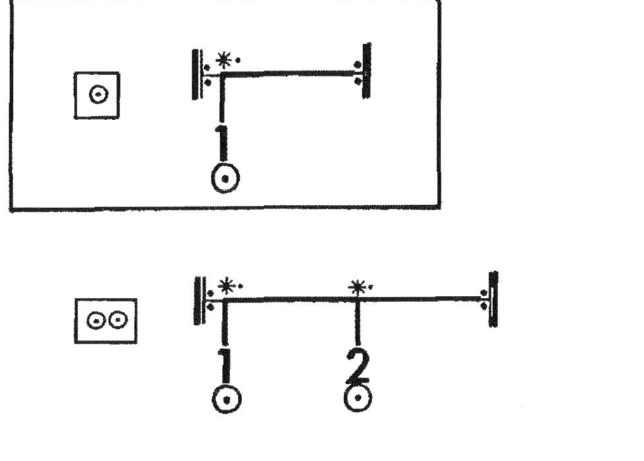

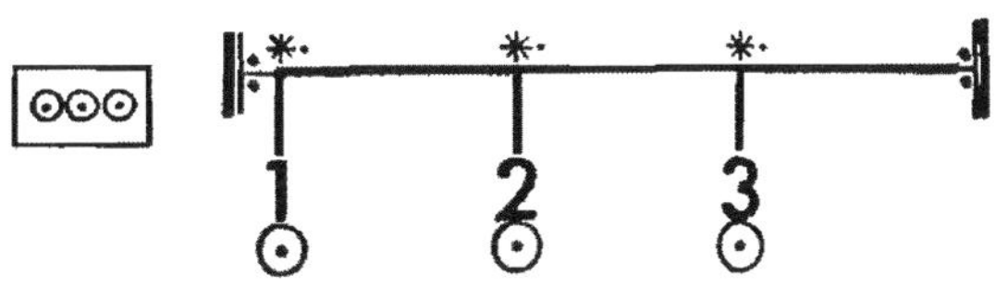

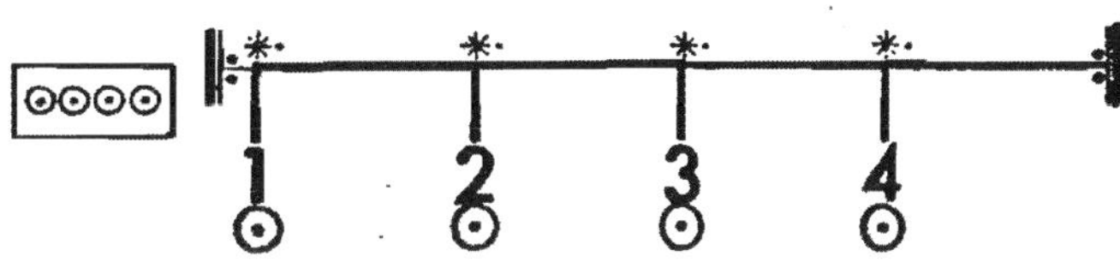

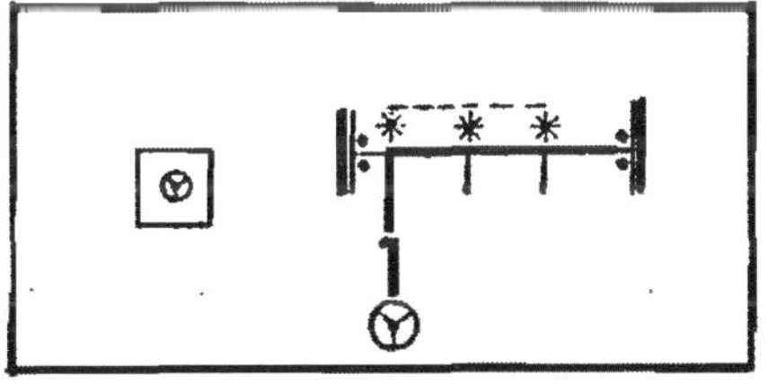

**2**

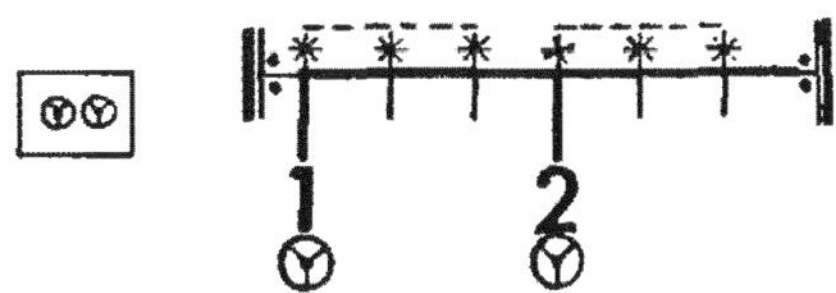

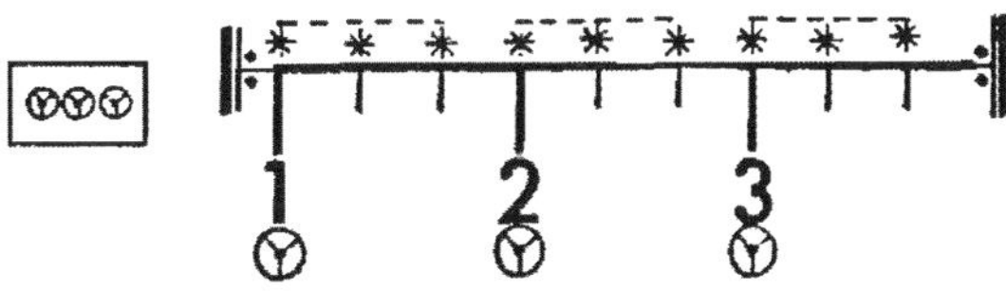

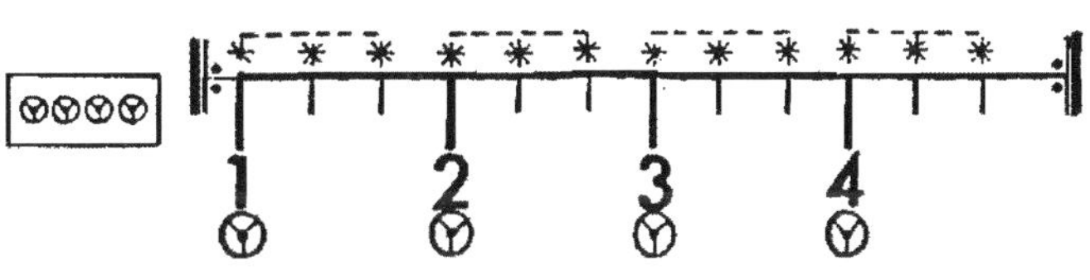

**3**

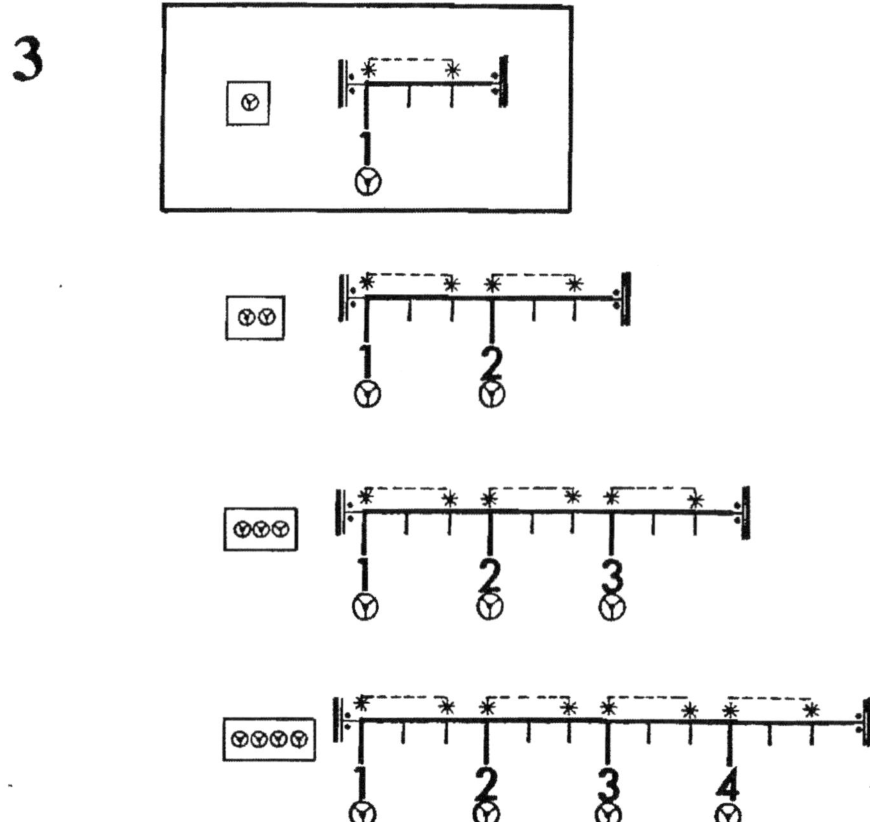

**4**

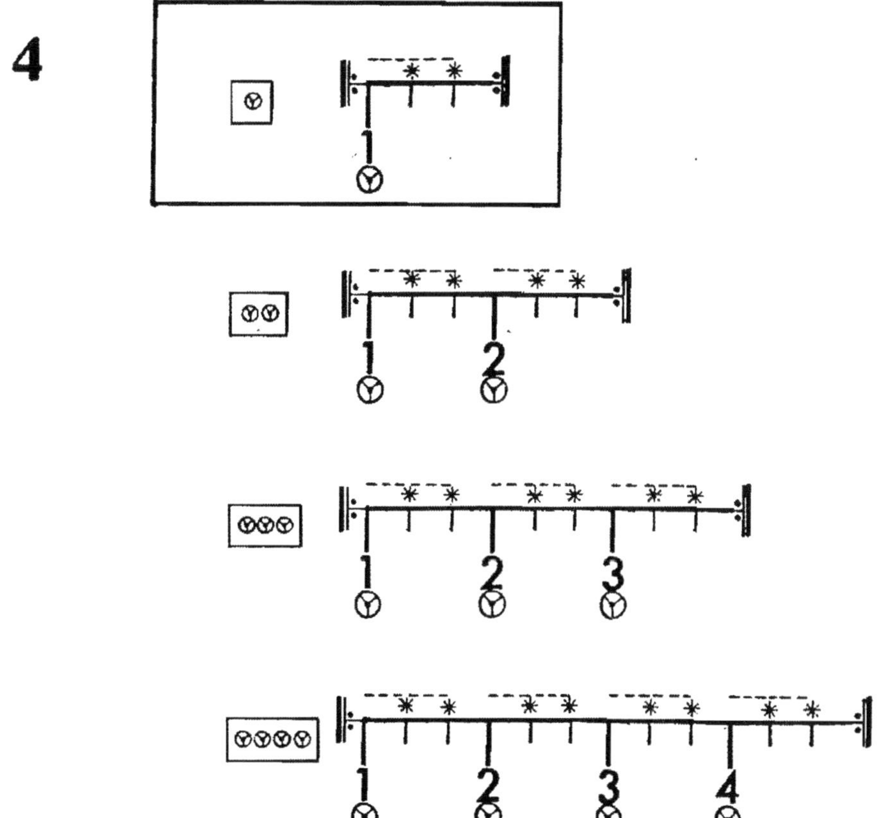

5

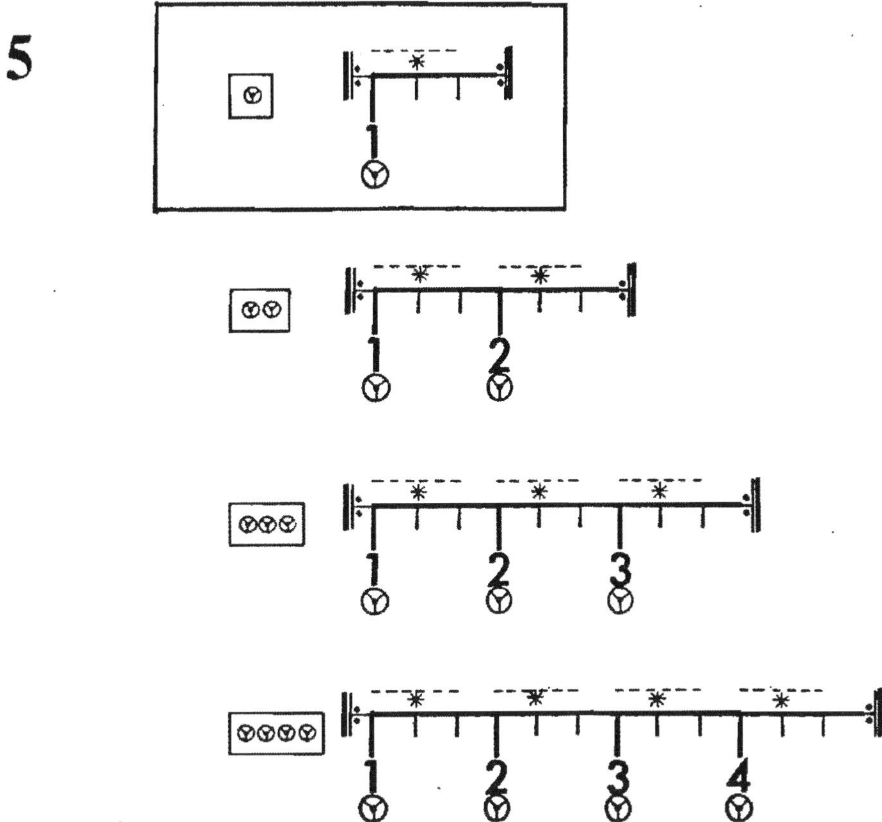

6

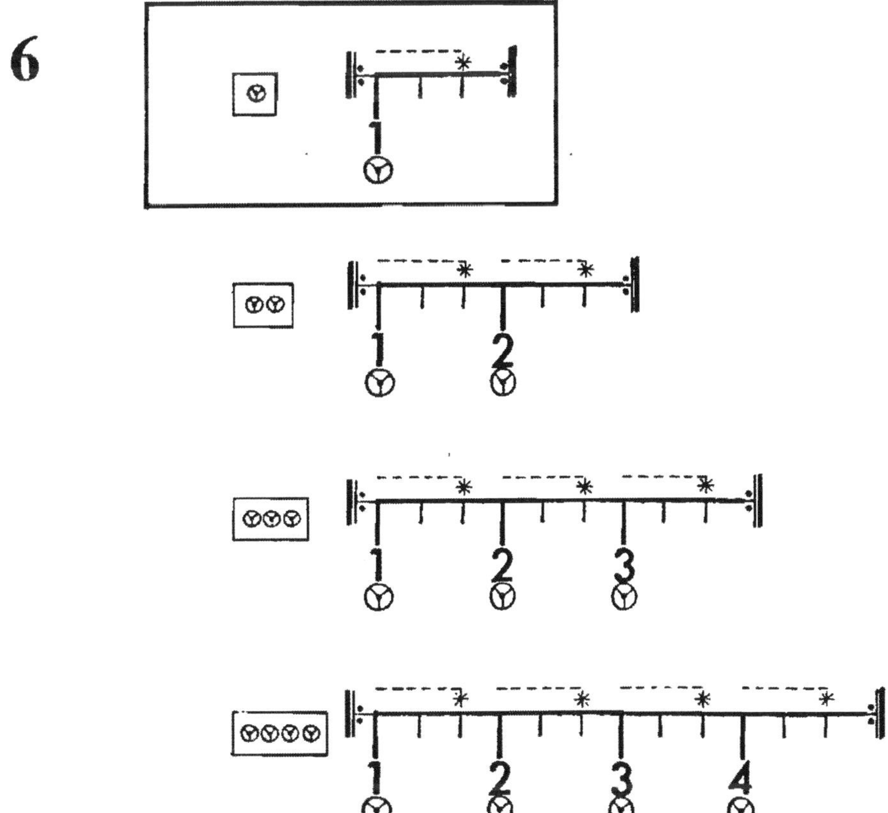

# BEAT, COMPOUND DIVISION AND SUBDIVISION

On a rhythm ruler subdivision of compound division looks like this:

Subdivision adds the syllable "ta" (tah) between the beat and divisions:

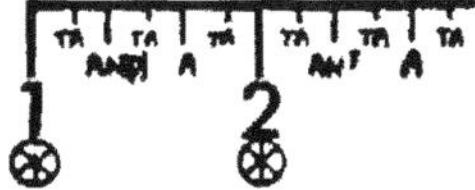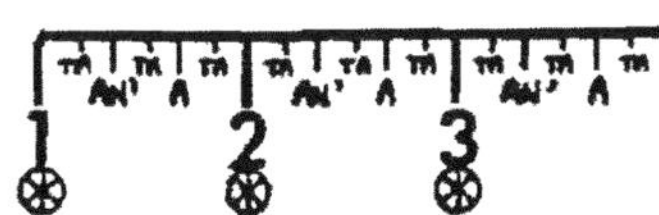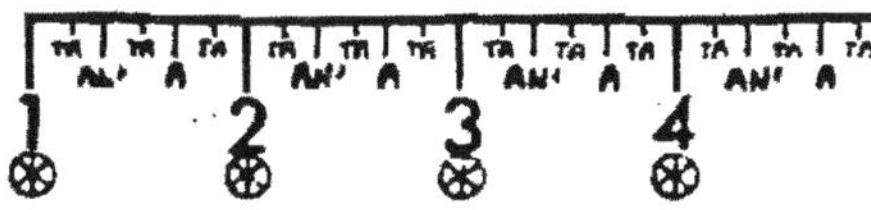

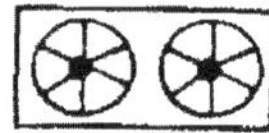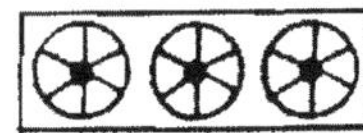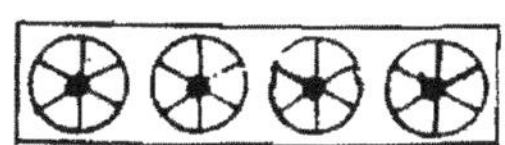

**1**

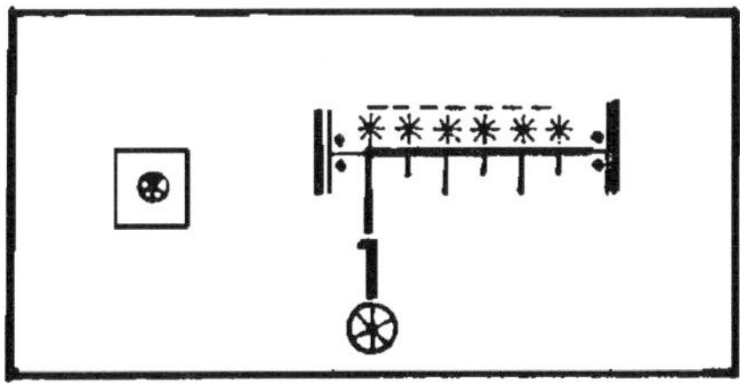

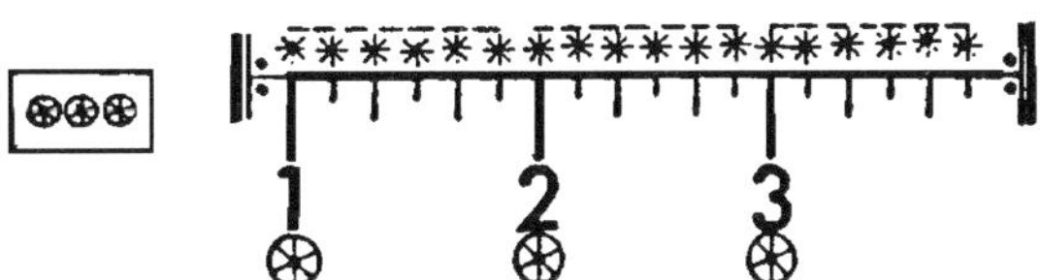

**2**

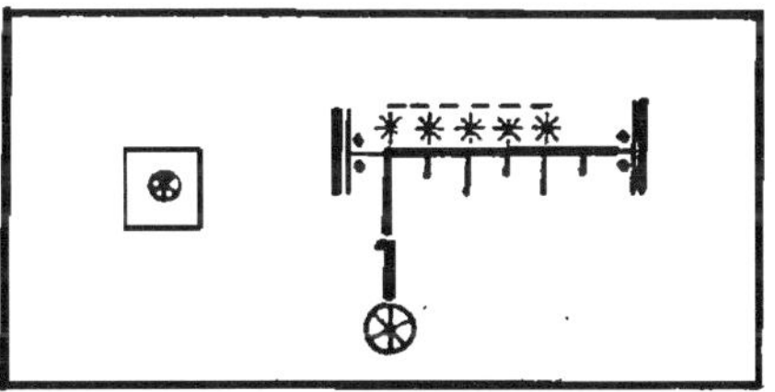

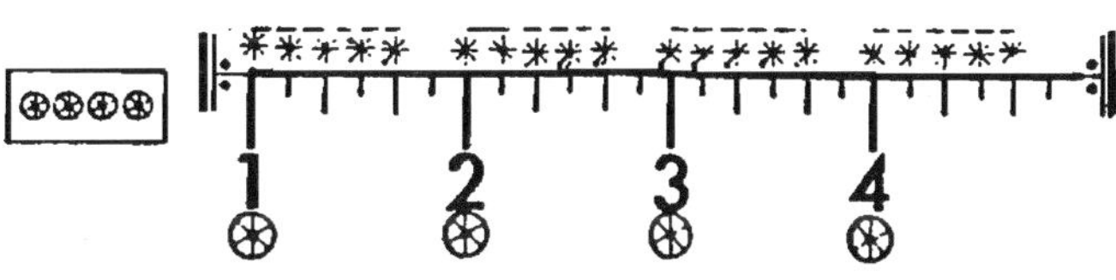

**3**

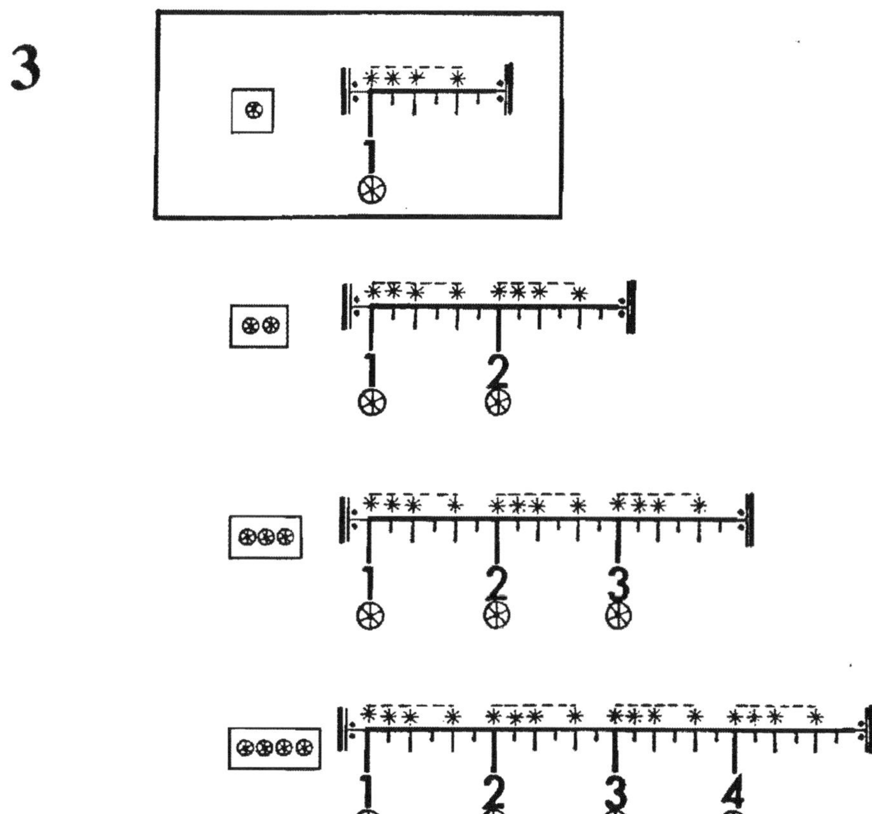

**4**

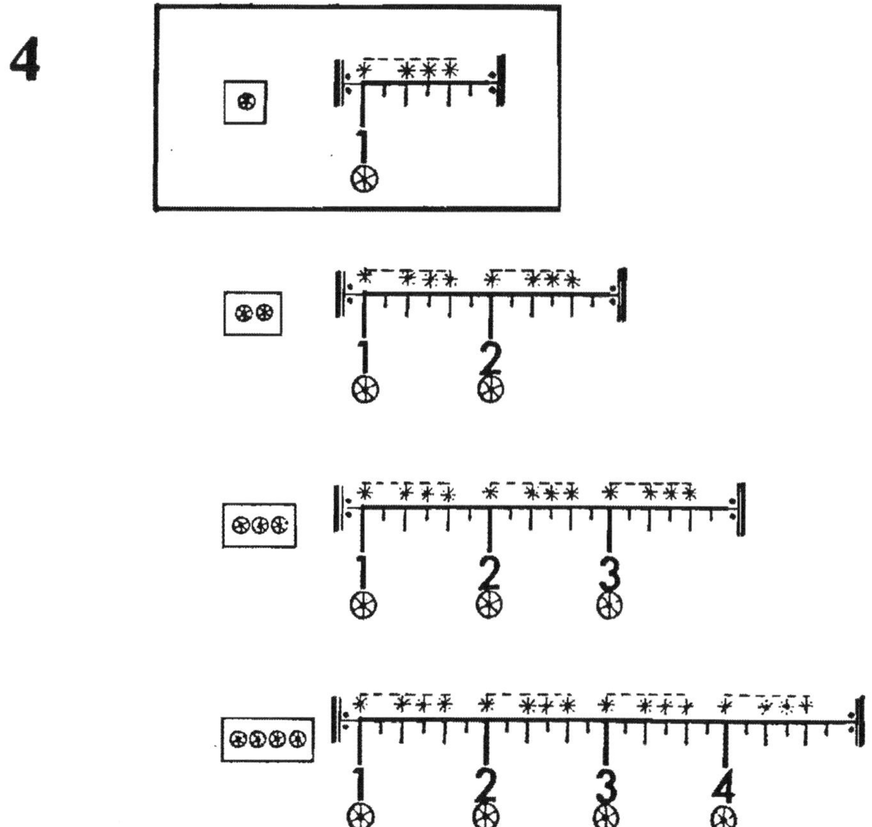

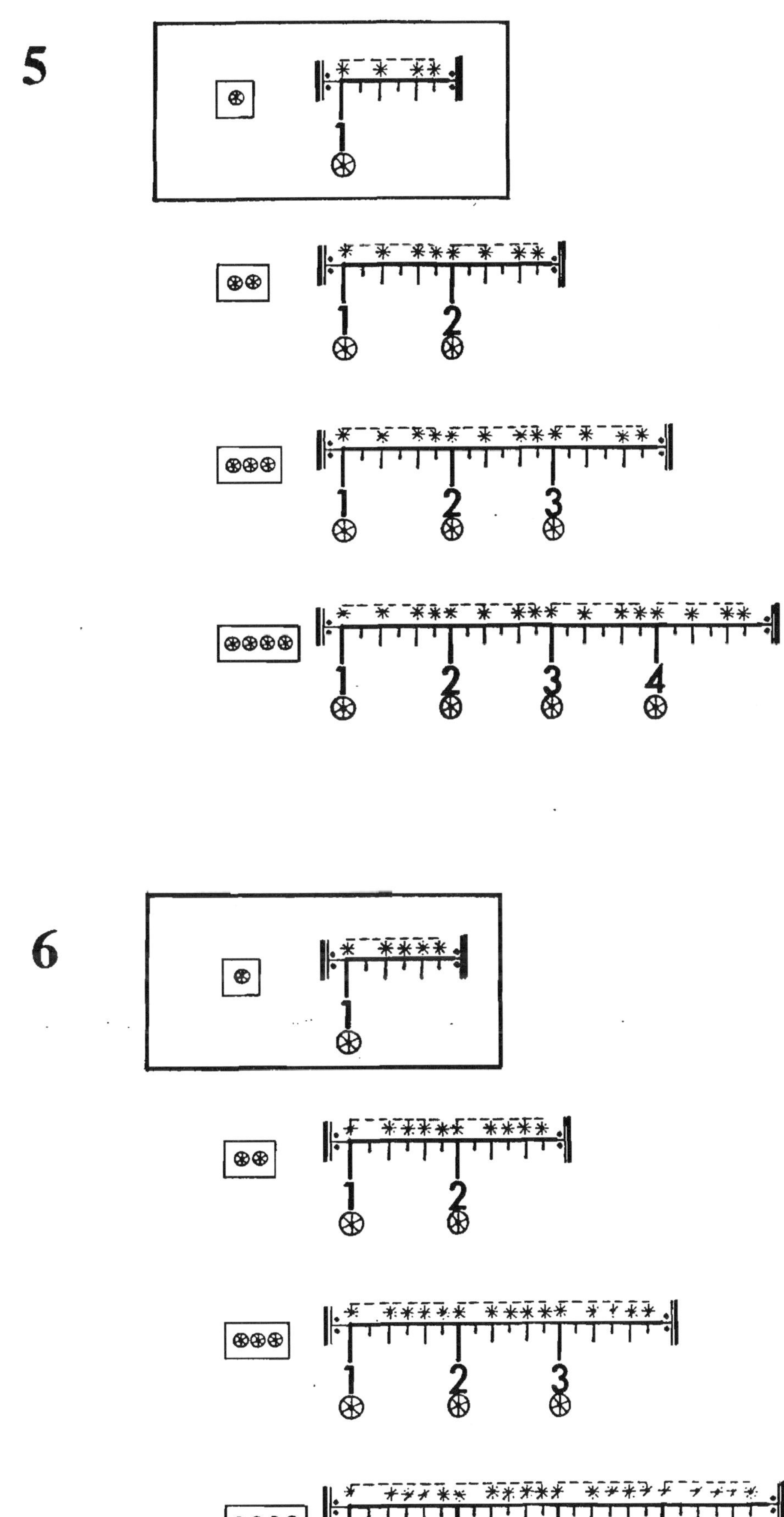

**7**

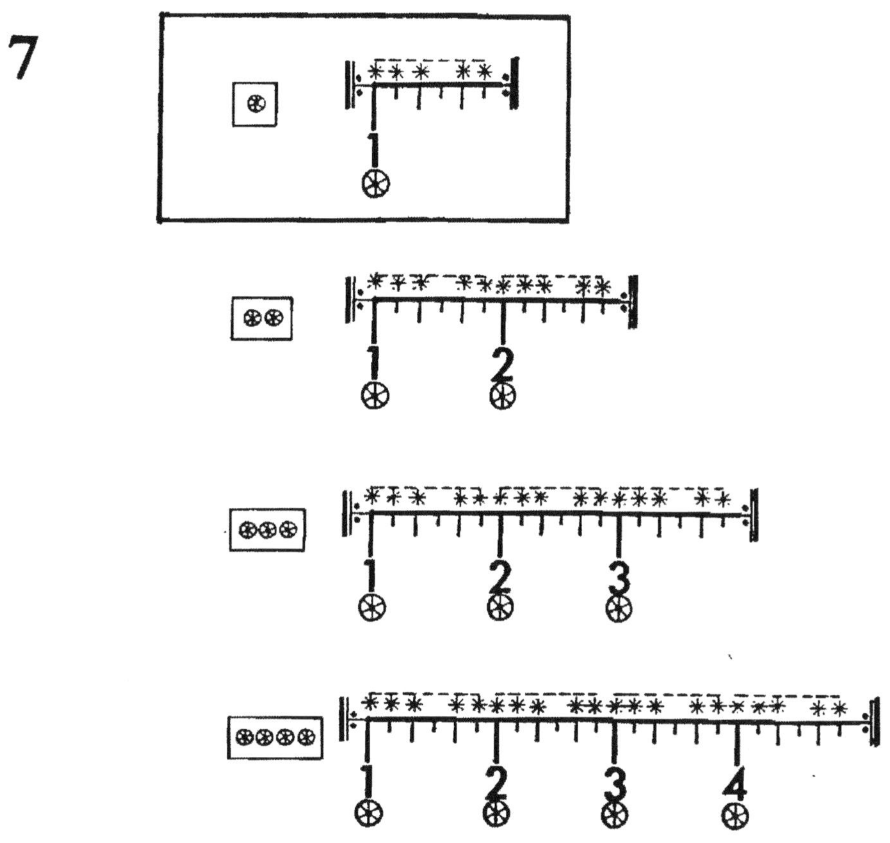

**8**

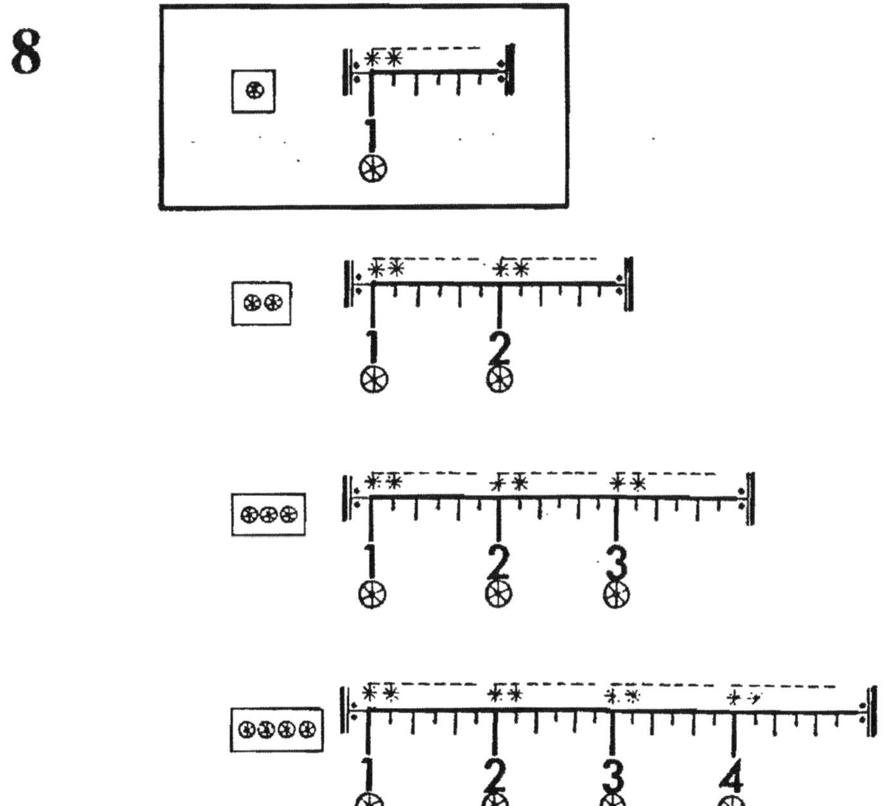

**11**

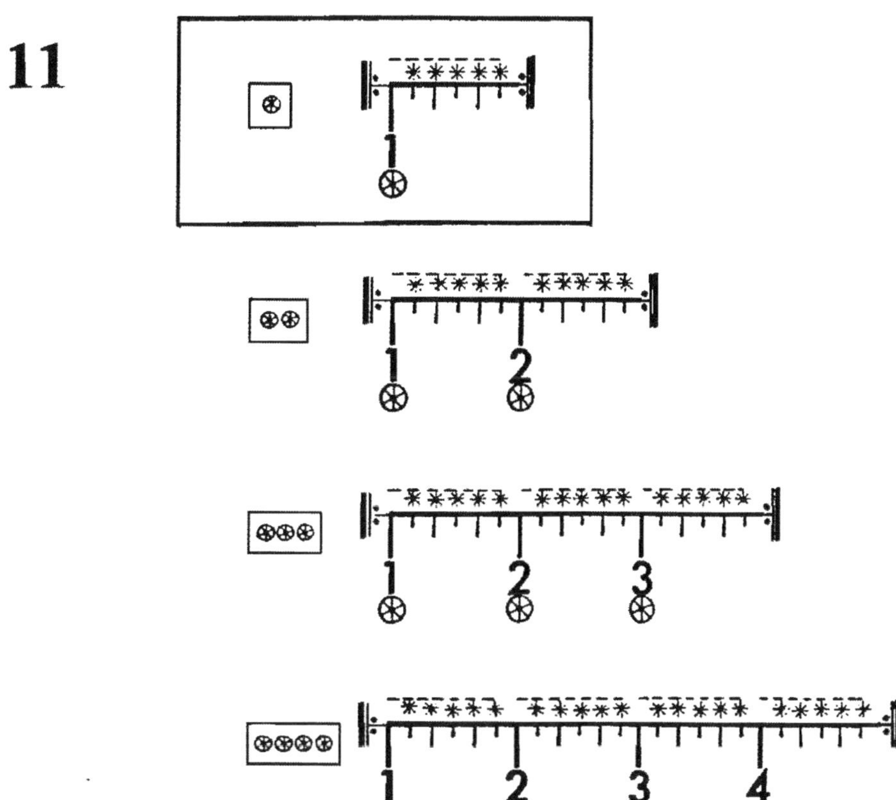

**12**

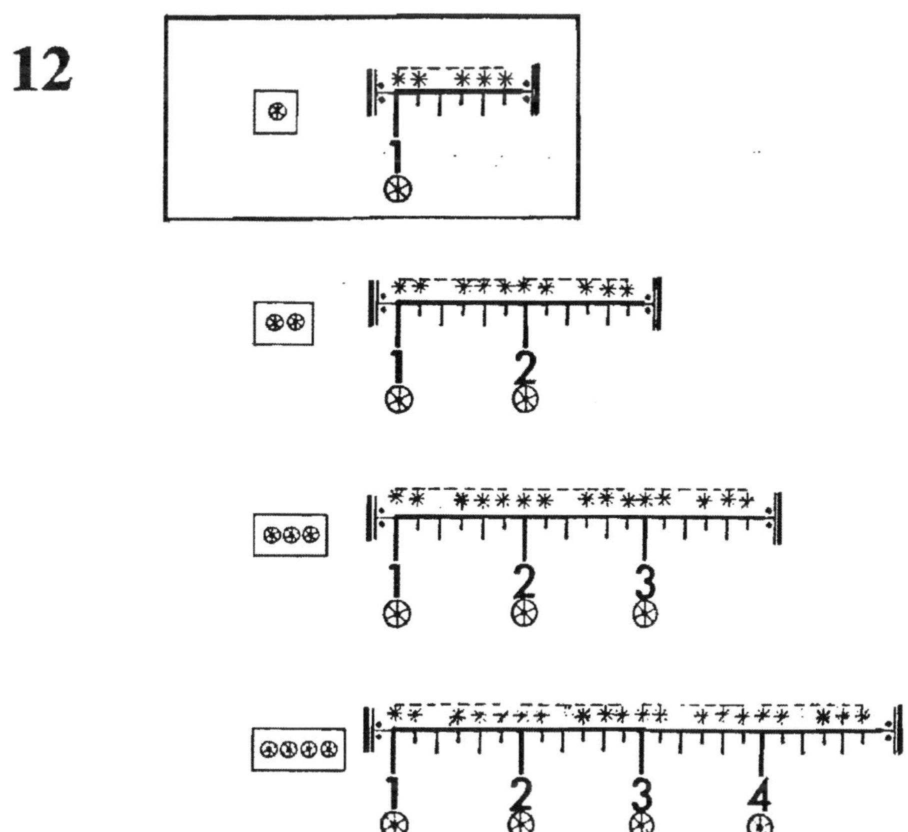

**13**

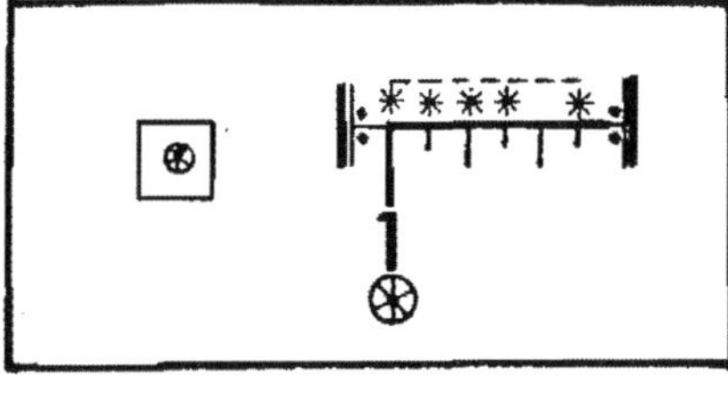

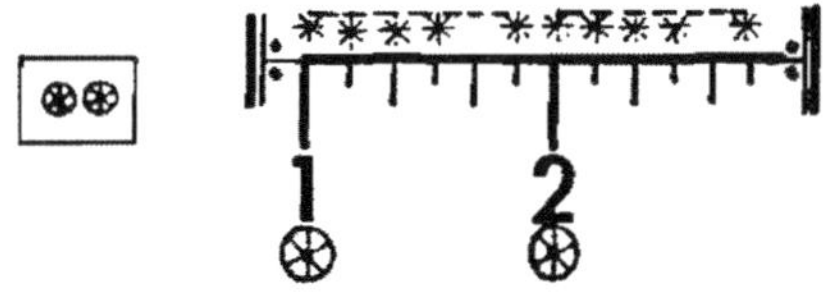

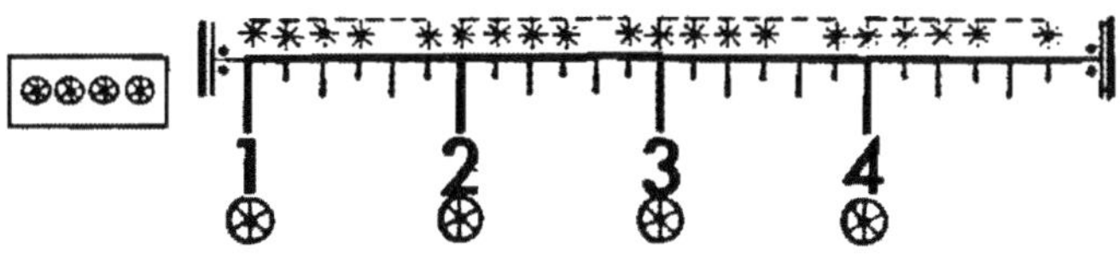

**14**

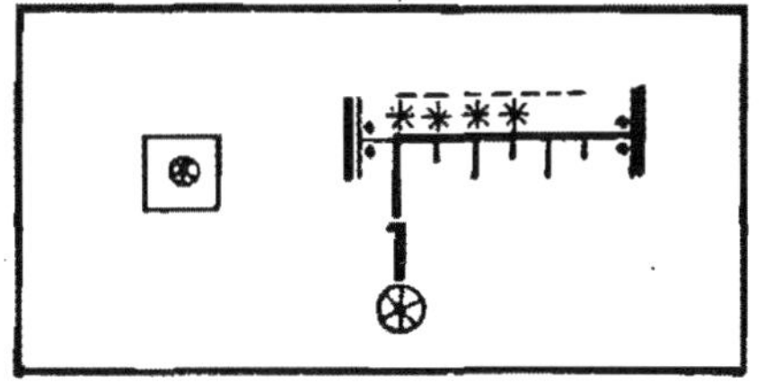

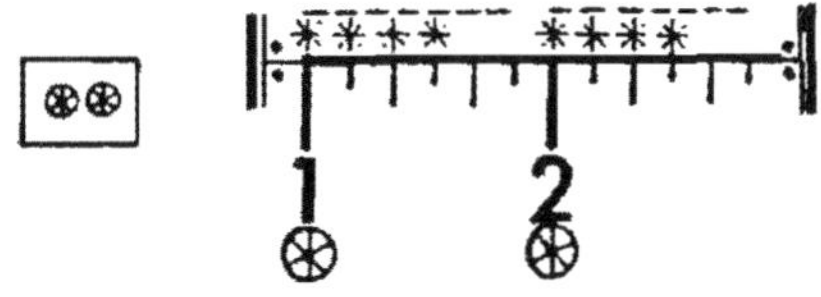

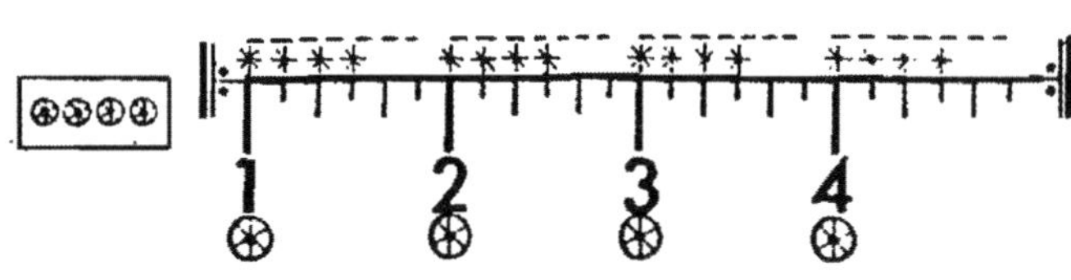

**15**

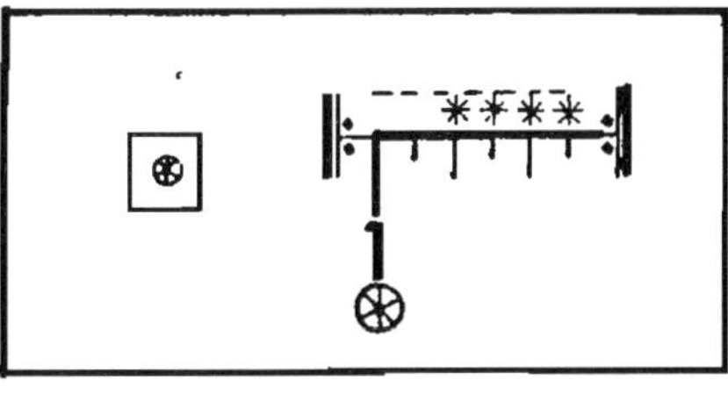

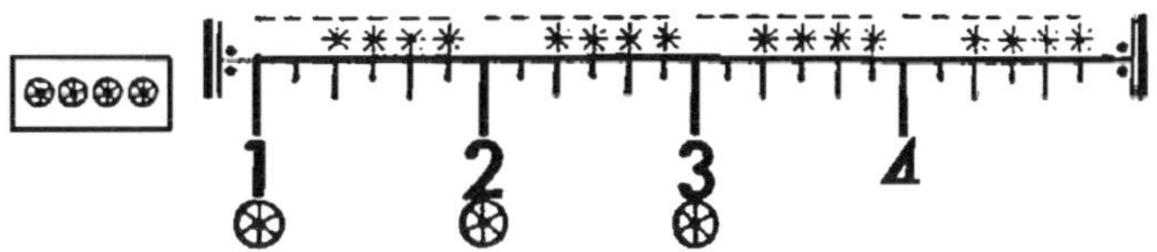

**16**

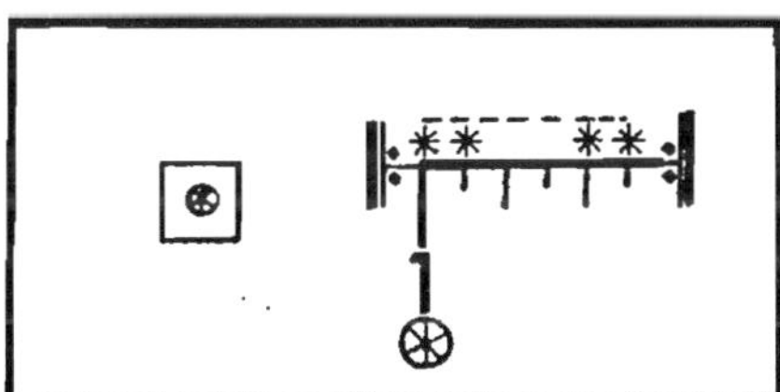

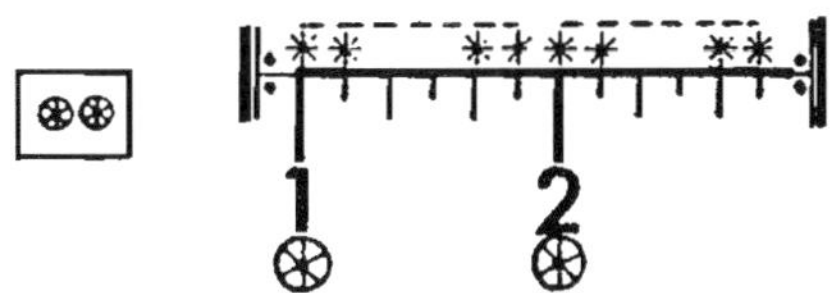

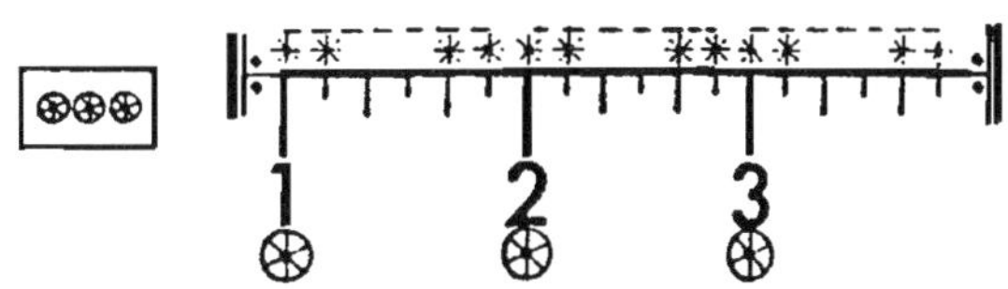

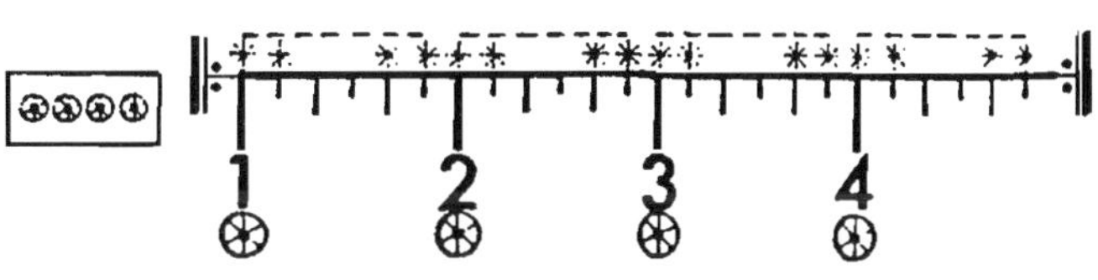

**19**

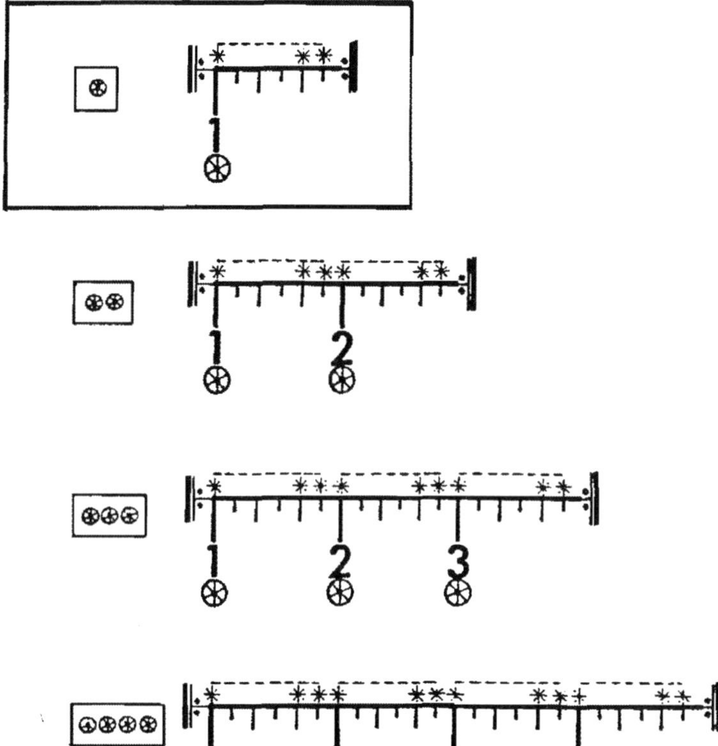

# ETUDES USING BEAT, SIMPLE DIVISION AND SUBDIVISION

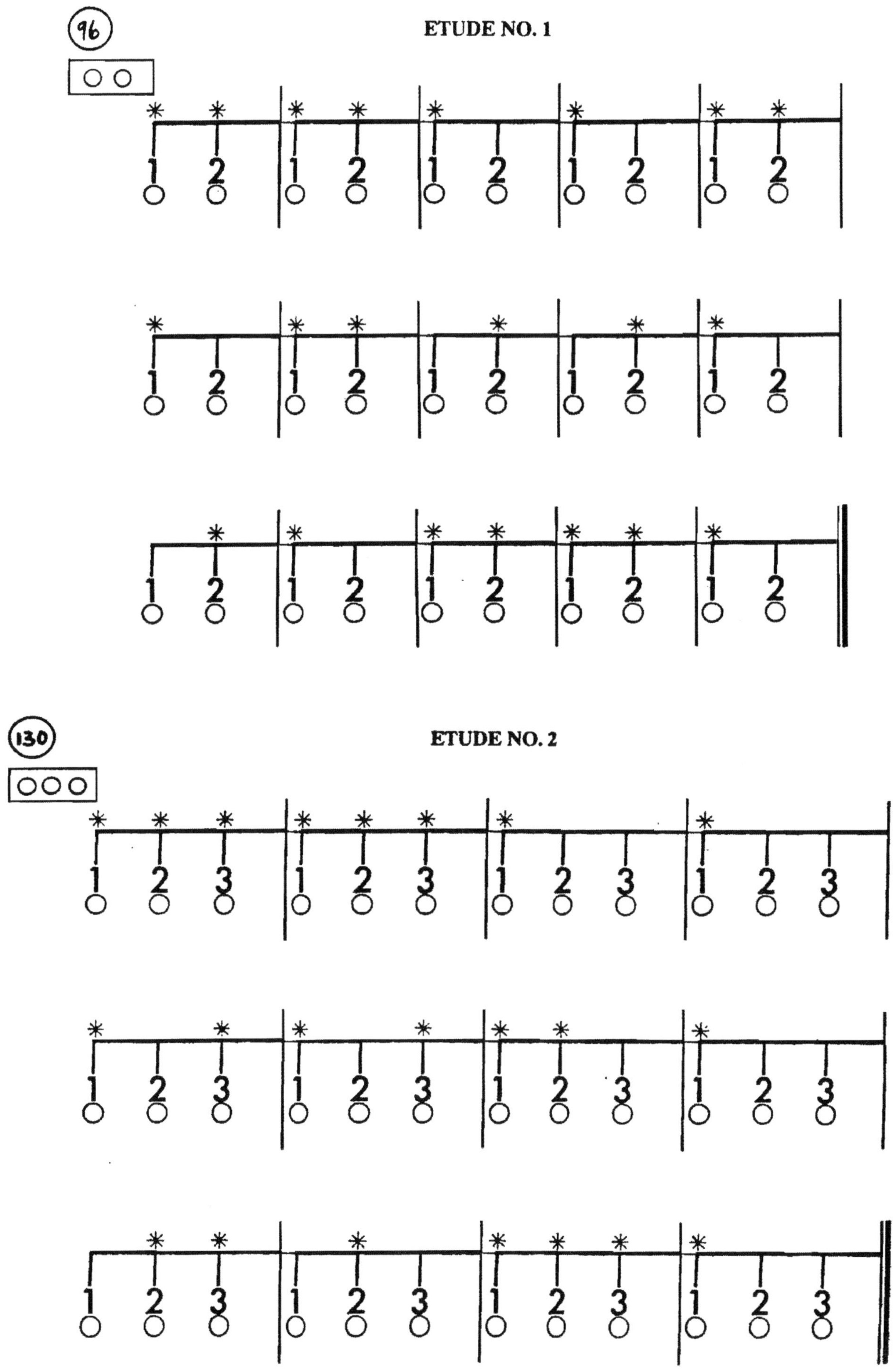
ETUDE NO. 1
96
ETUDE NO. 2
130

**ETUDE NO. 3**

**ETUDE NO. 4**

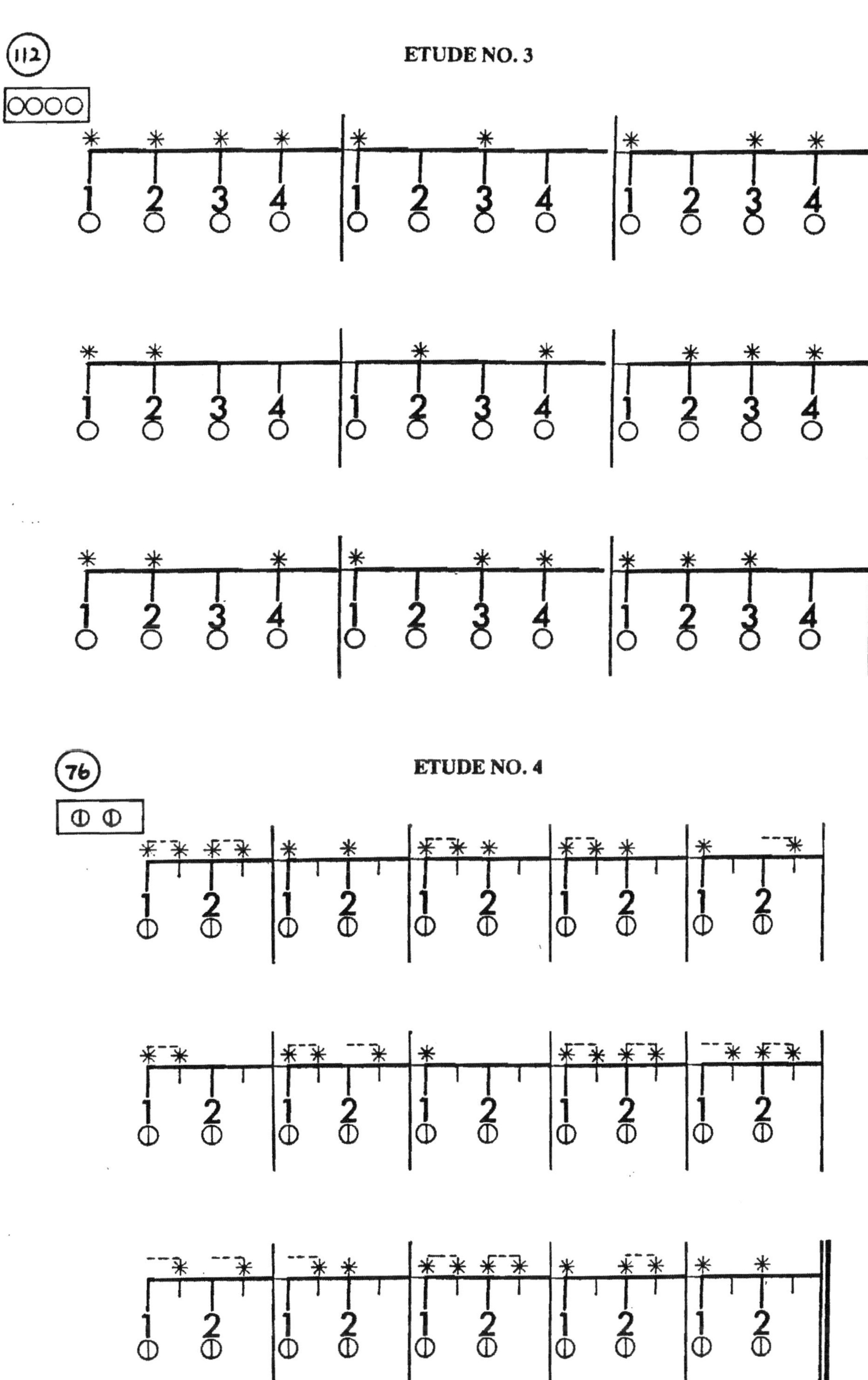

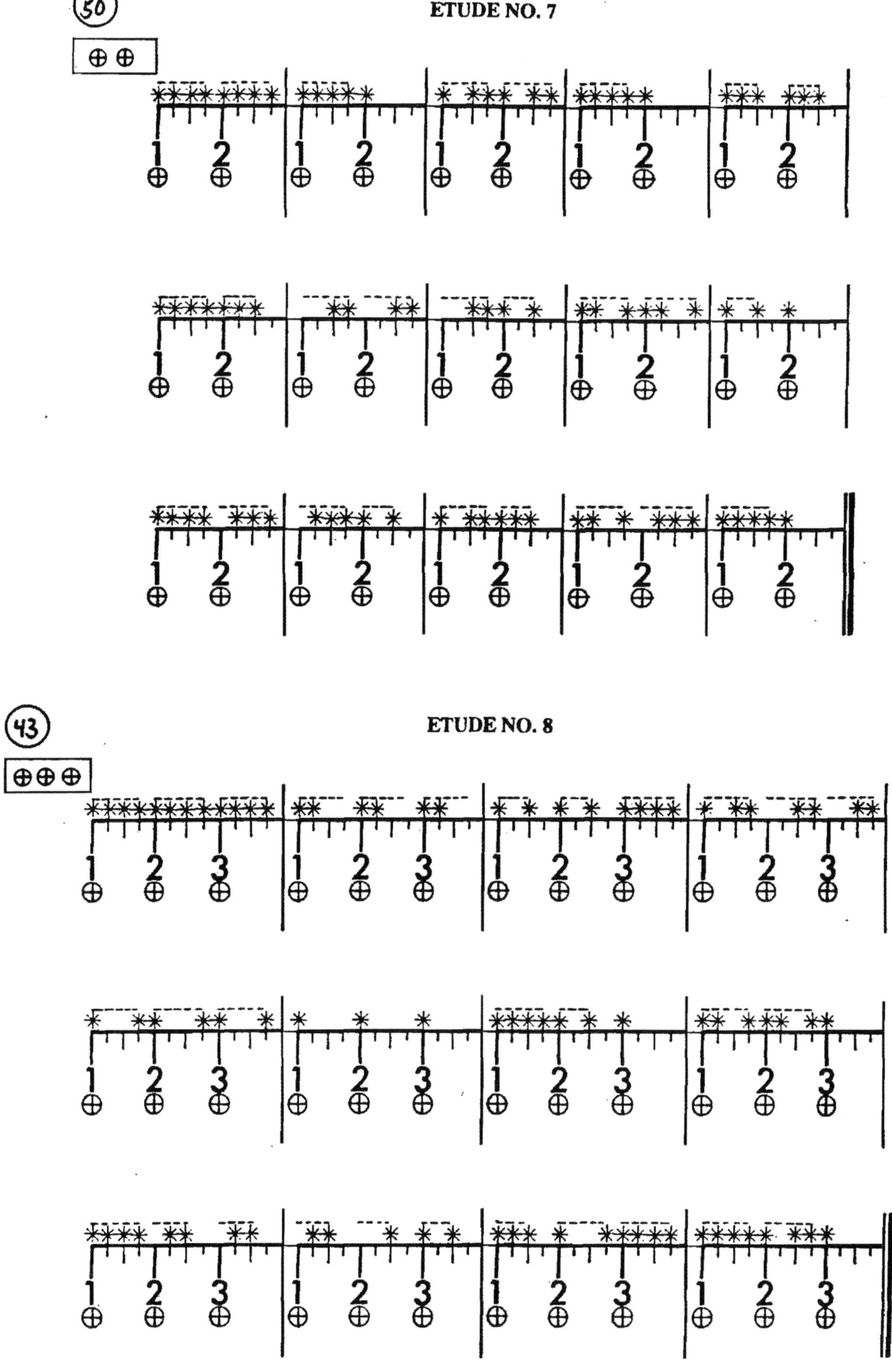
ETUDE NO. 7
ETUDE NO. 8

## ETUDE NO. 9

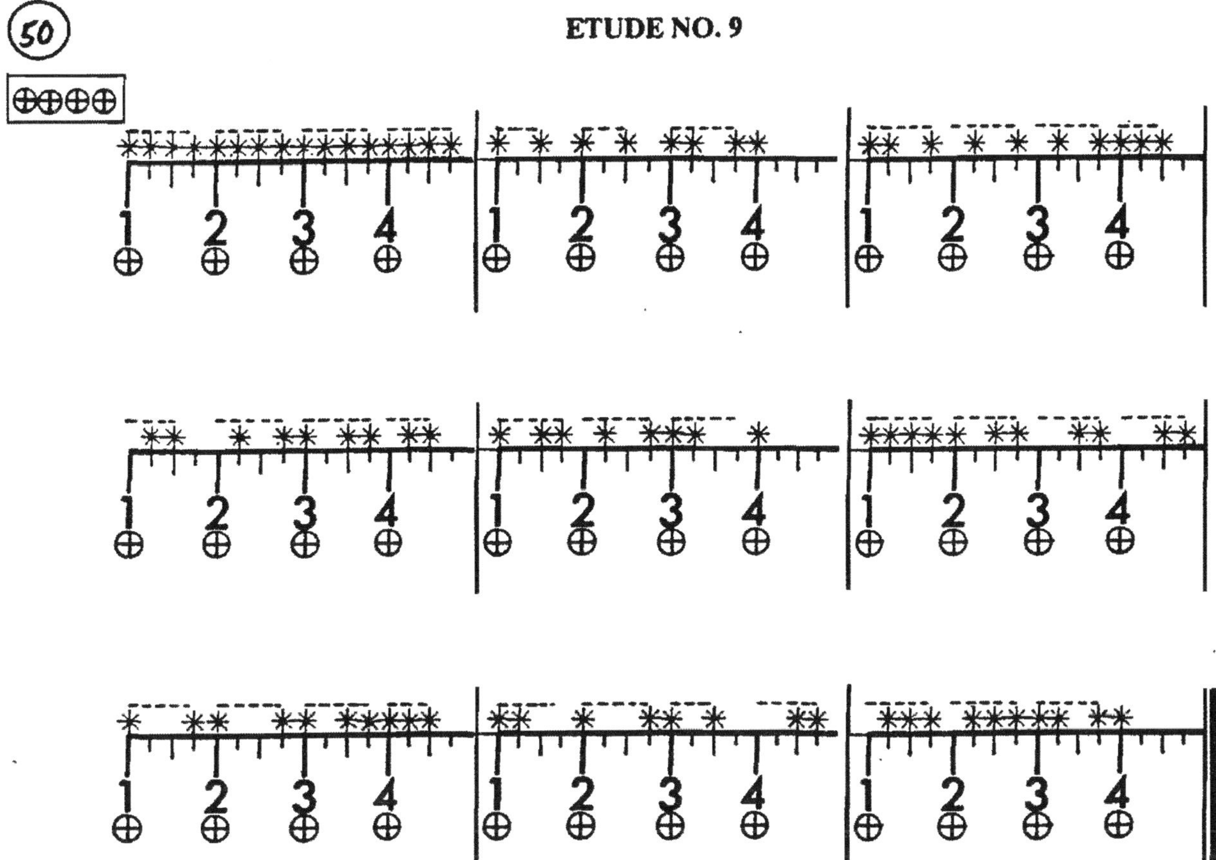

# ETUDES USING BEAT, COMPOUND DIVISION AND SUBDIVISION

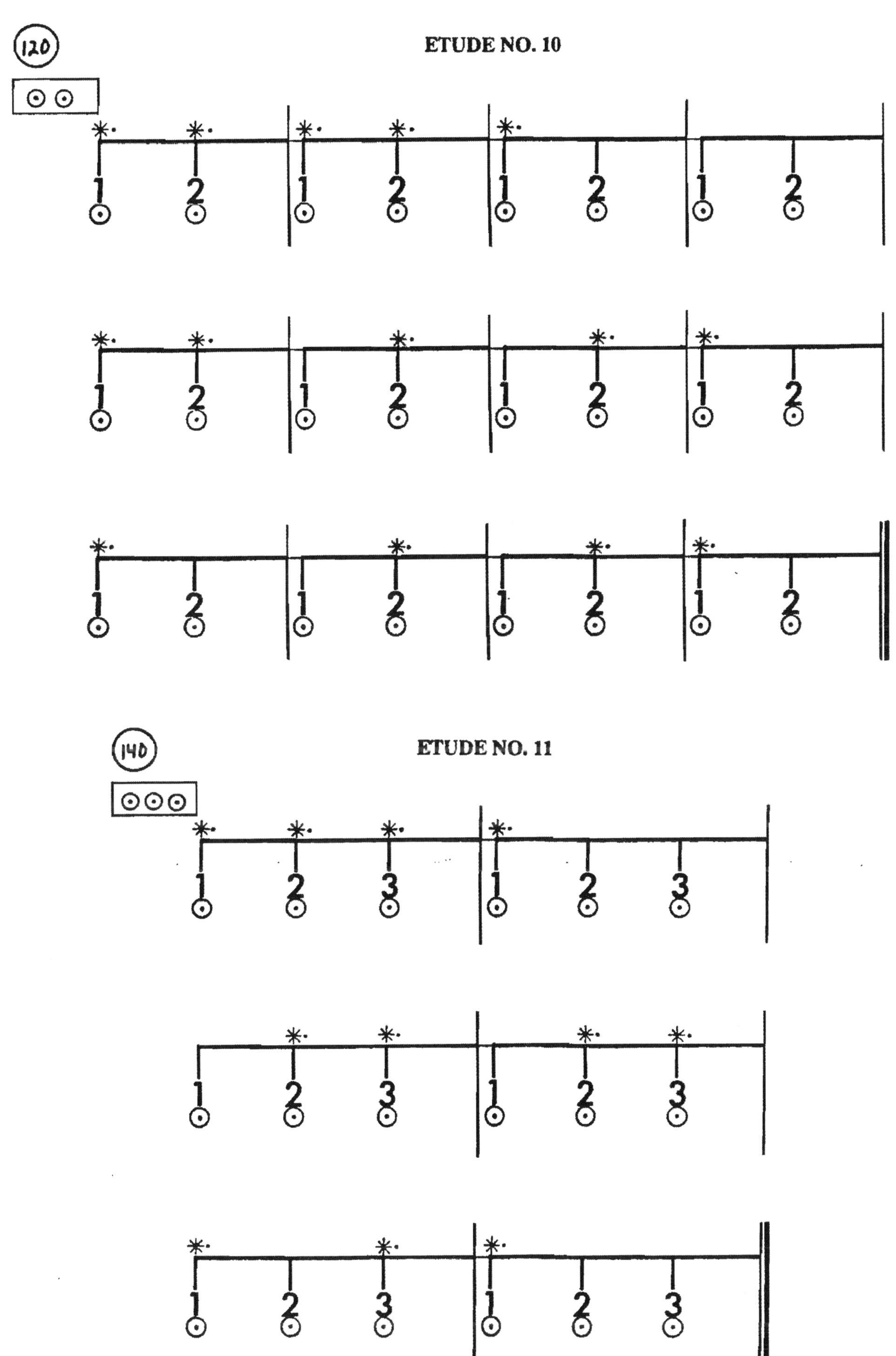
120
ETUDE NO. 10
140
ETUDE NO. 11

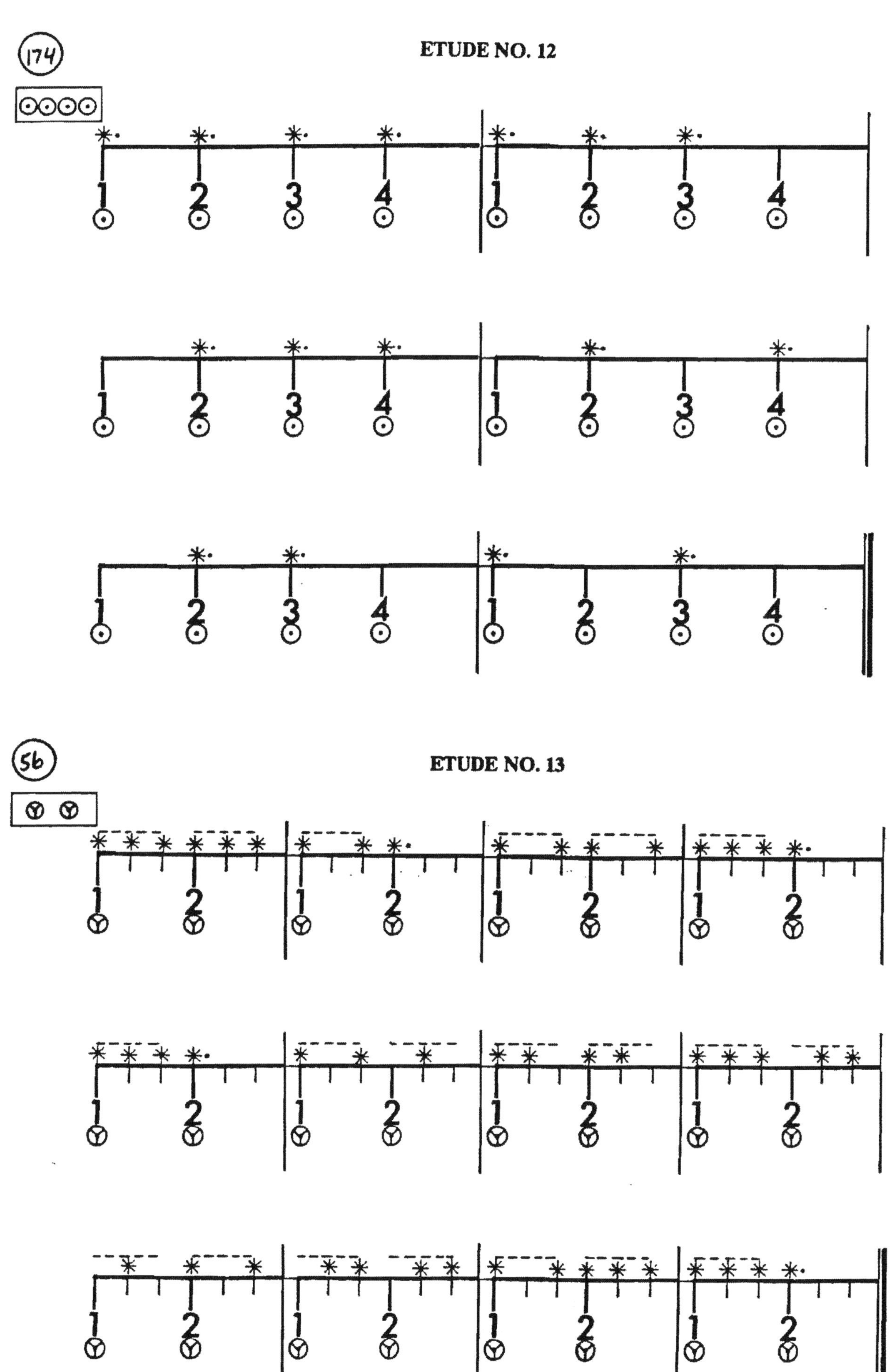
174
ETUDE NO. 12
56
ETUDE NO. 13

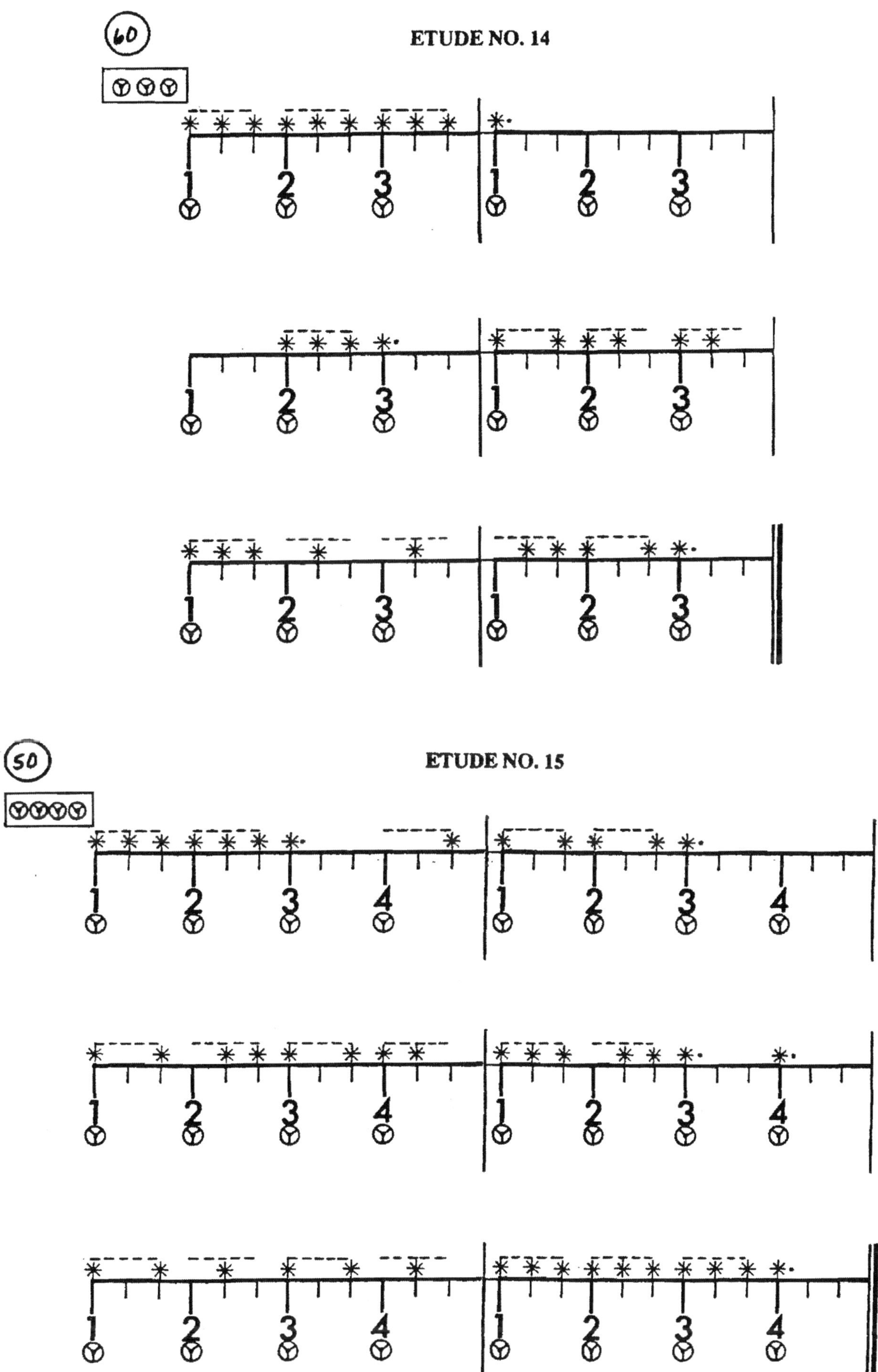


ETUDE NO. 14
60
ETUDE NO. 15
50

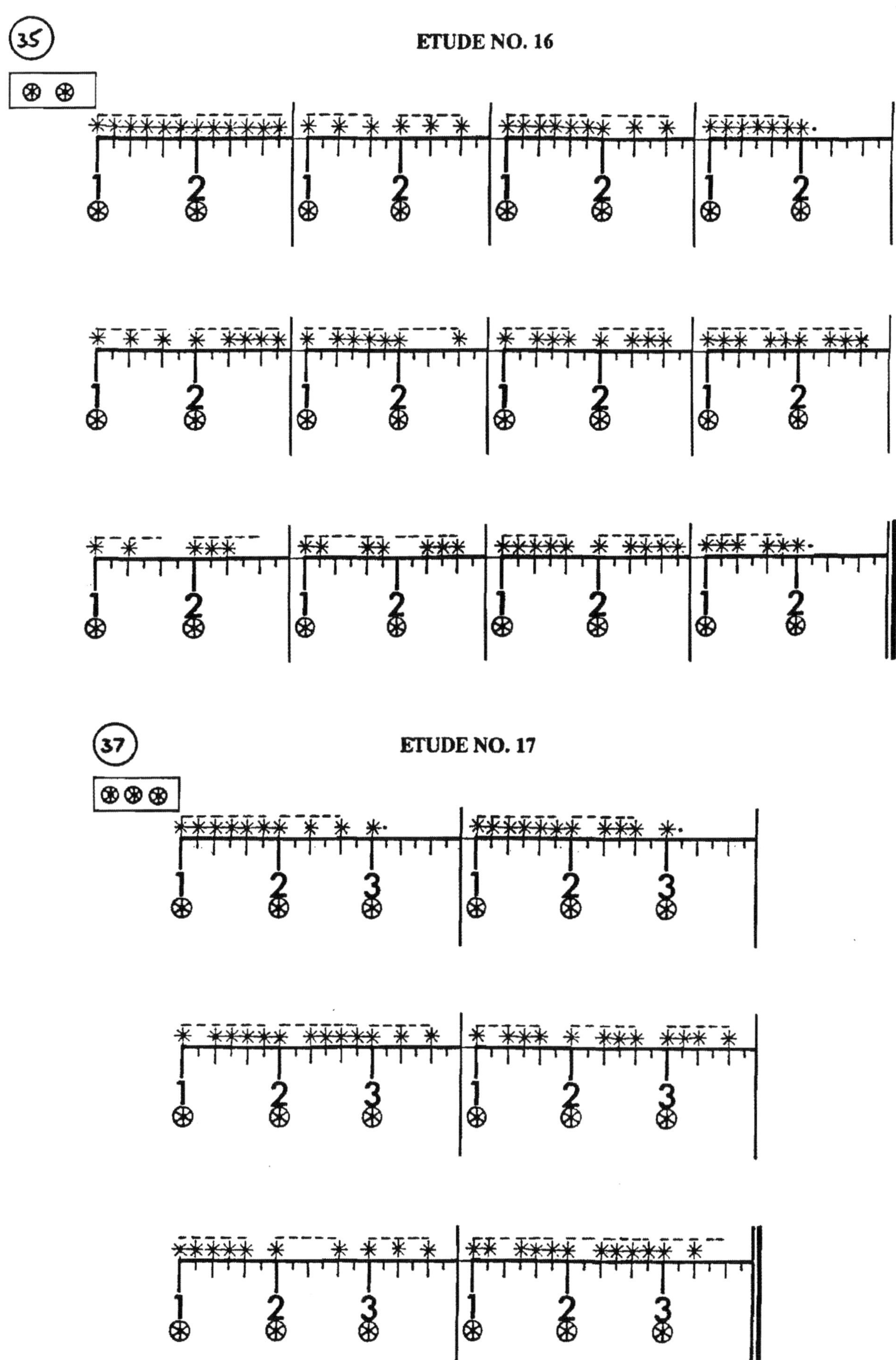
ETUDE NO. 16
ETUDE NO. 17

## ETUDE NO. 18

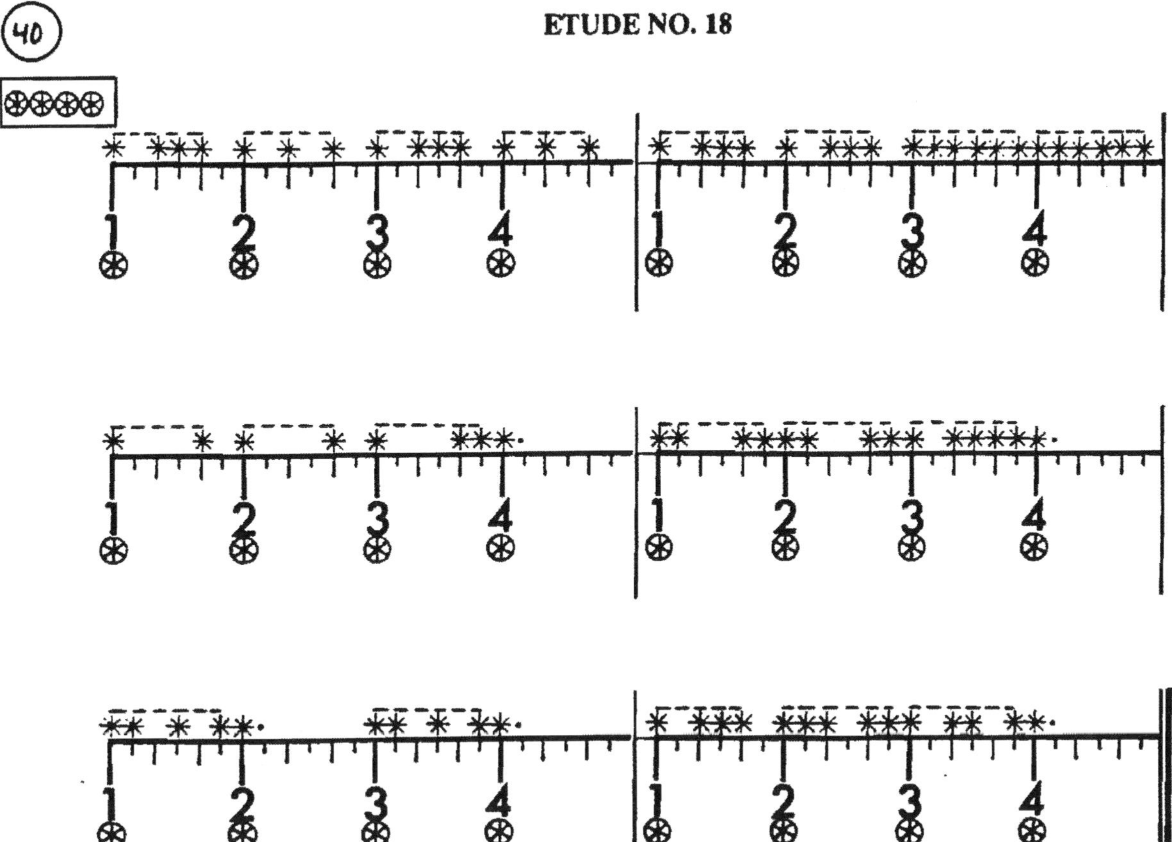

# STANDARD RHYTHMIC NOTATION

The following etudes use standard musical notation.  For the time being, use the following names when referring to these symbols:

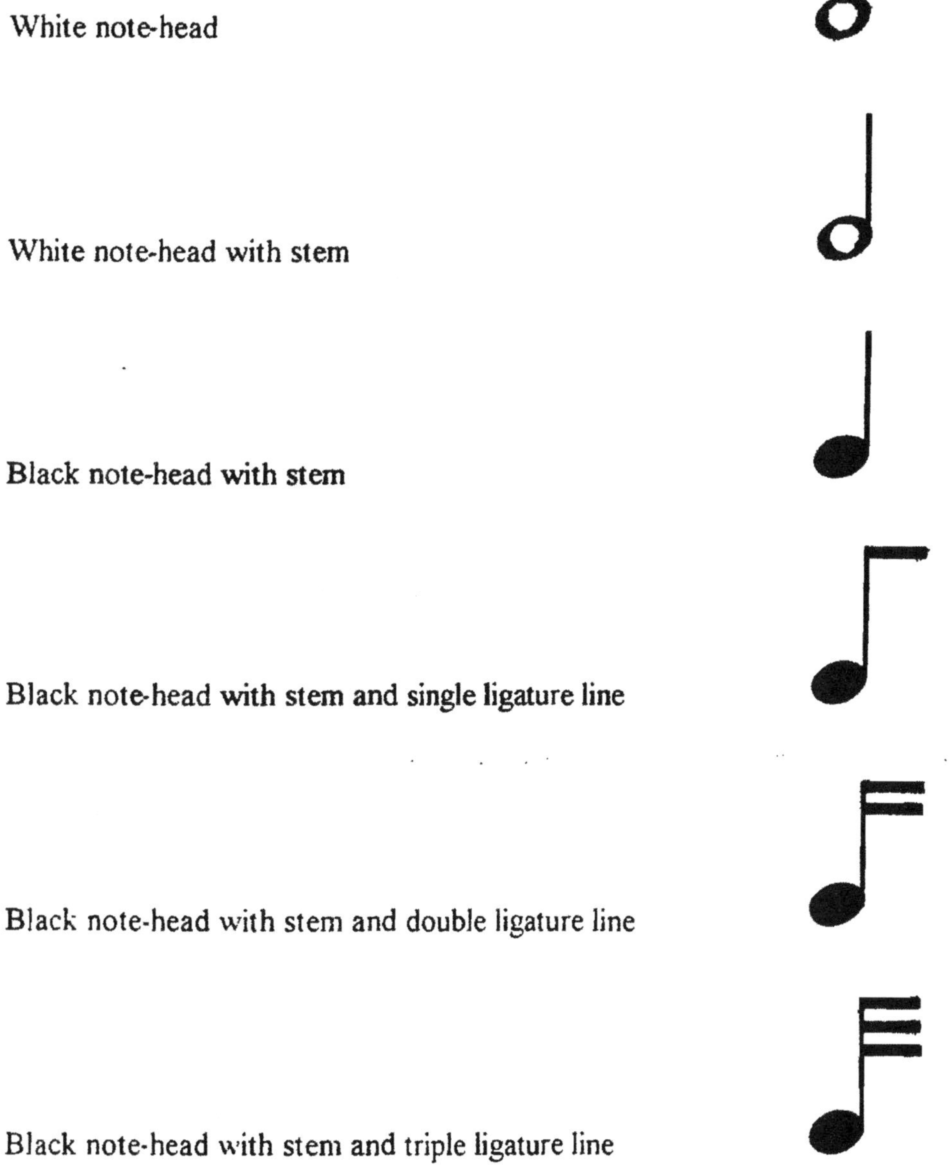

White note-head

White note-head with stem

Black note-head with stem

Black note-head with stem and single ligature line

Black note-head with stem and double ligature line

Black note-head with stem and triple ligature line

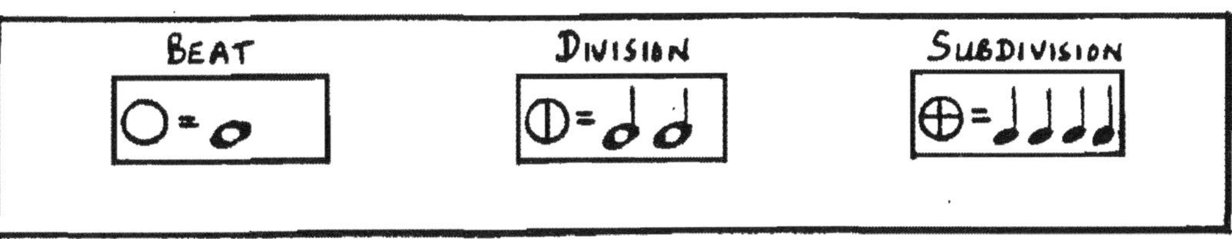

**a.**

**b.**

**c.**

**d.**

**e.**

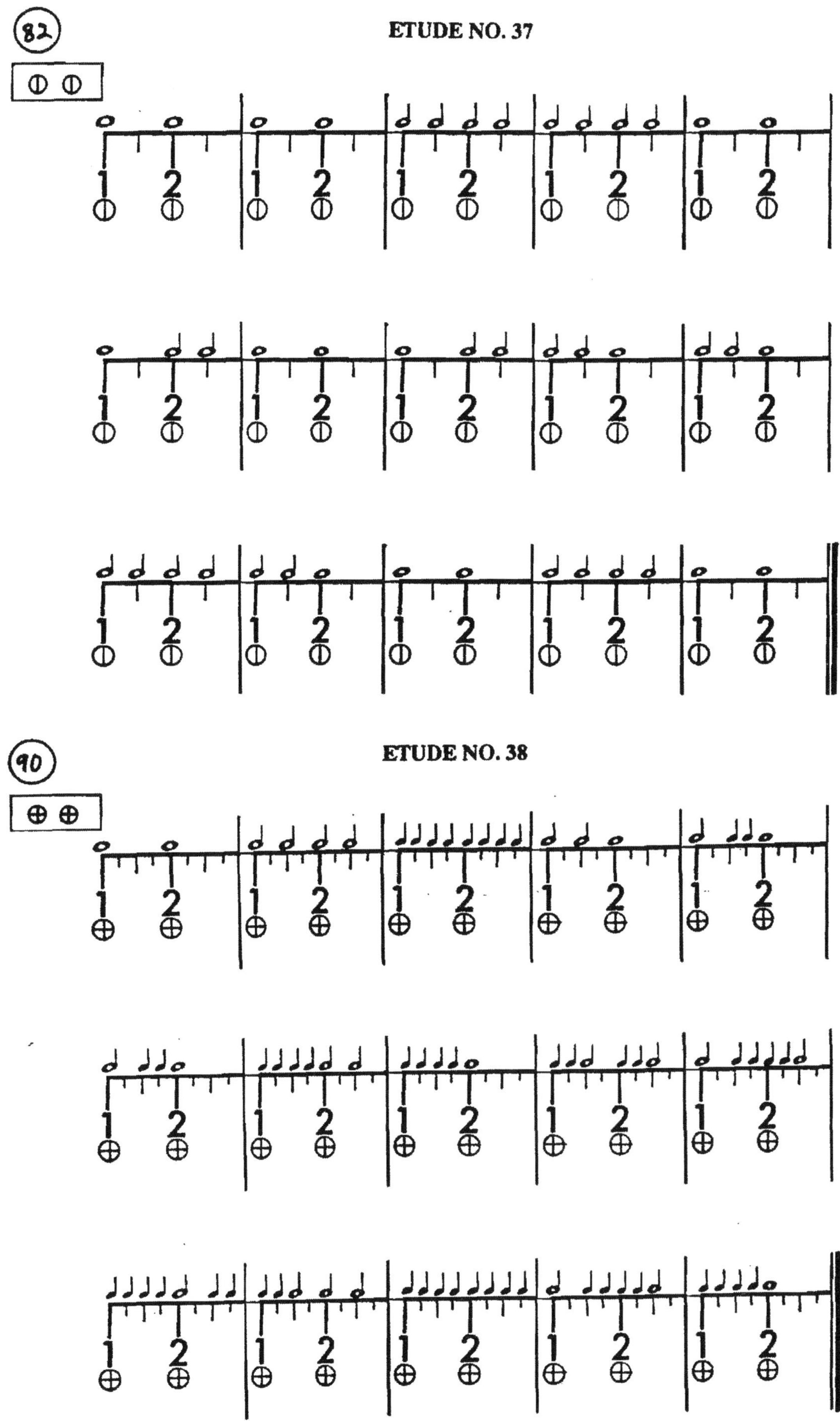
82
ETUDE NO. 37
90
ETUDE NO. 38

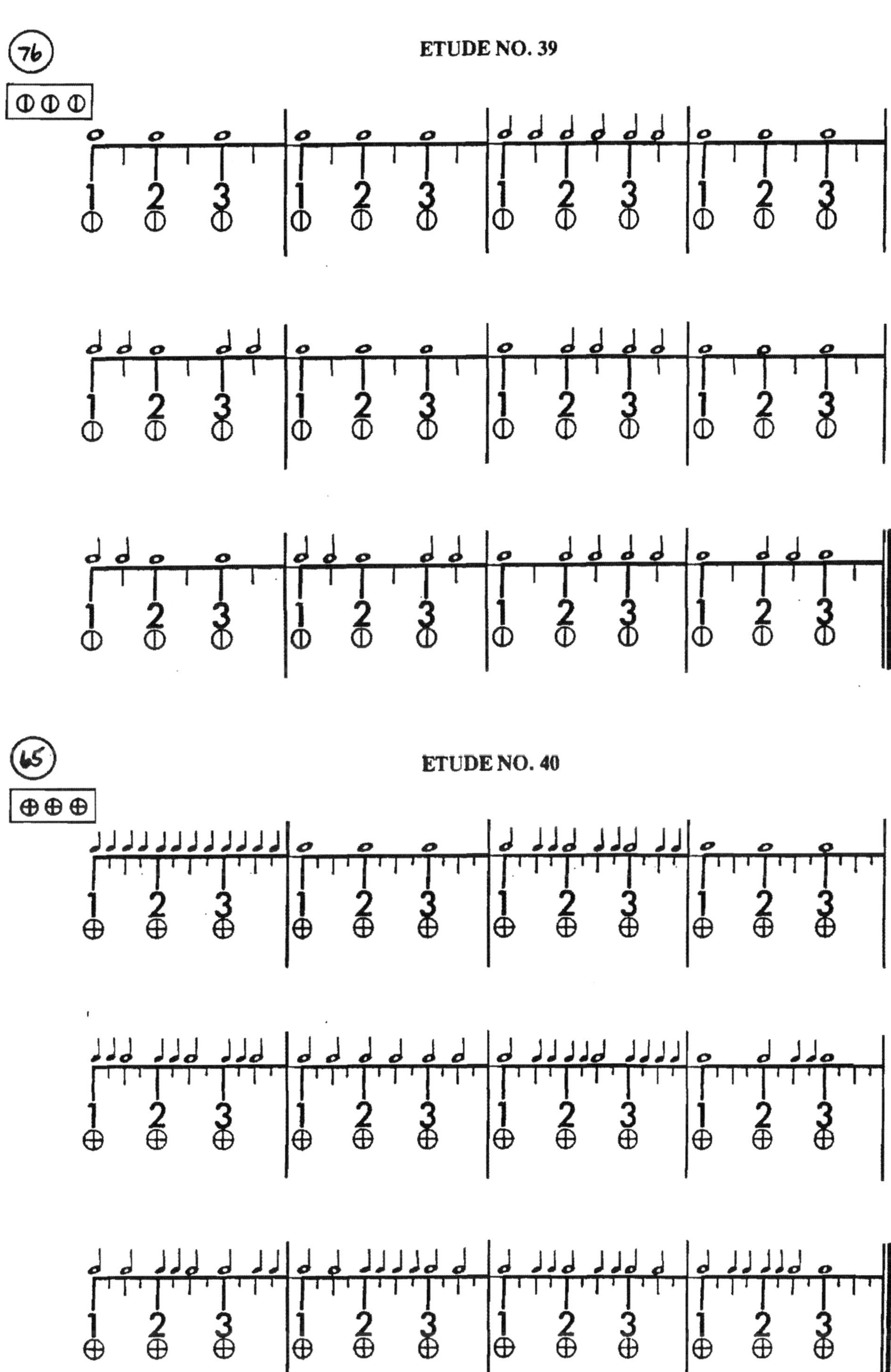
ETUDE NO. 39
76
1 2 3 1 2 3 1 2 3 1 2 3
1 2 3 1 2 3 1 2 3 1 2 3
1 2 3 1 2 3 1 2 3 1 2 3
ETUDE NO. 40
65
1 2 3 1 2 3 1 2 3 1 2 3
1 2 3 1 2 3 1 2 3 1 2 3
1 2 3 1 2 3 1 2 3 1 2 3

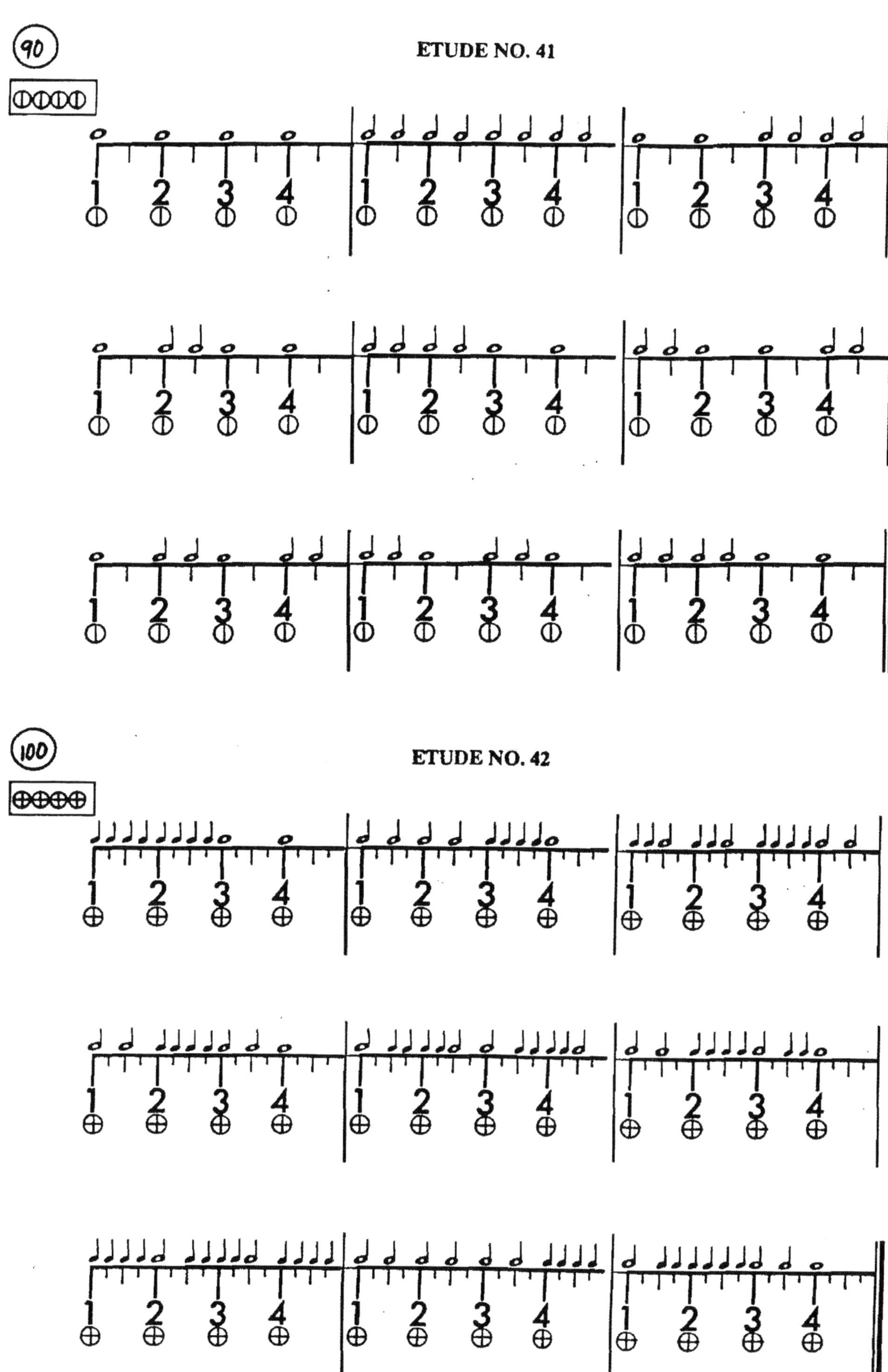
90
ETUDE NO. 41
100
ETUDE NO. 42

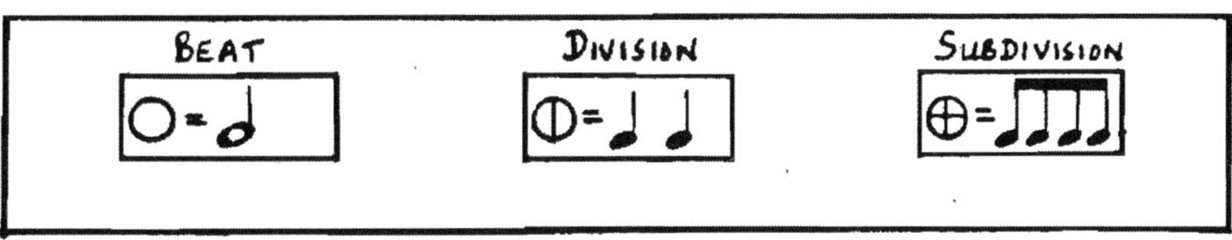


**a.**

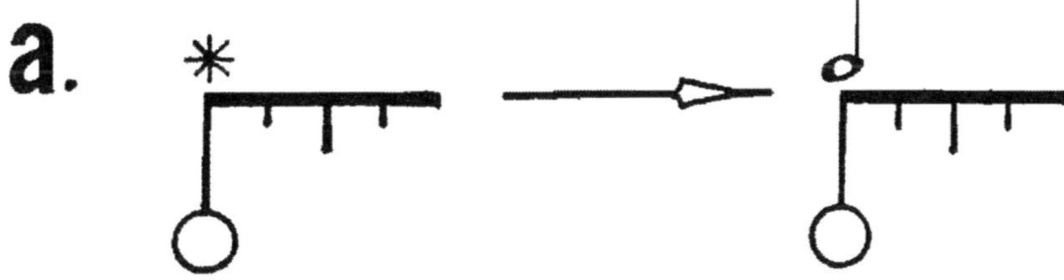

**b.**

**c.**

**d.**

**e.**

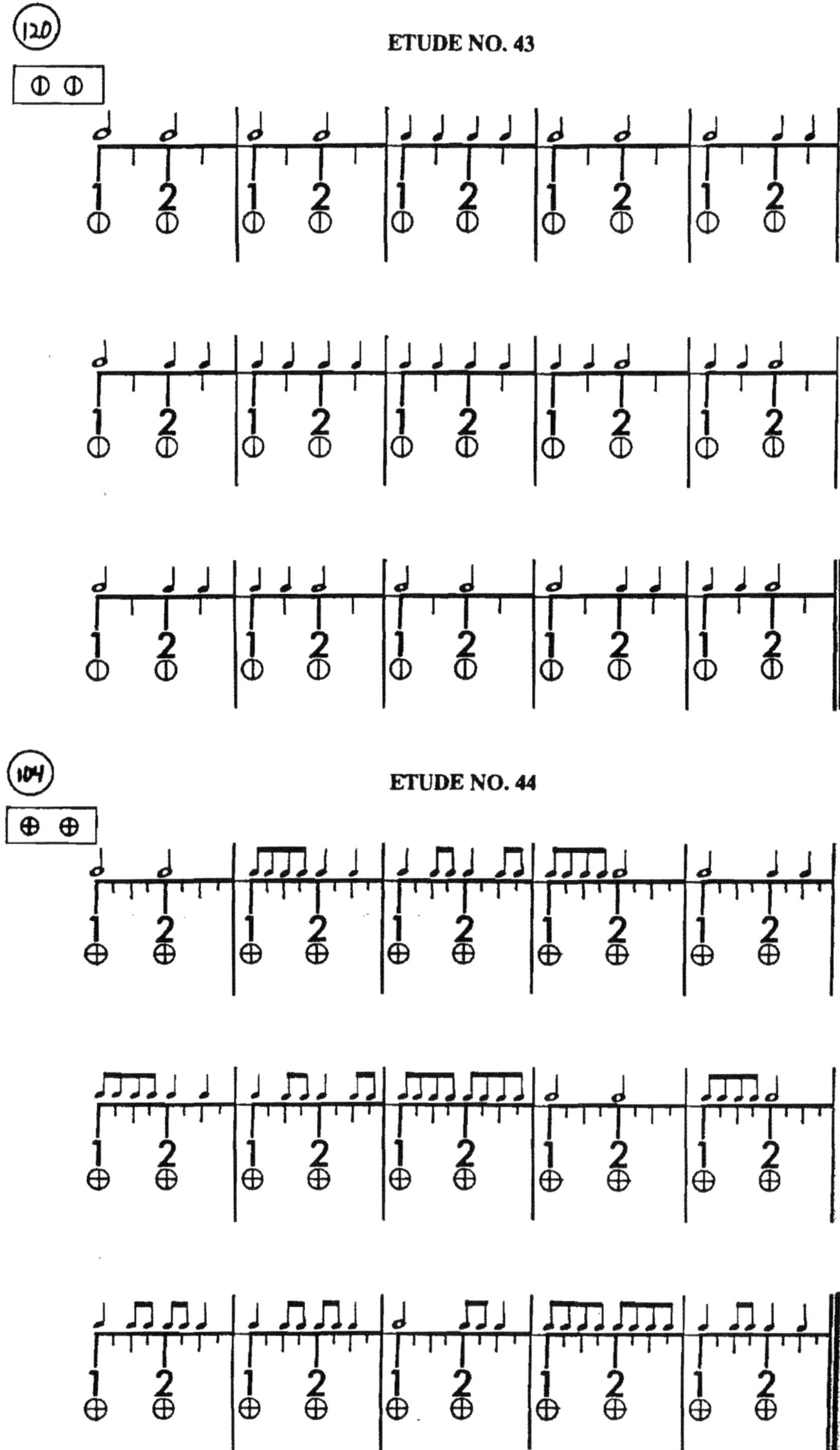
ETUDE NO. 43
ETUDE NO. 44

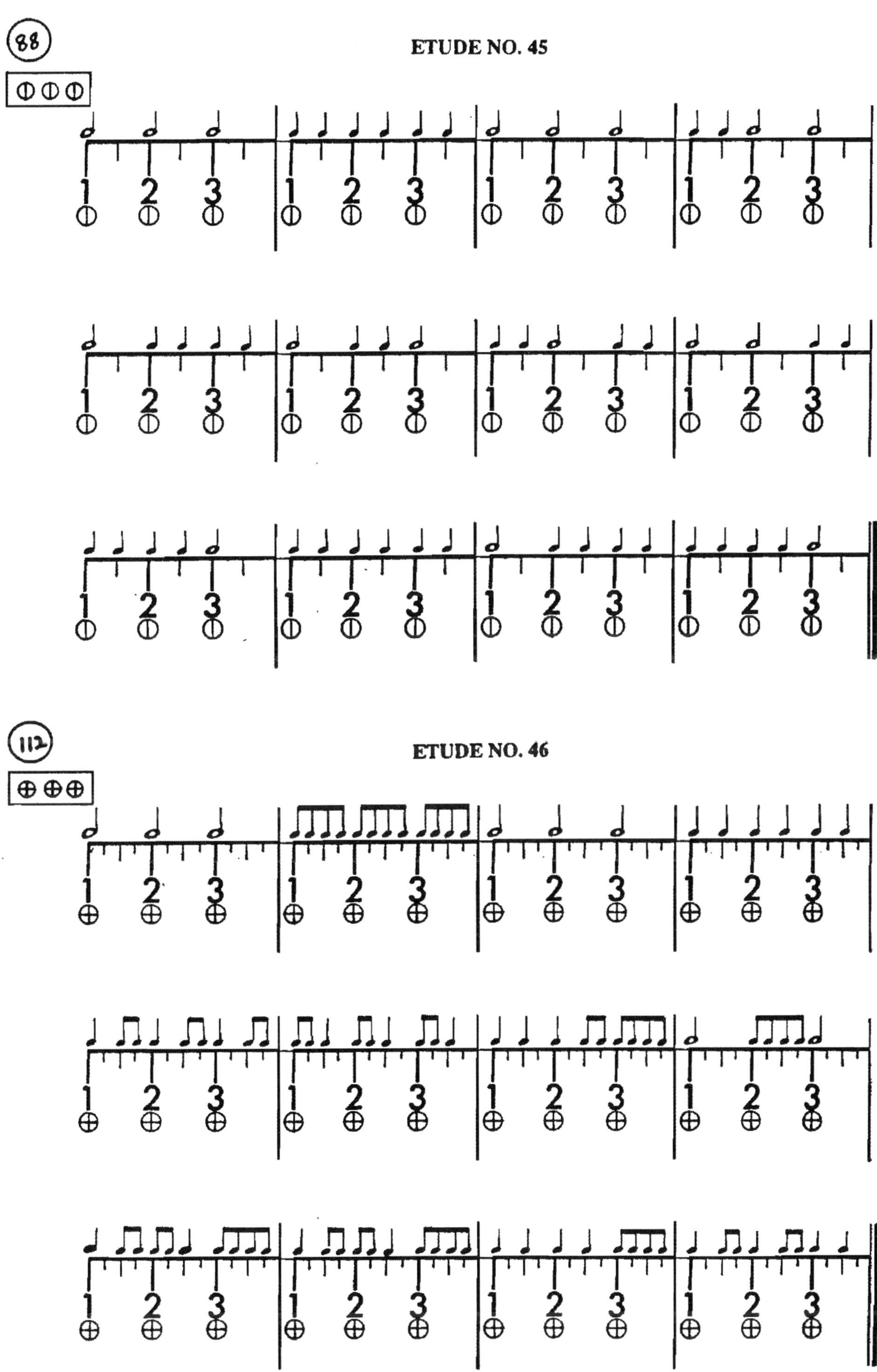


ETUDE NO. 45
ETUDE NO. 46

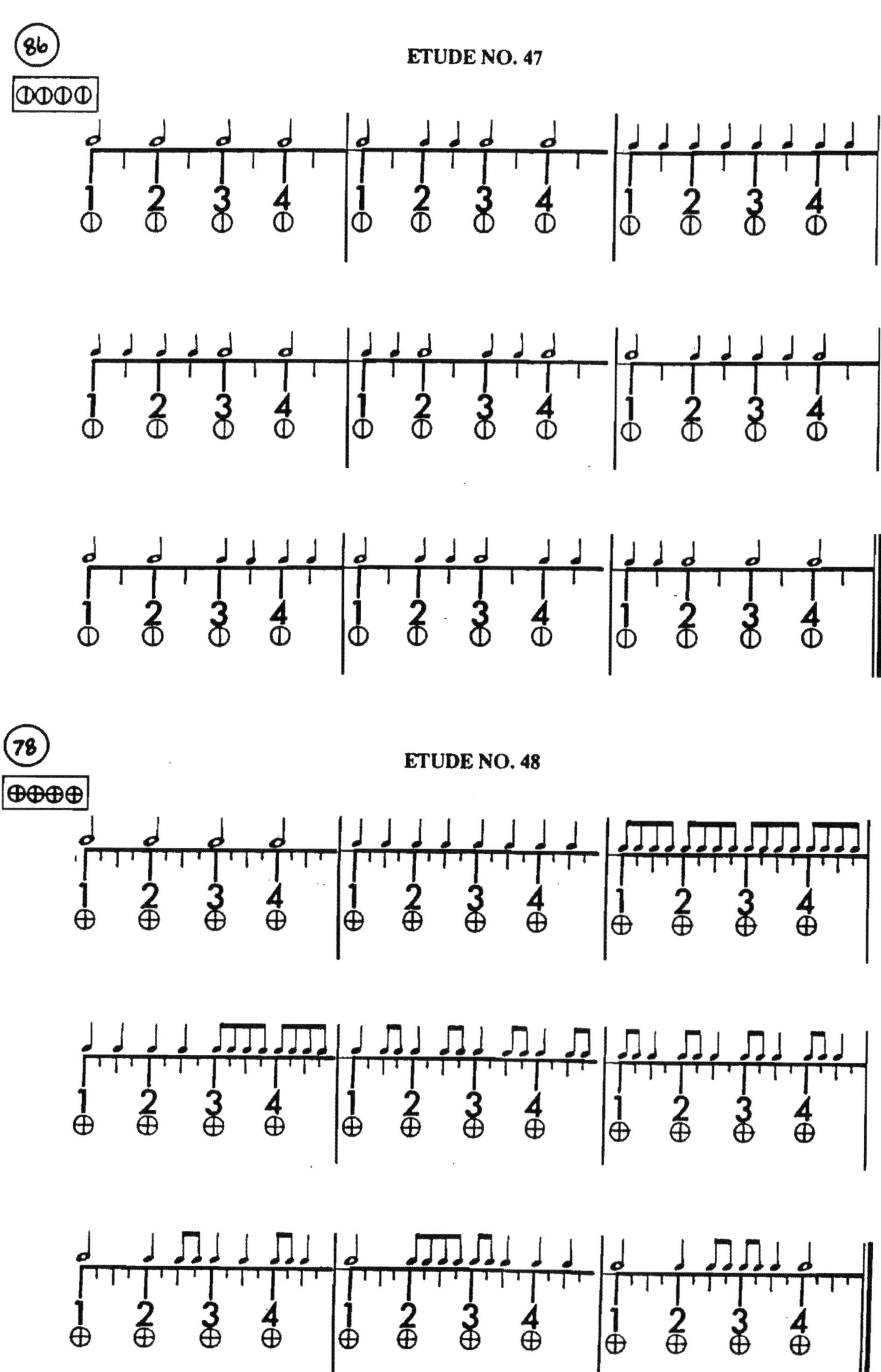
ETUDE NO. 47
ETUDE NO. 48

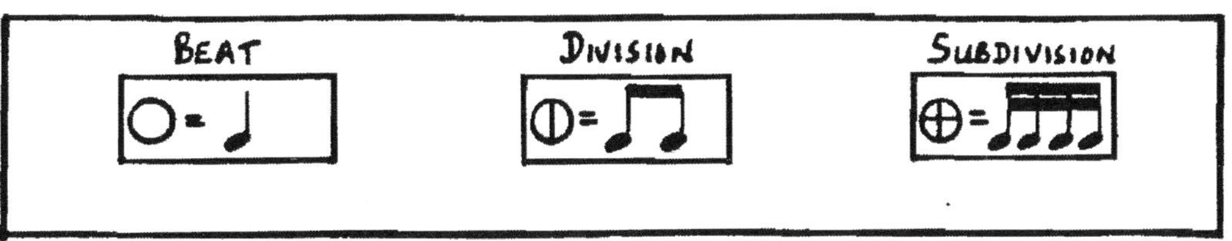


**a.**

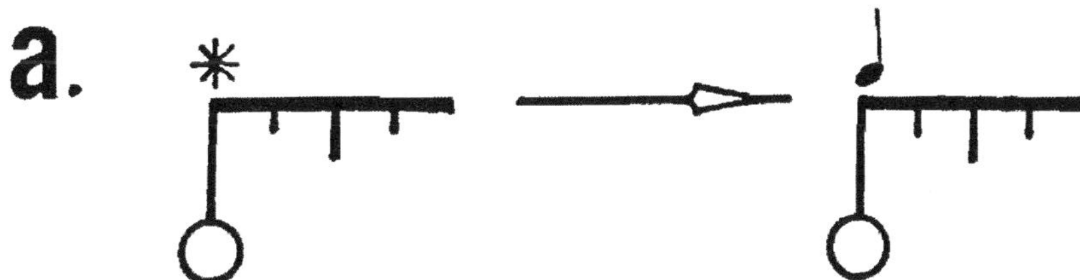

**b.**

**c.**

**d.**

**e.**

ETUDE NO. 49

ETUDE NO. 50

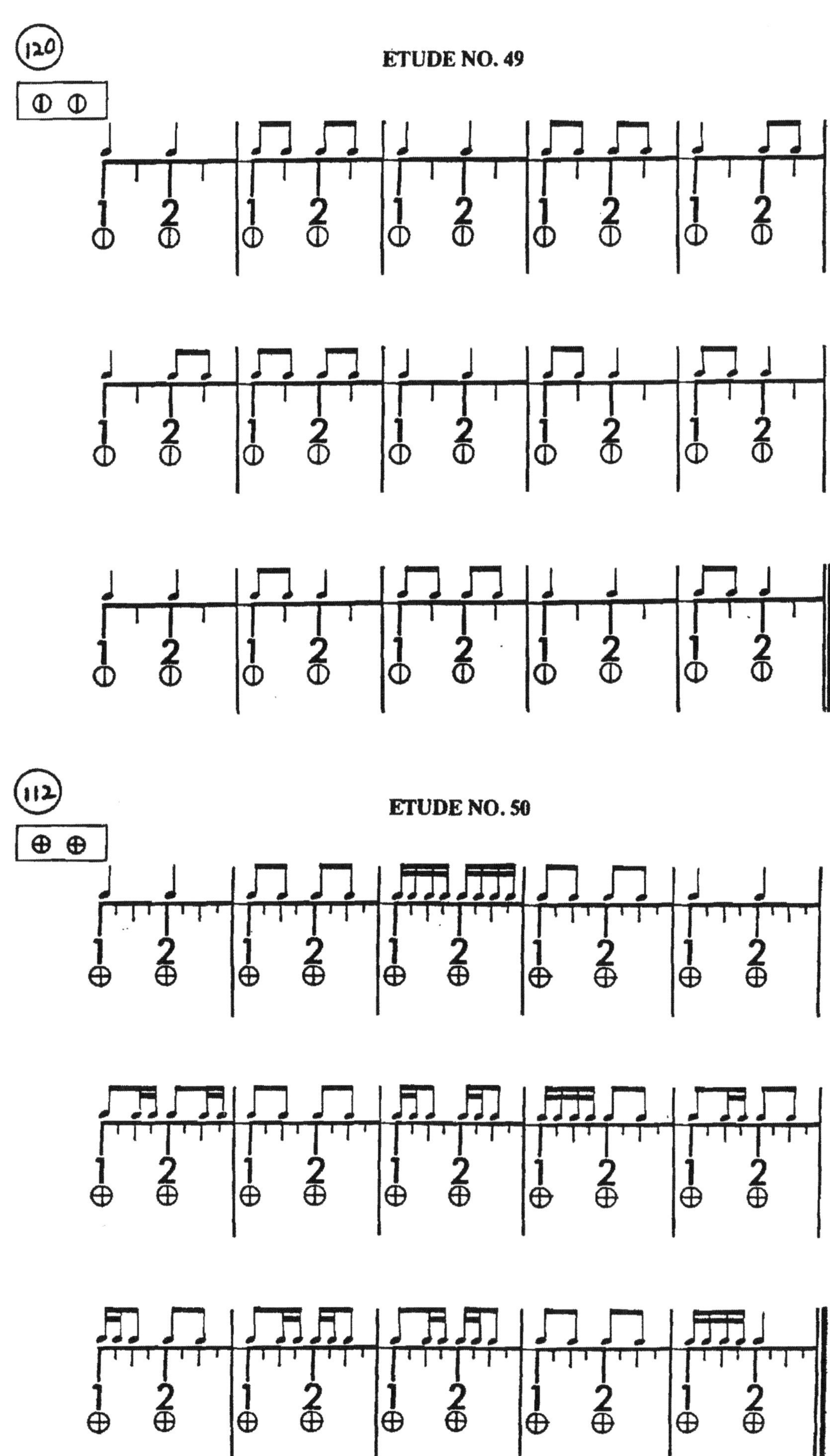

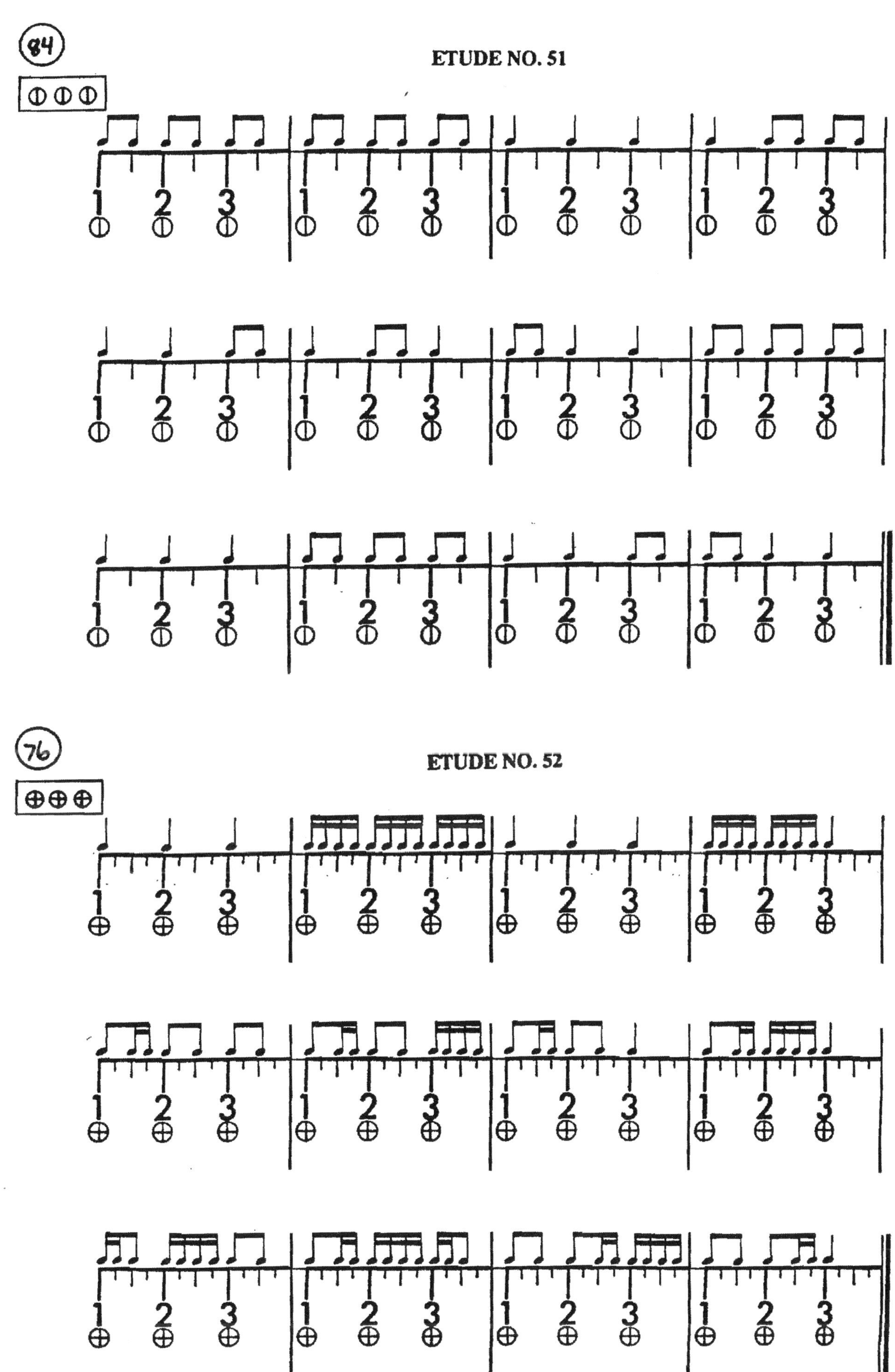
84
ETUDE NO. 51
76
ETUDE NO. 52

**ETUDE NO. 53**

**ETUDE NO. 54**

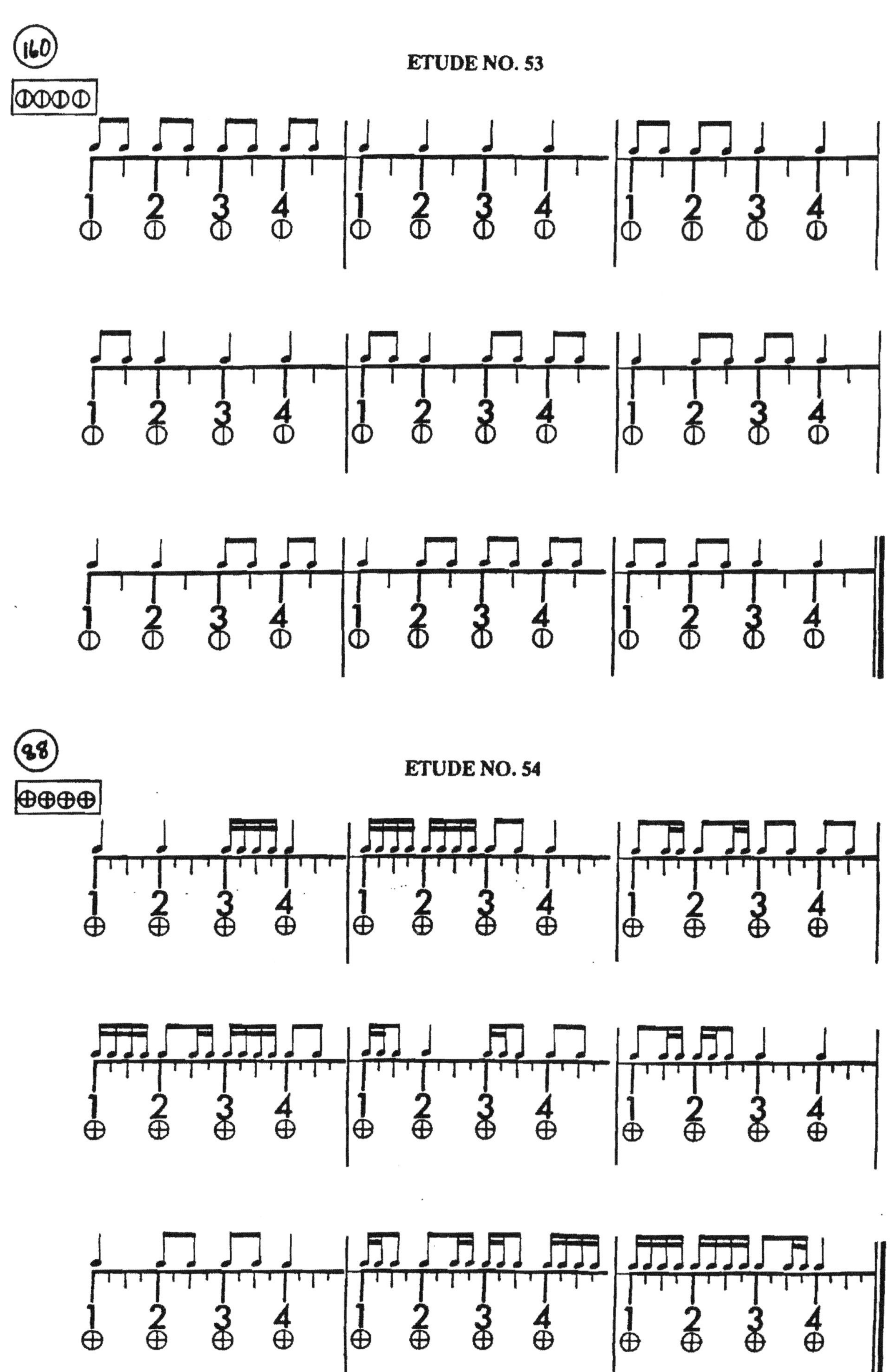

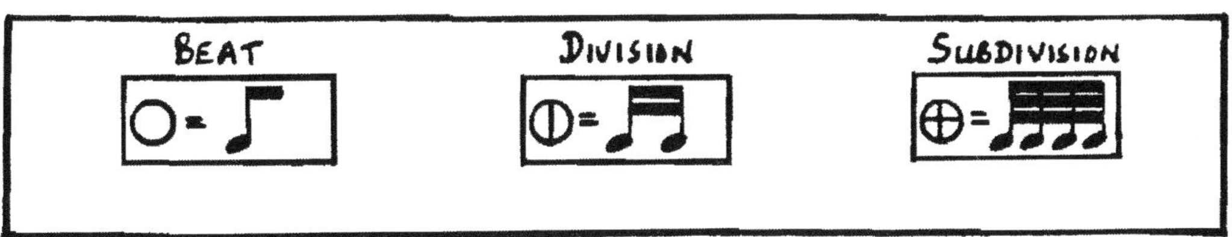


**a.**

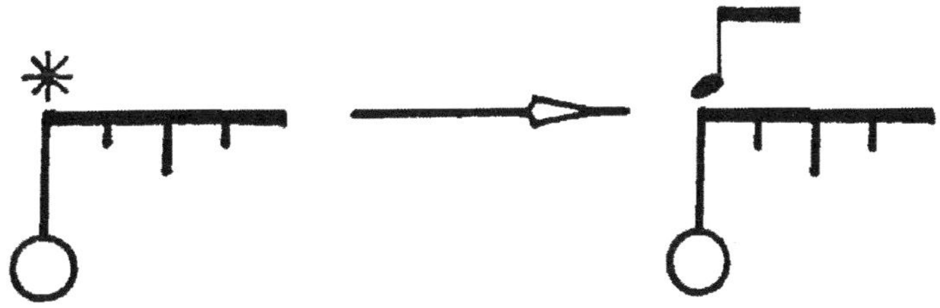

**b.**

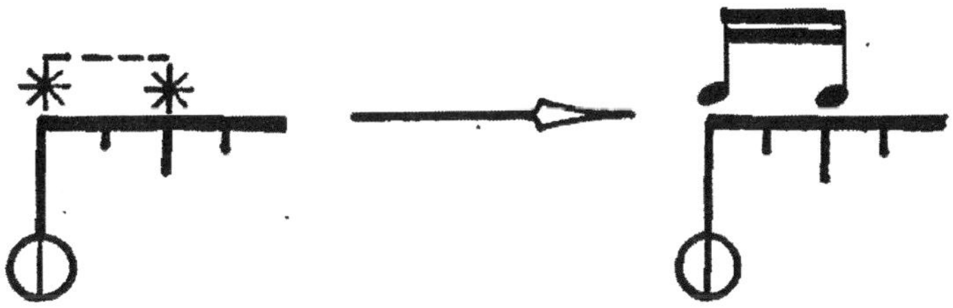

**c.**

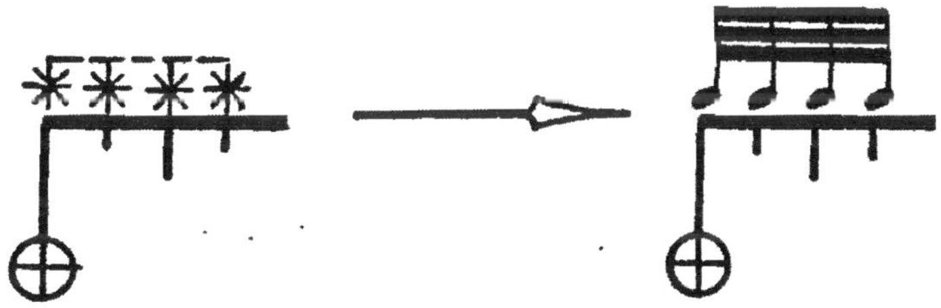

**d.**

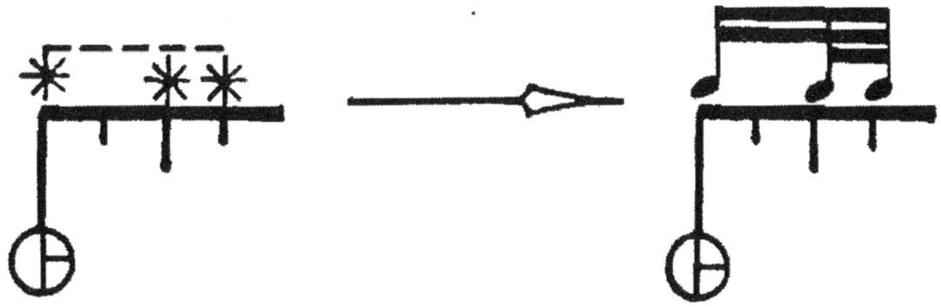

**e.**

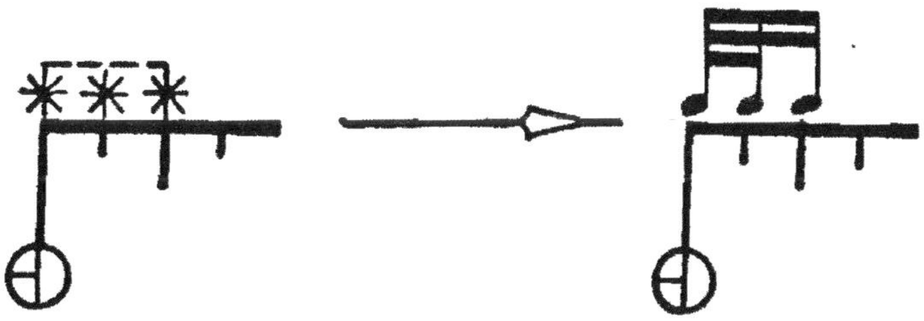

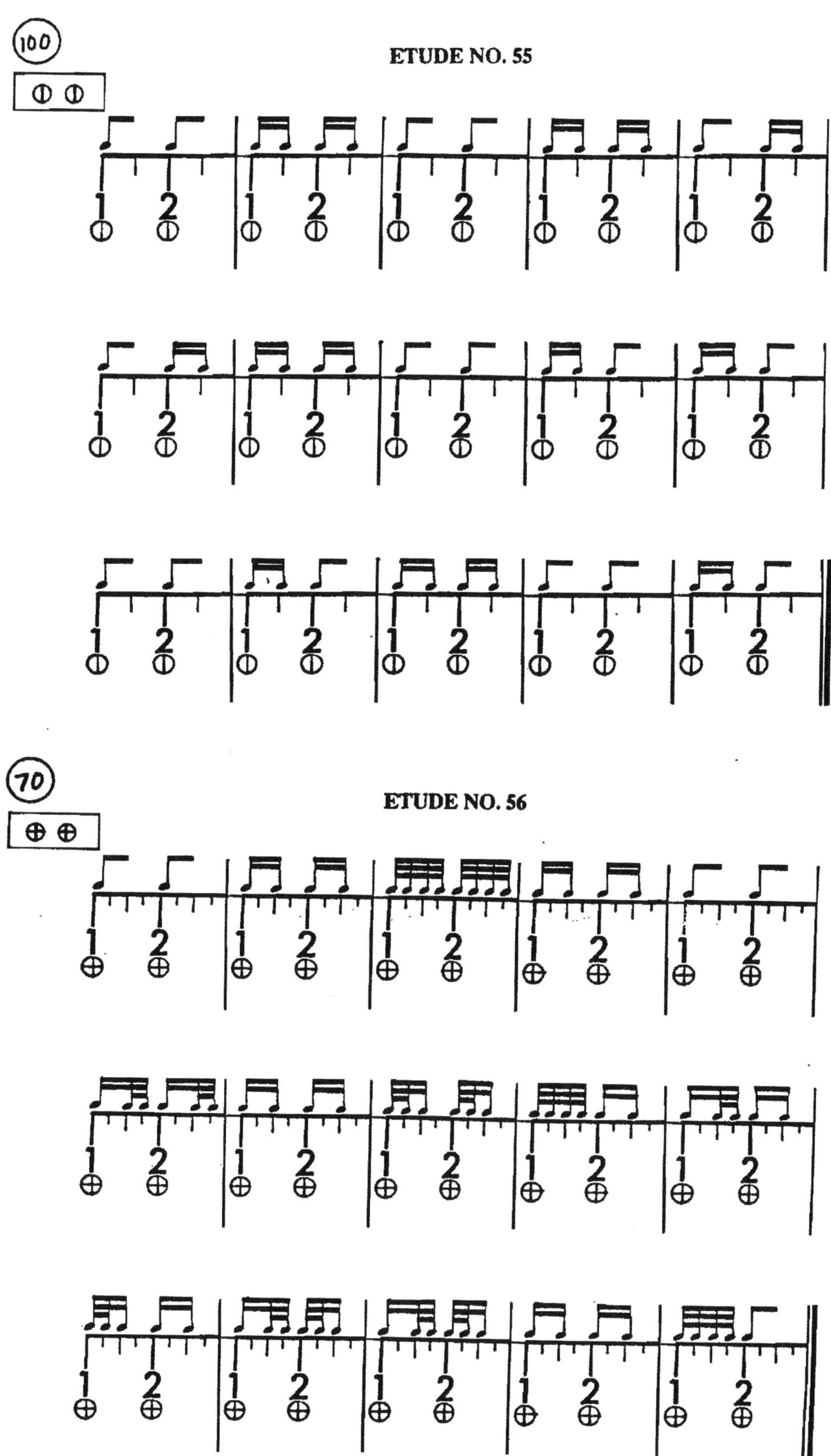
100
ETUDE NO. 55
70
ETUDE NO. 56

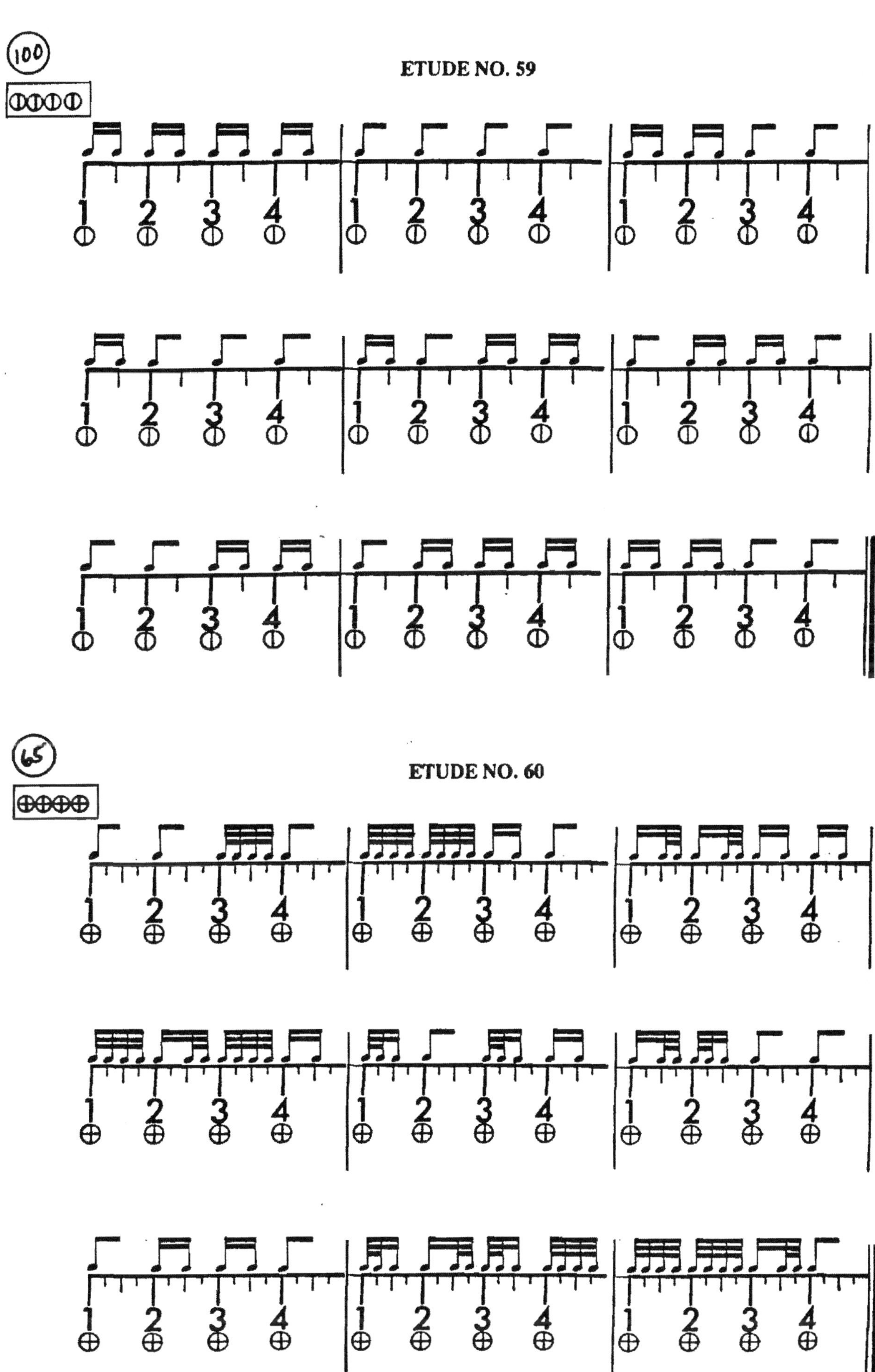
ETUDE NO. 59
ETUDE NO. 60

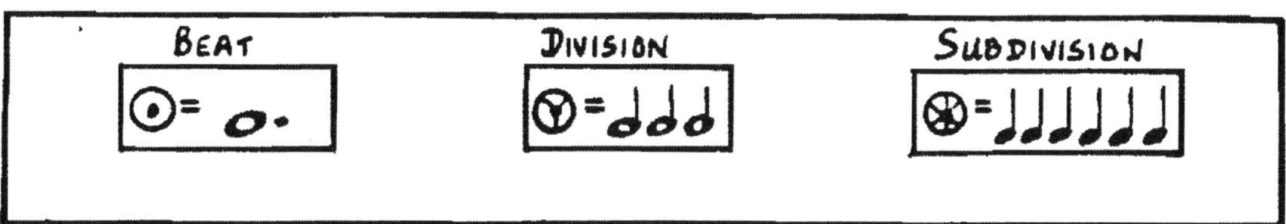


a.

b.

c.

d.

e.

**f.**

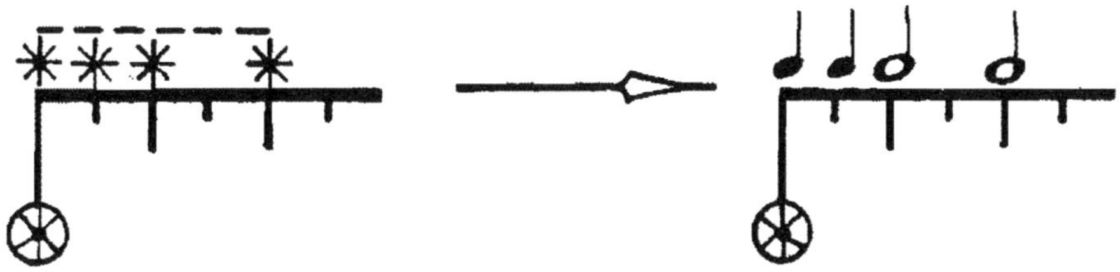

**g.**

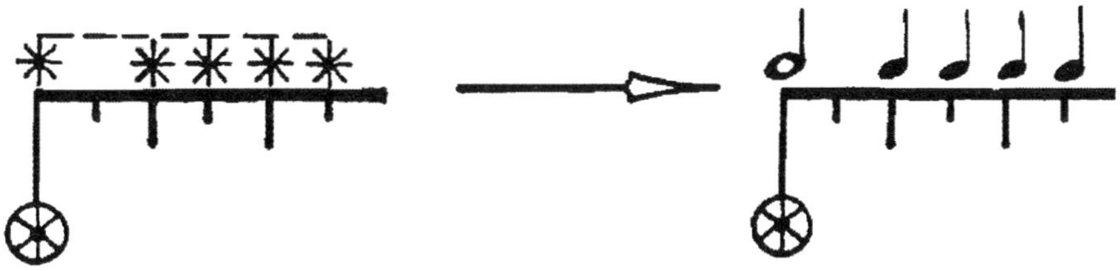

**h.**

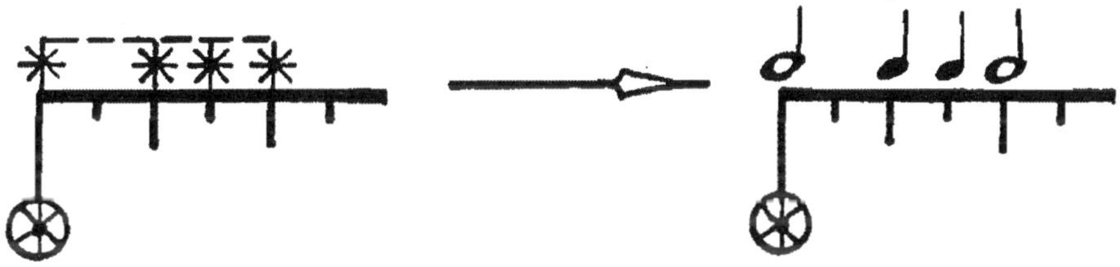

**i.**

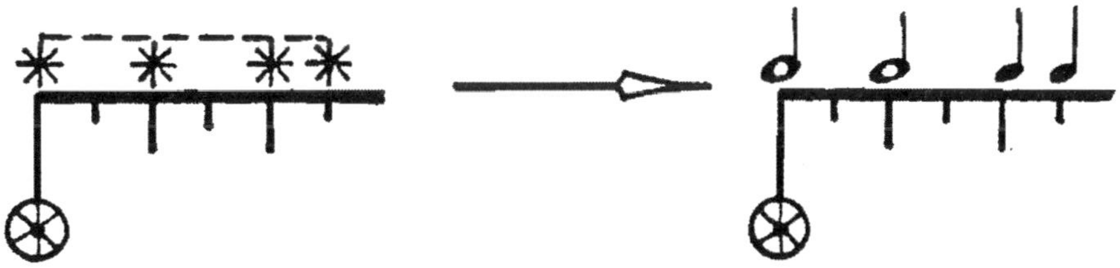

**j.**

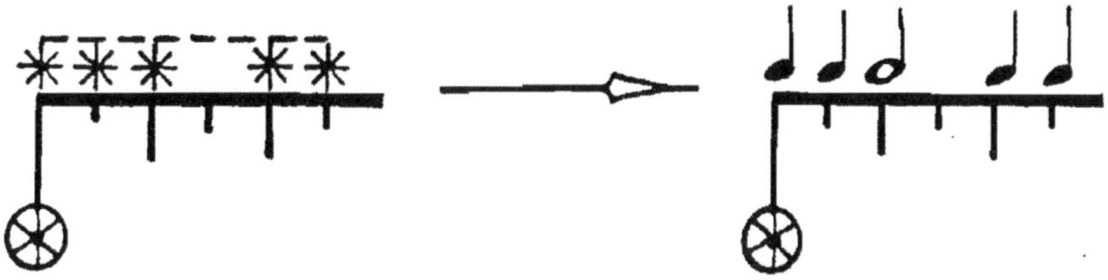

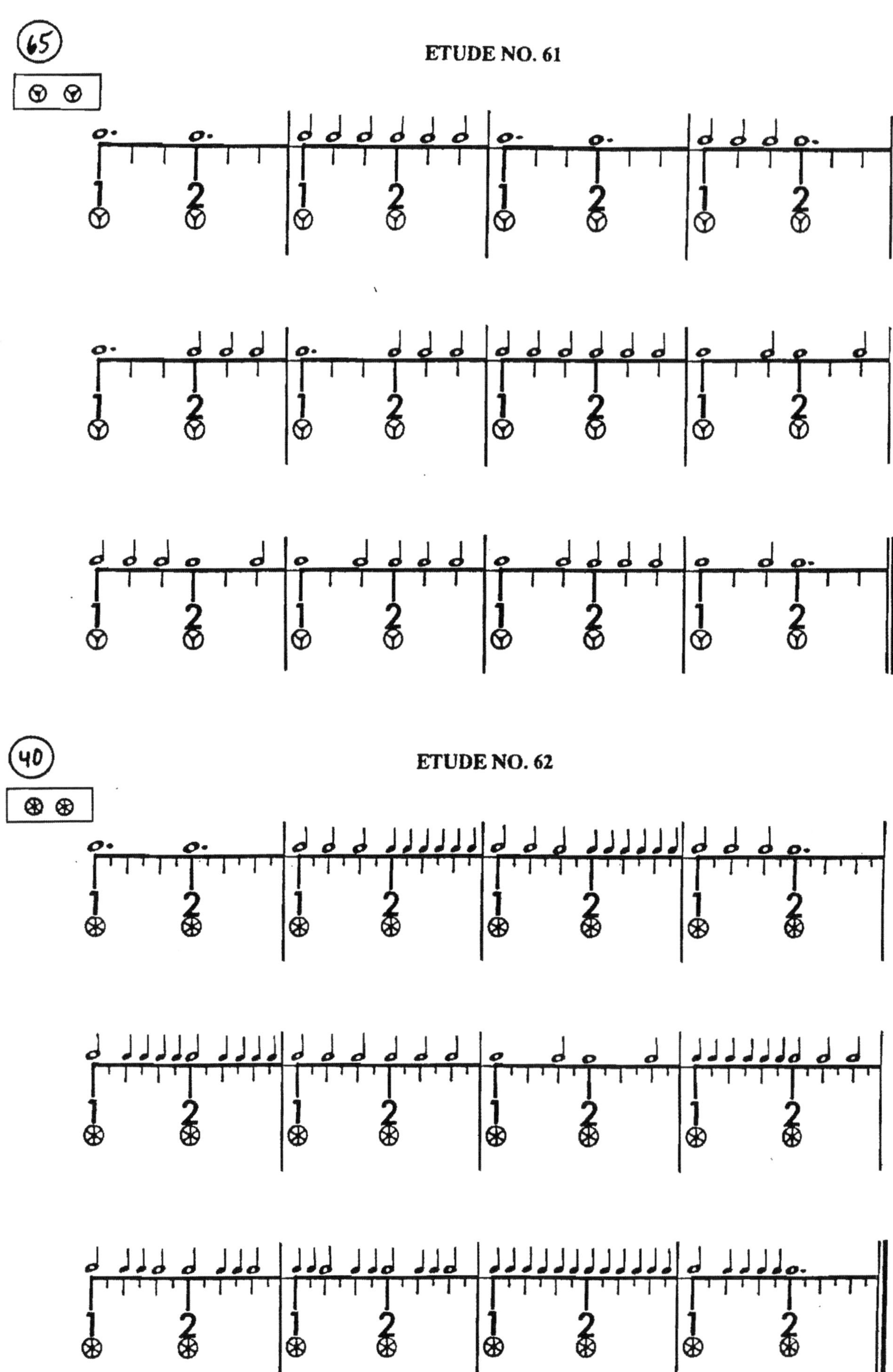
ETUDE NO. 61
ETUDE NO. 62

**ETUDE NO. 63**

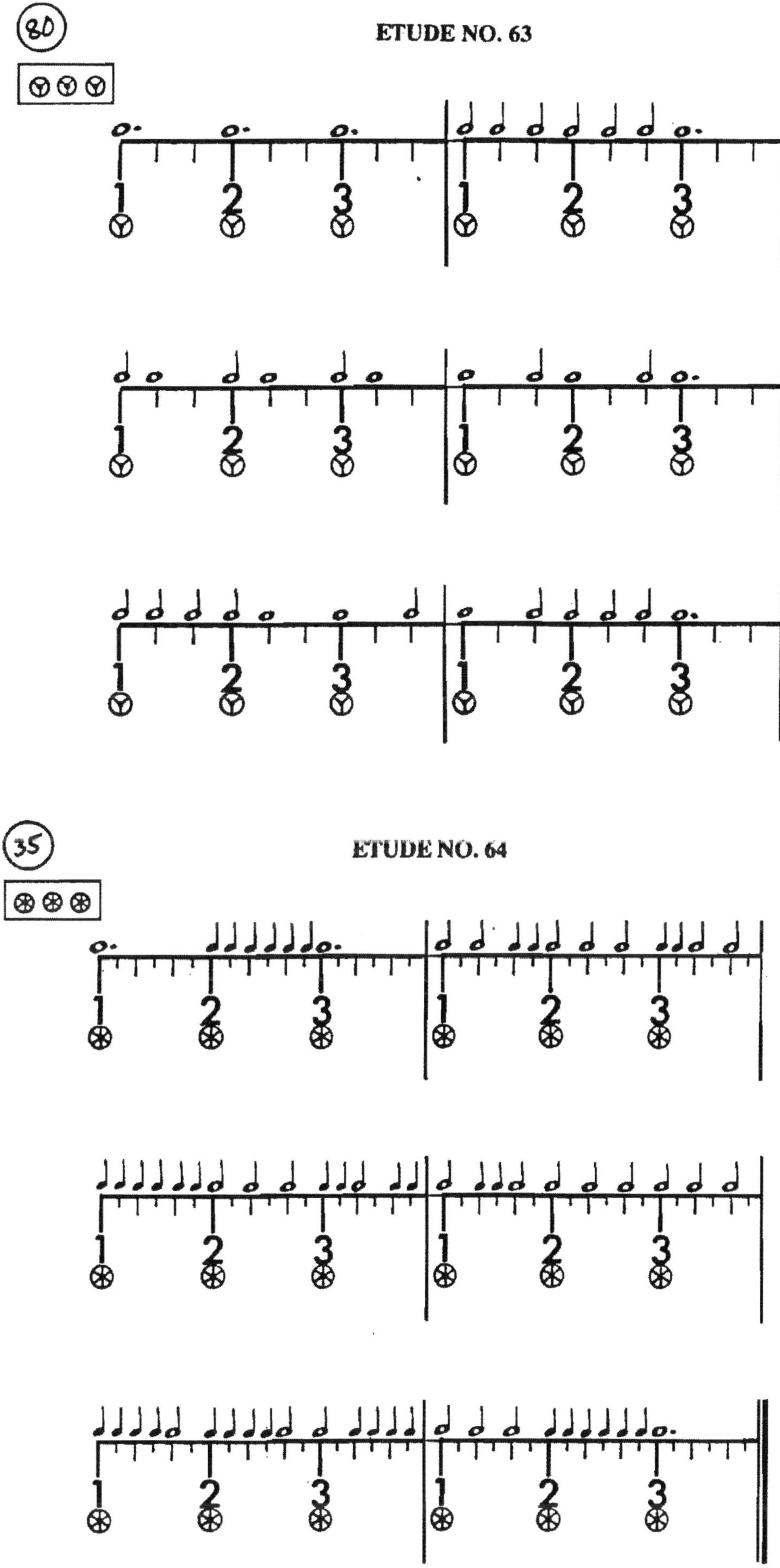

**ETUDE NO. 64**

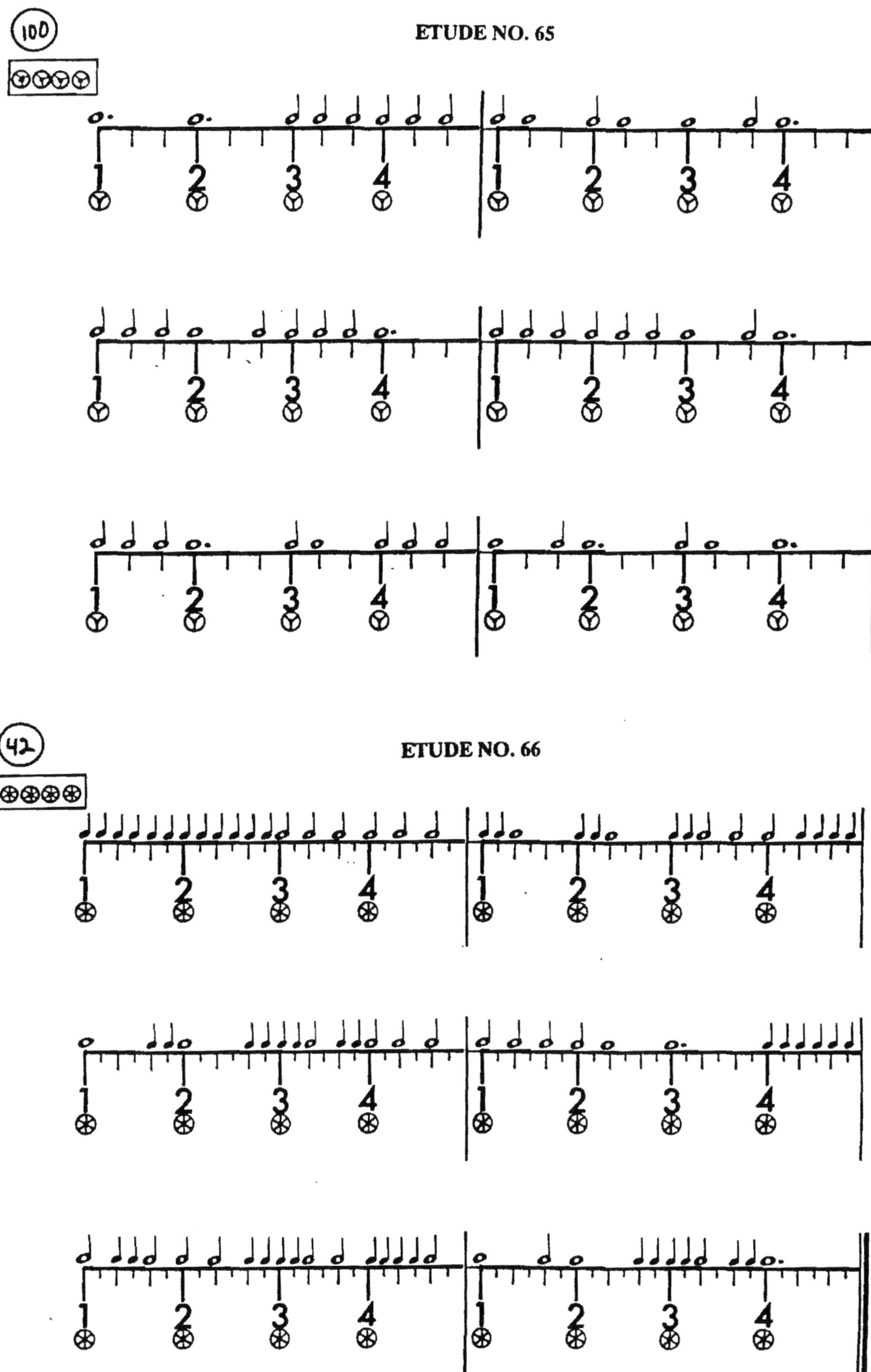
ETUDE NO. 65
ETUDE NO. 66

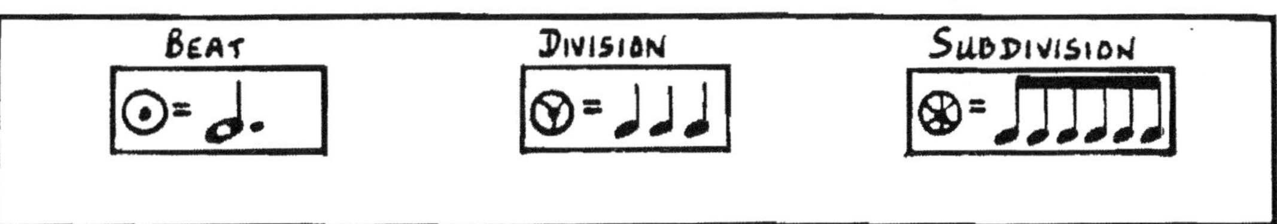

BEAT
DIVISION
SUBDIVISION


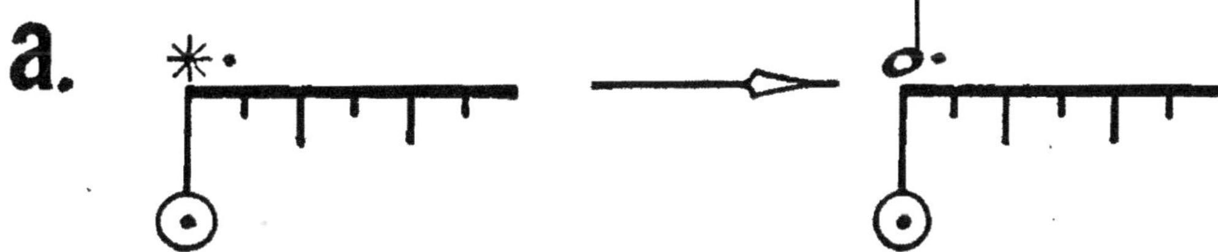


a.

b.

c.

d.

e.

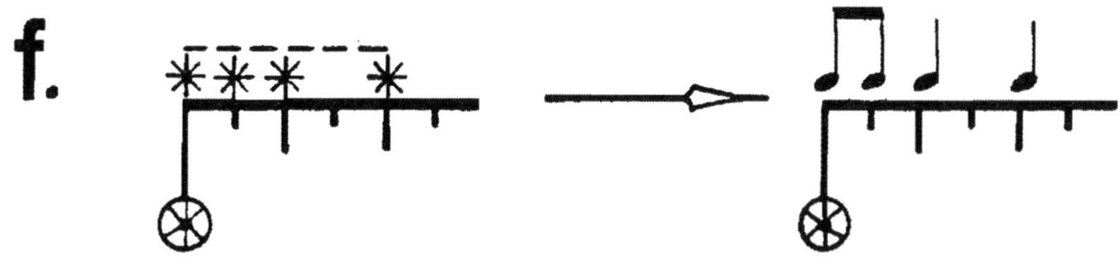

**ETUDE NO. 67**

**ETUDE NO. 68**

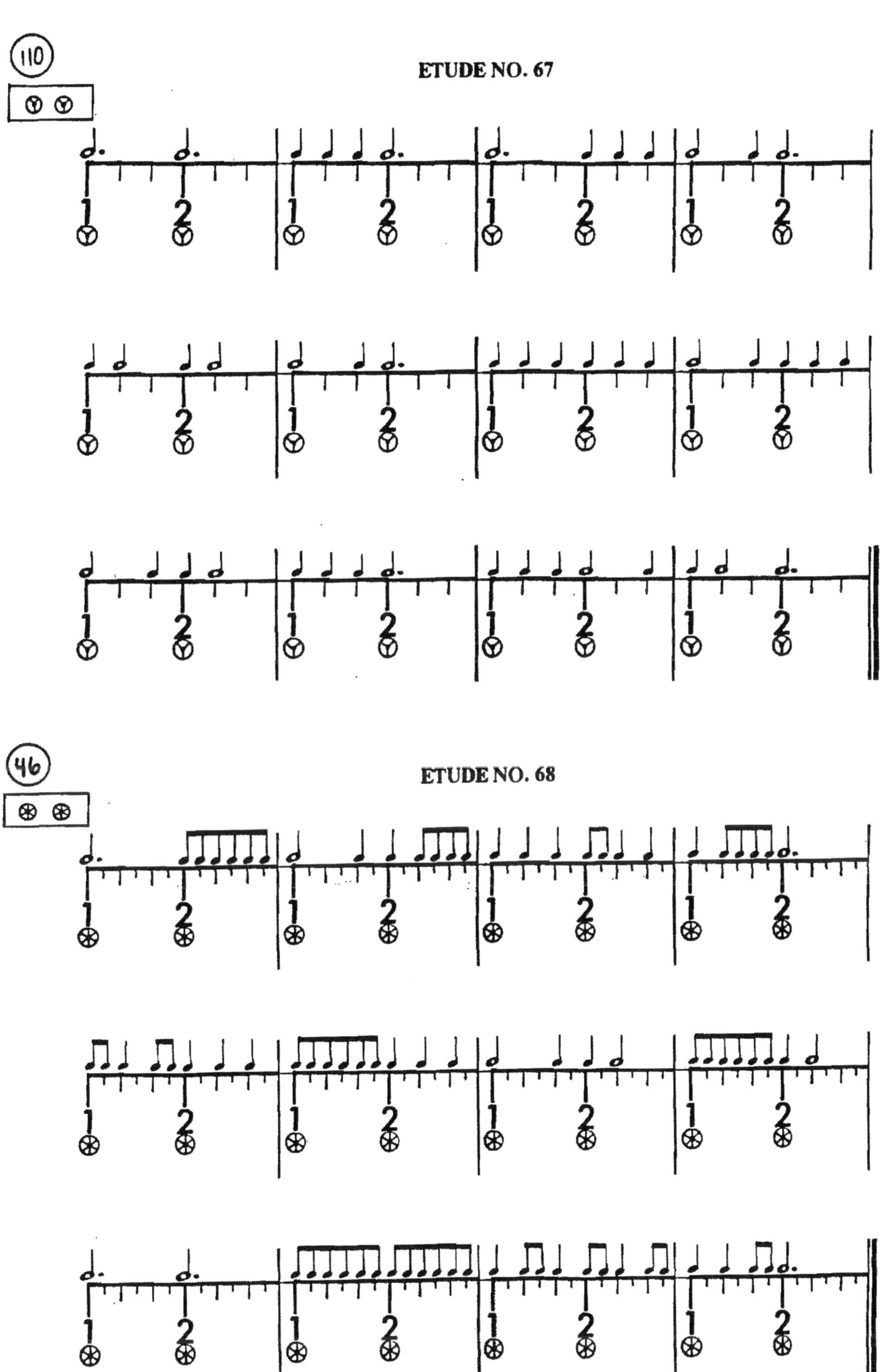

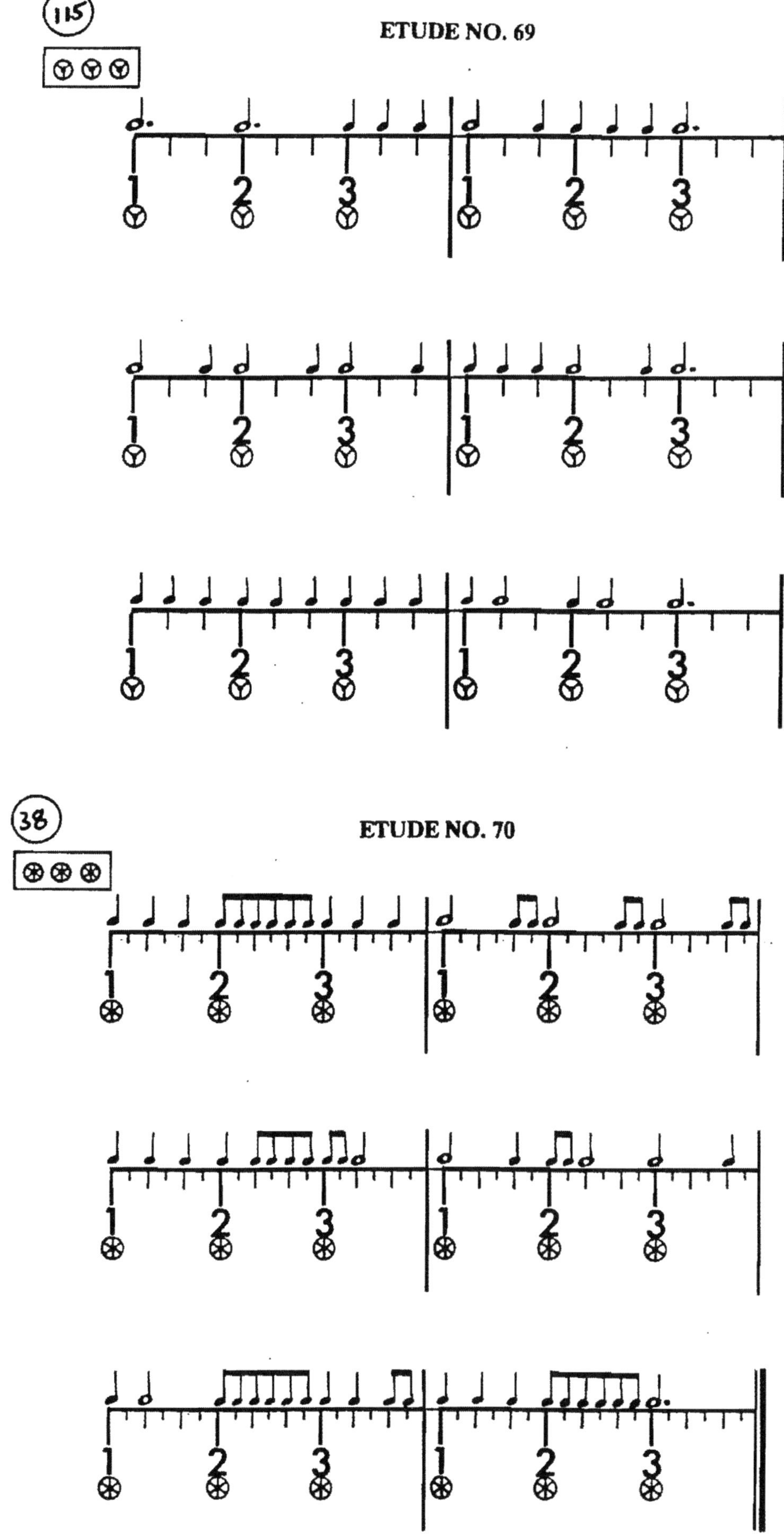
115
ETUDE NO. 69
1 2 3 1 2 3
1 2 3 1 2 3
1 2 3 1 2 3
38
ETUDE NO. 70
1 2 3 1 2 3
1 2 3 1 2 3
1 2 3 1 2 3

ETUDE NO. 71

ETUDE NO. 72

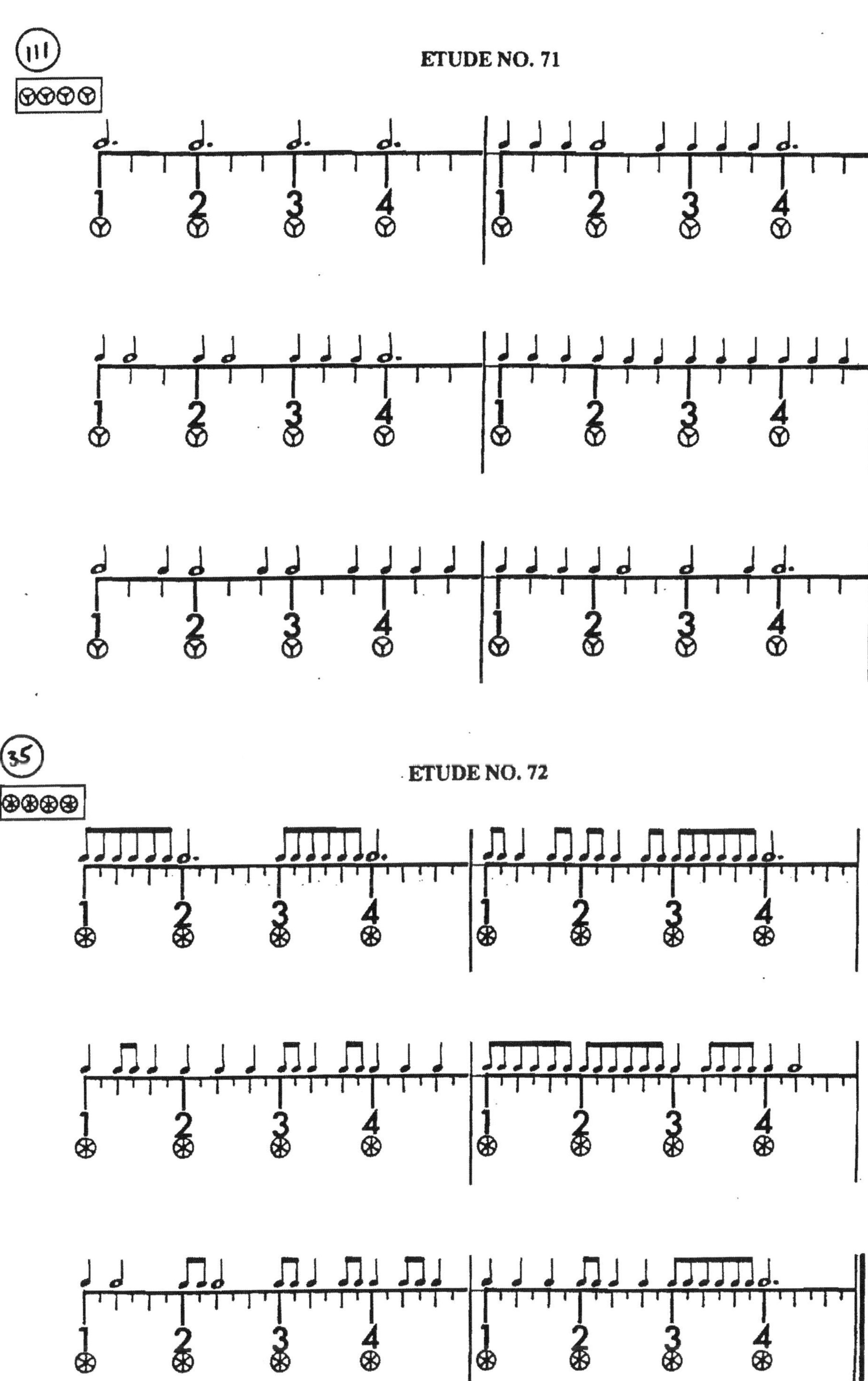

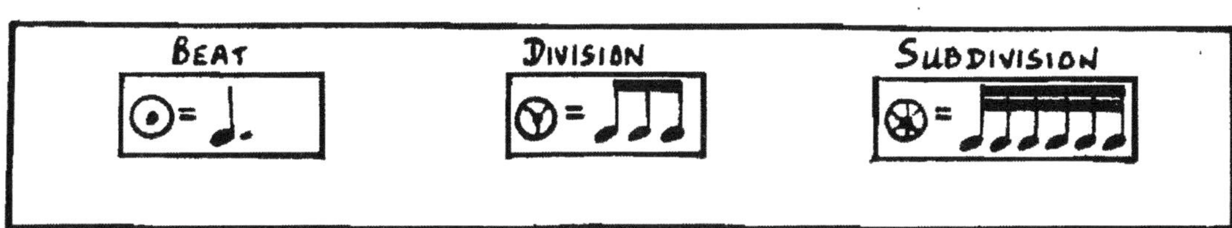

BEAT
DIVISION
SUBDIVISION


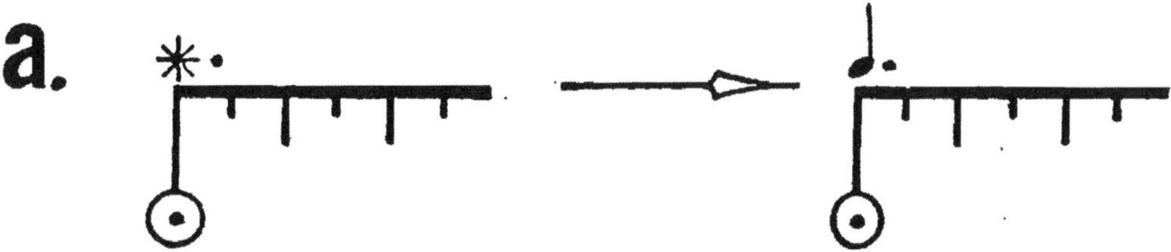

a.
b.
c.
d.
e.

**f.**

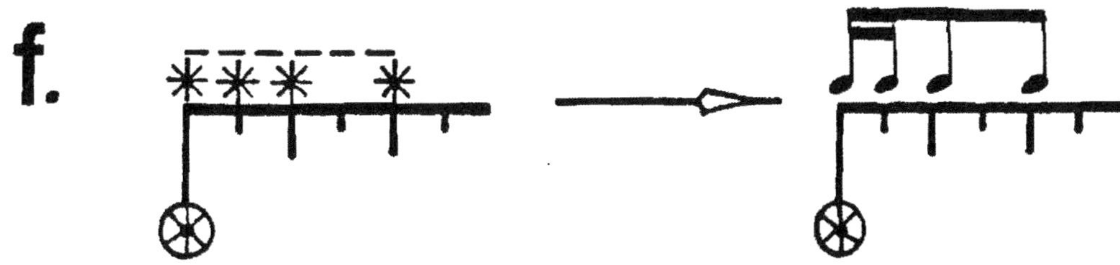

**g.**

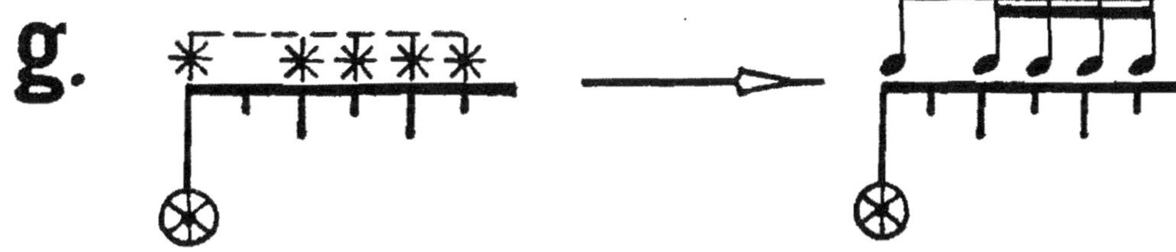

**h.**

**i.**

**j.**

**Measured Music**

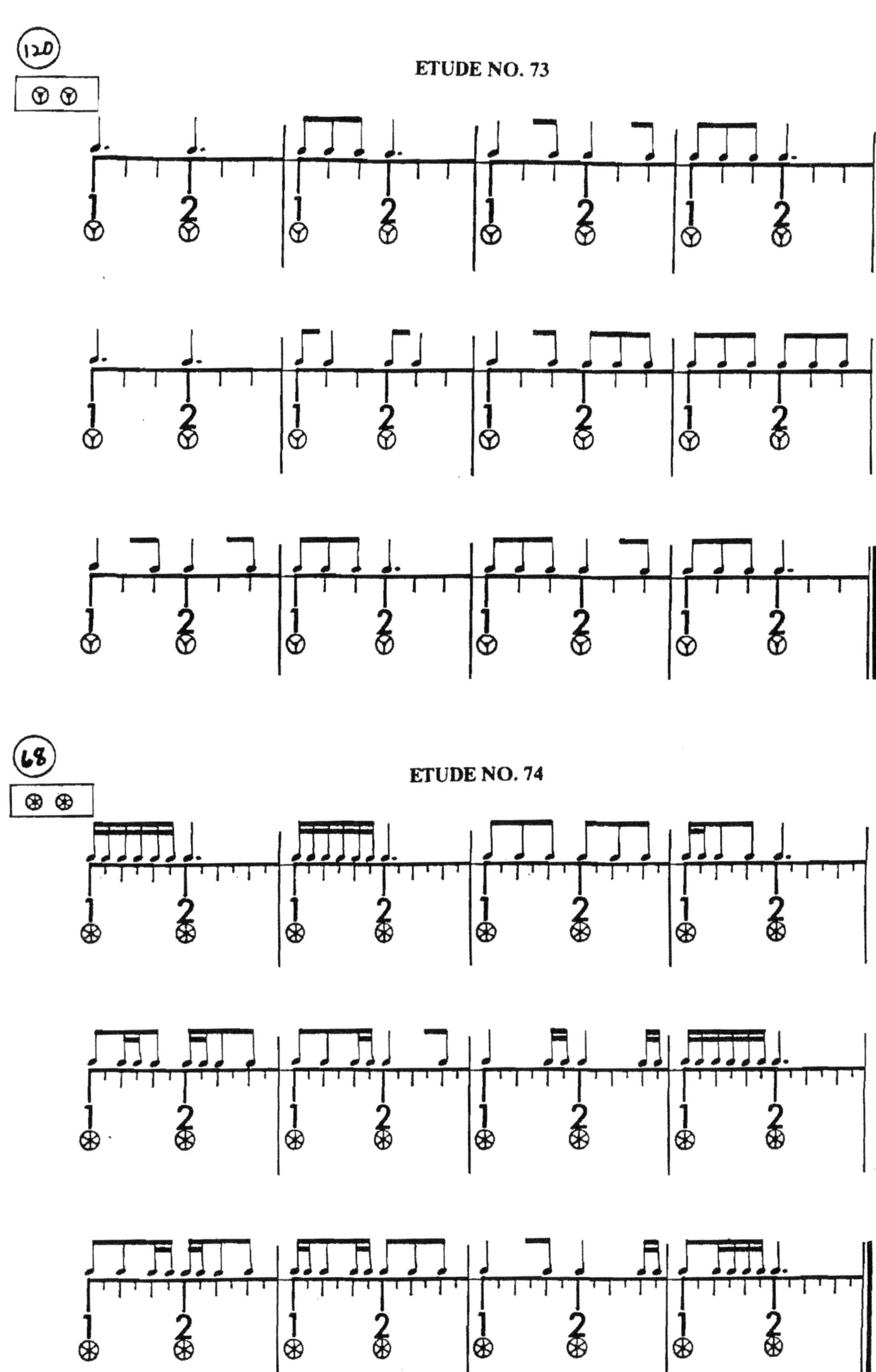

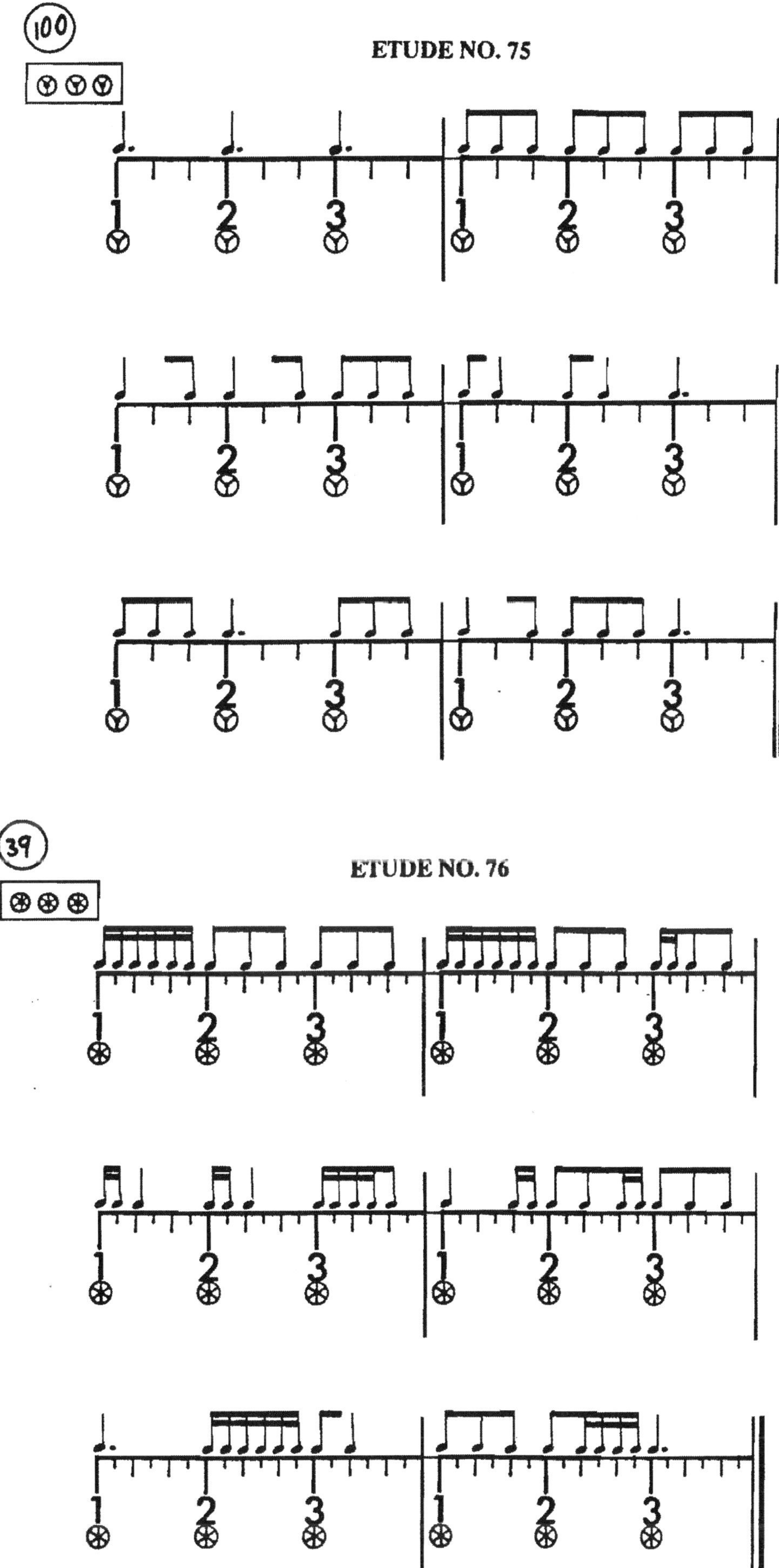
ETUDE NO. 75
ETUDE NO. 76

## ETUDE NO. 77

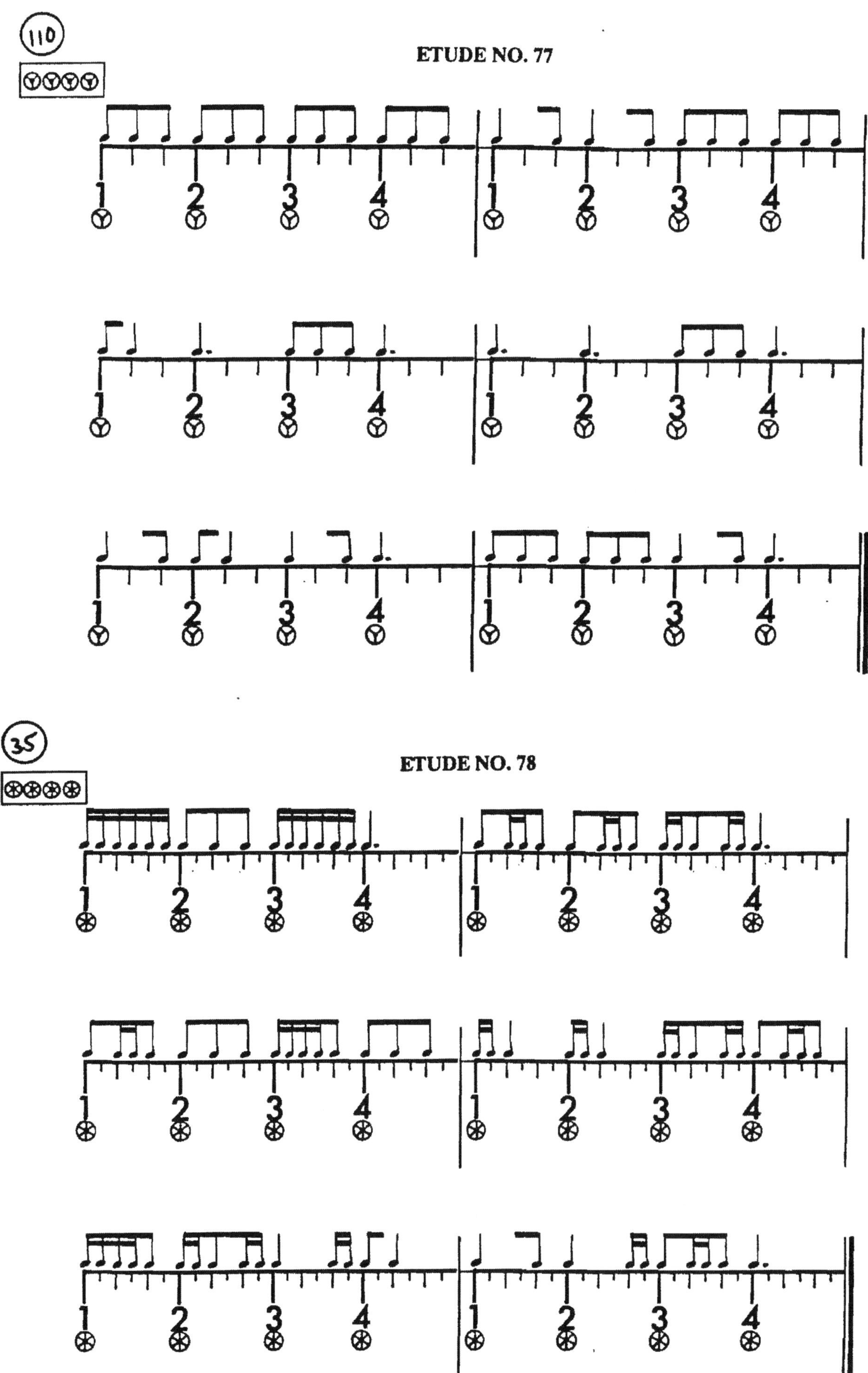

## ETUDE NO. 78

**a.**

**b.**

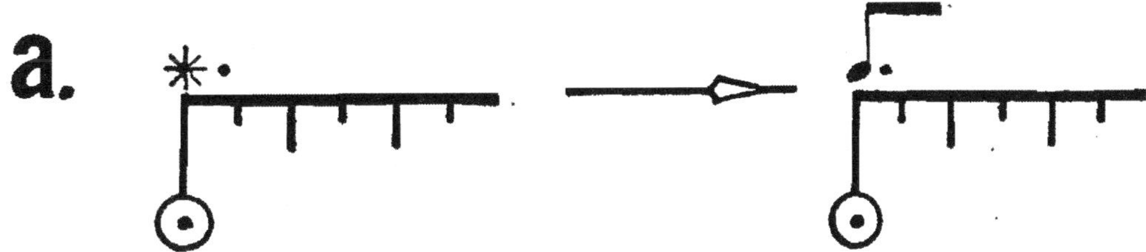

**c.**

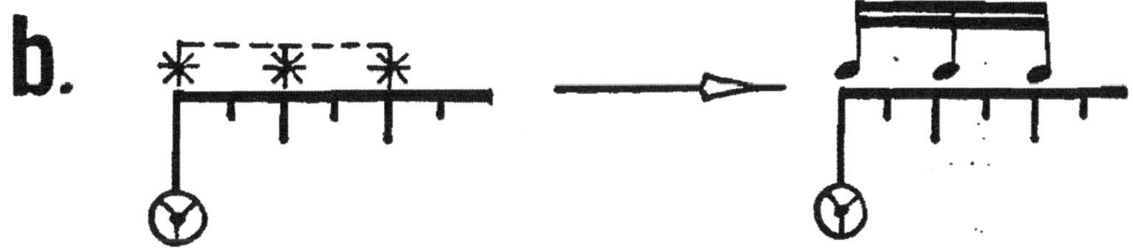

**d.**

**e.**

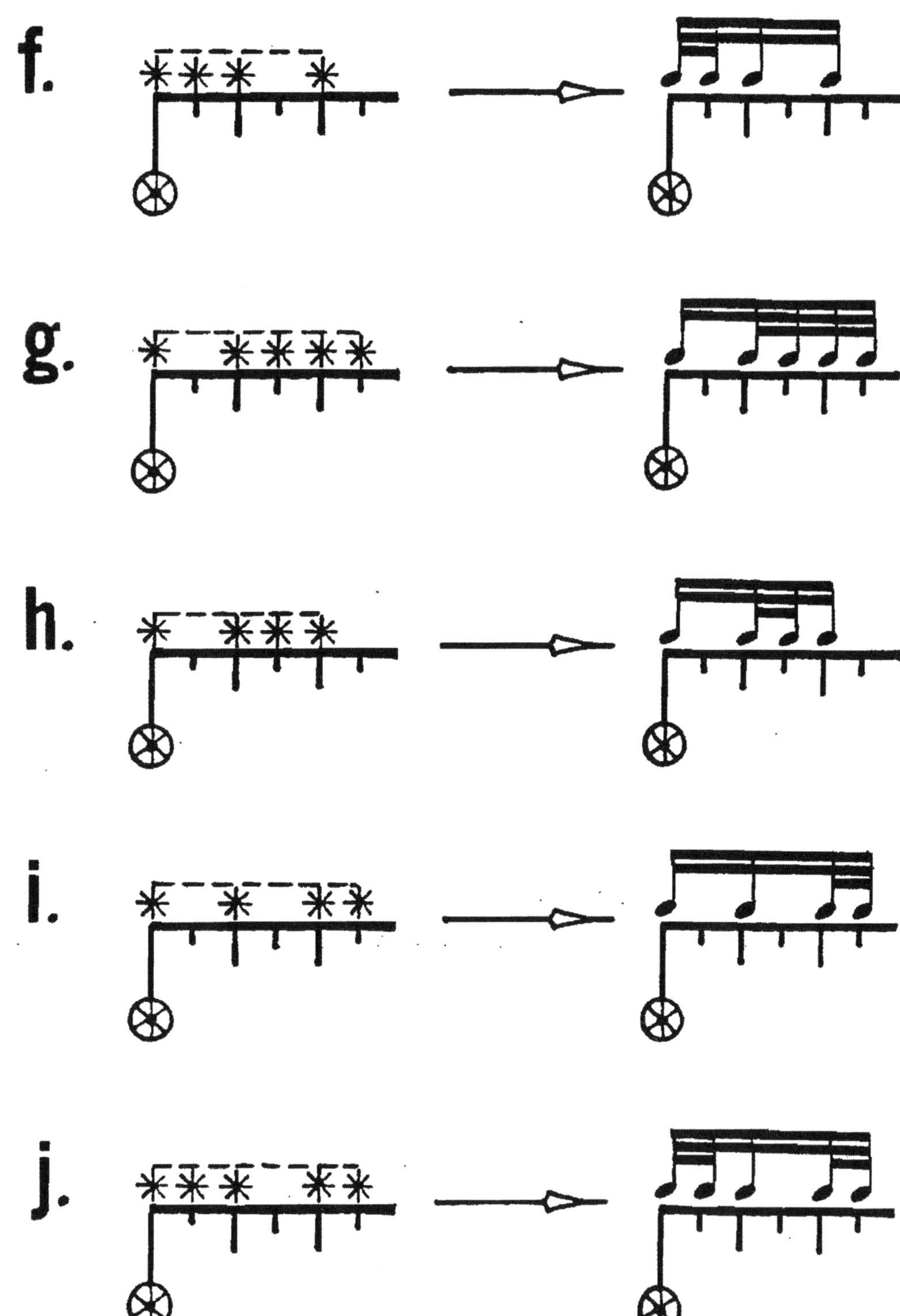


f.
g.
h.
i.
j.

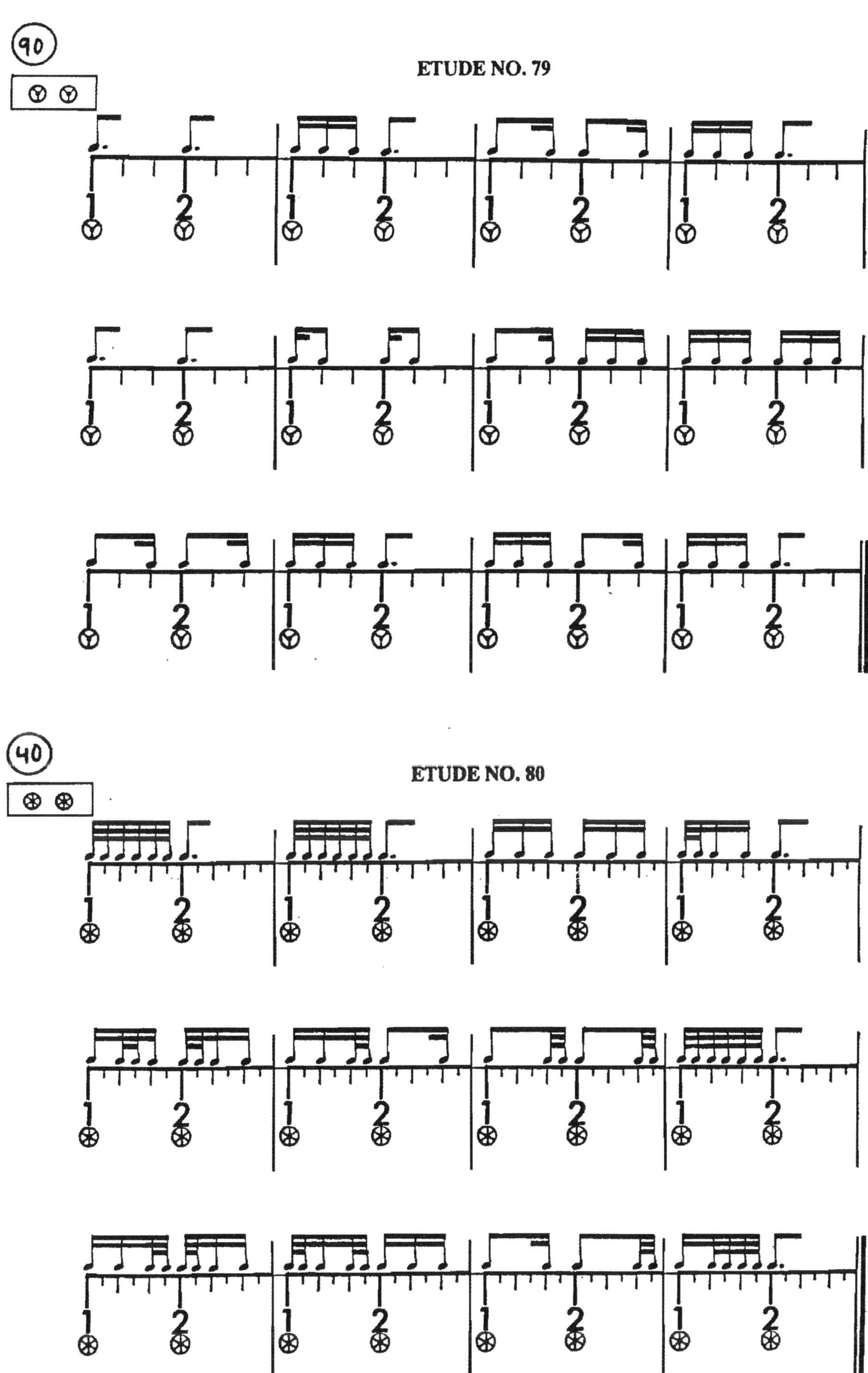

ETUDE NO. 79
ETUDE NO. 80

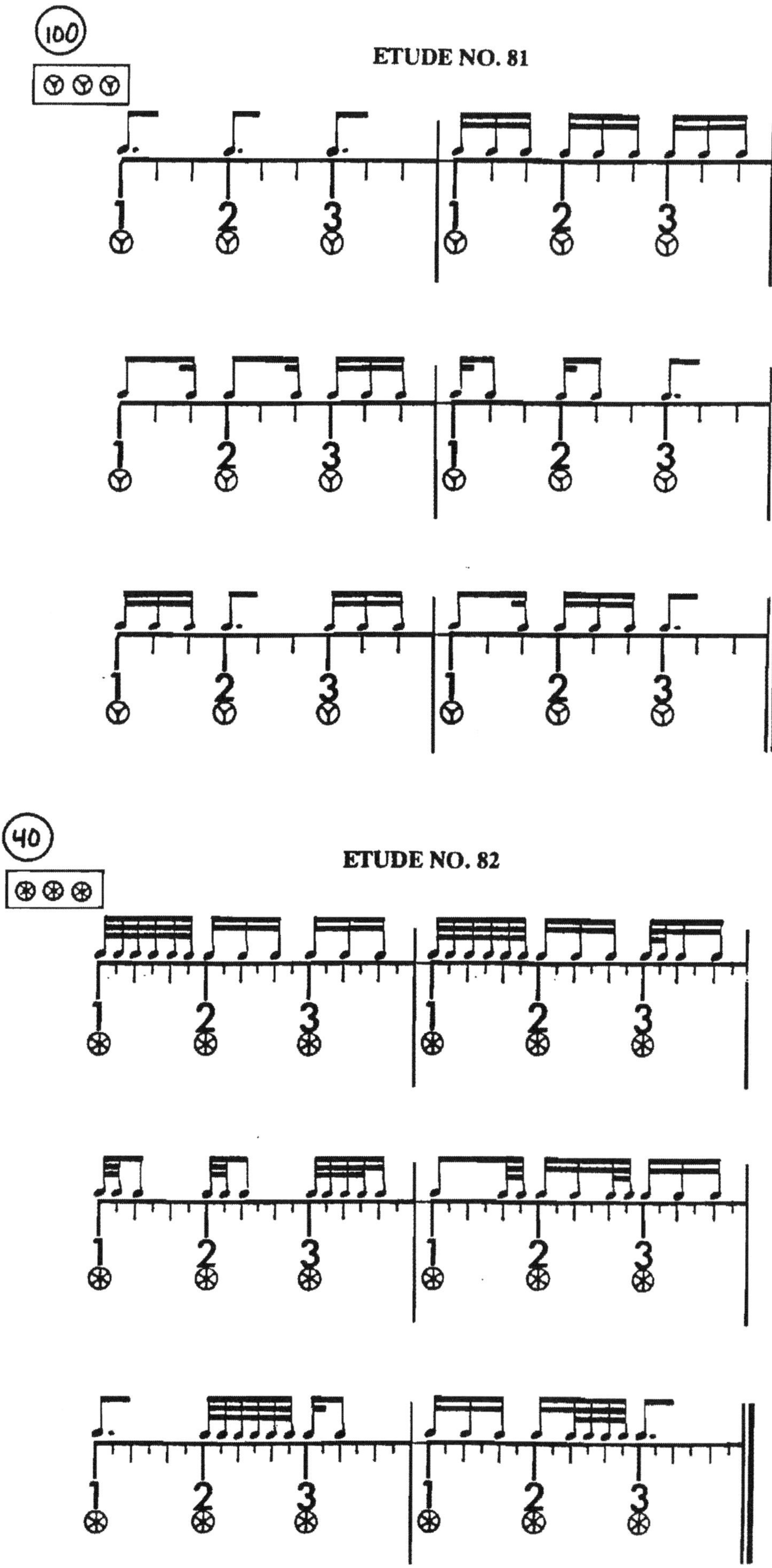
ETUDE NO. 81
100
ETUDE NO. 82
40

### ETUDE NO. 83

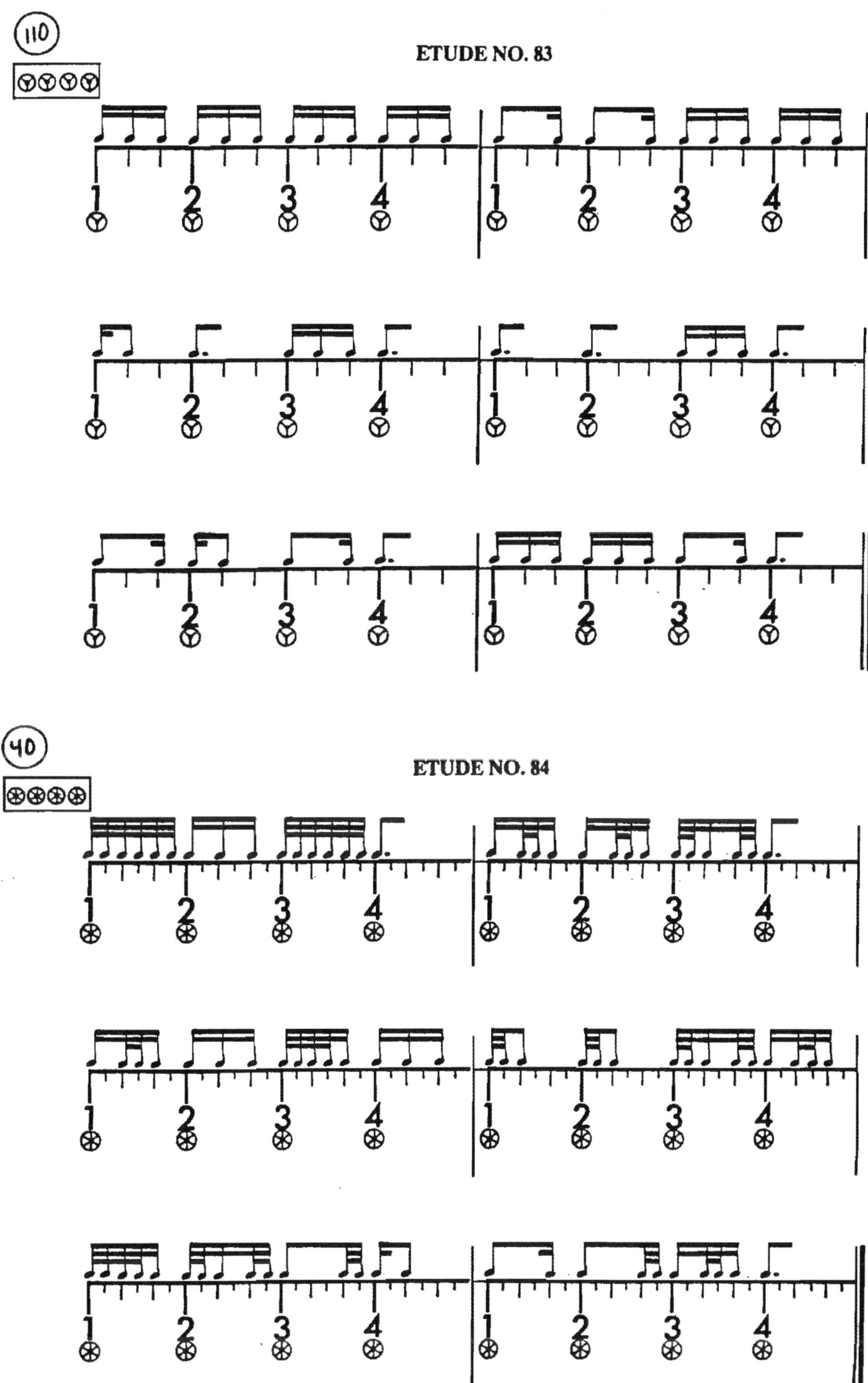

### ETUDE NO. 84

## ETUDE NO. 85

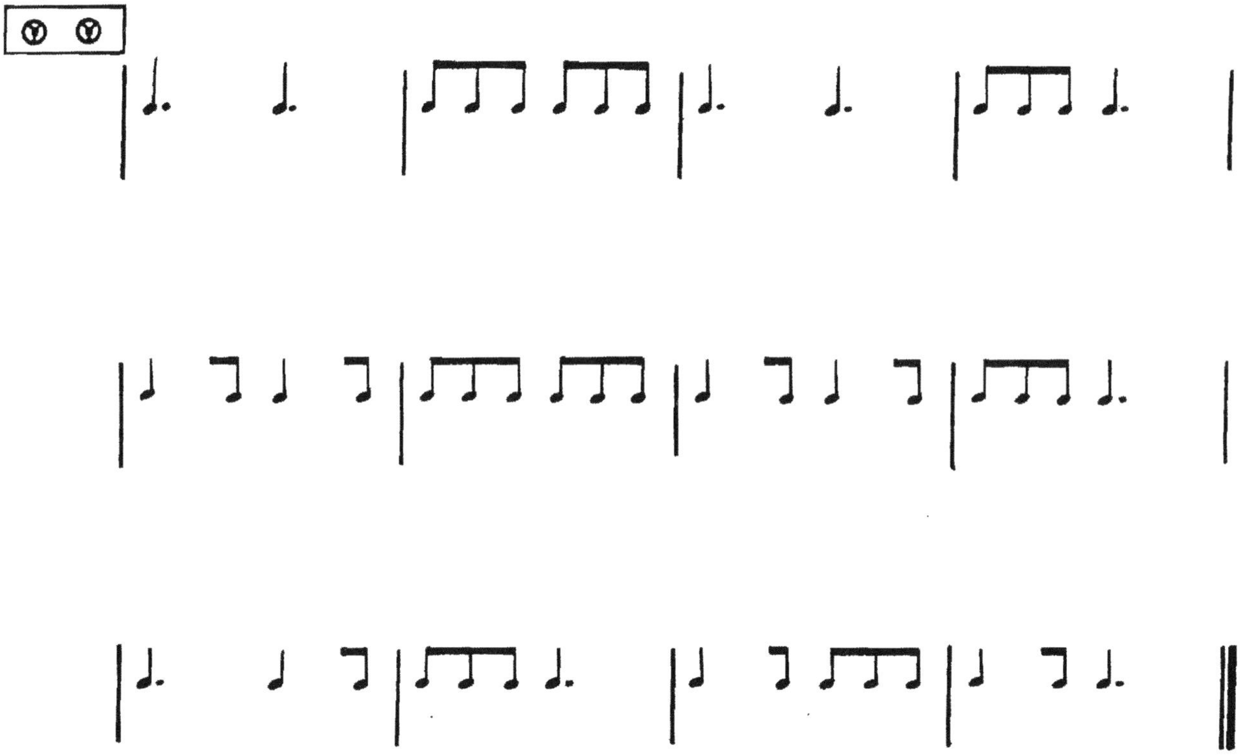

## ETUDE NO. 86

50
ETUDE NO. 87
40
ETUDE NO. 88

## ETUDE NO. 89

## ETUDE NO. 90

**Measured Music**

# ETUDE NO. 91

# ETUDE NO. 92

**ETUDE NO. 93**

**ETUDE NO. 94**

**ETUDE NO. 95**

**ETUDE NO. 96**

## ETUDE NO. 97

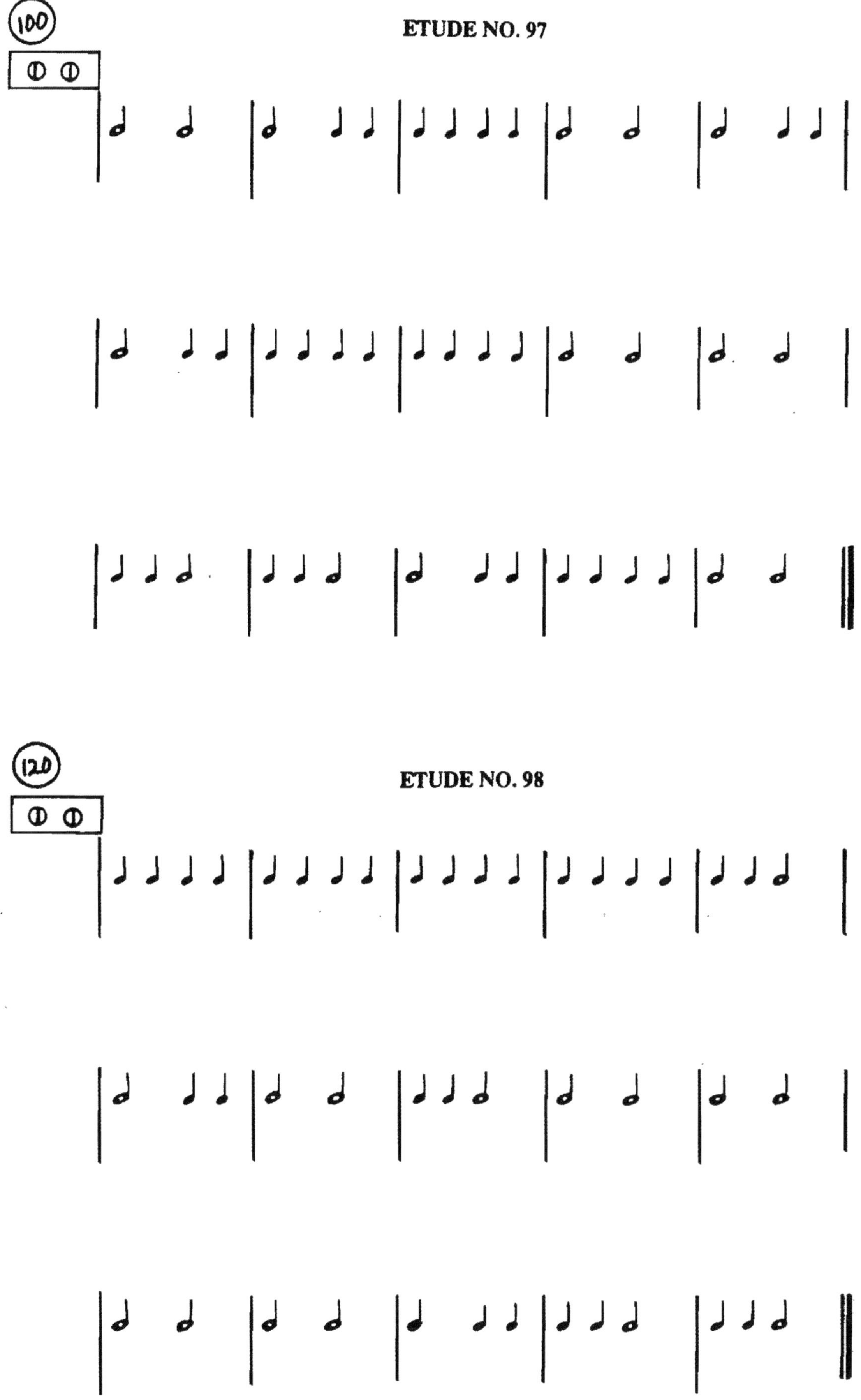

## ETUDE NO. 98

**ETUDE NO. 99**

**ETUDE NO. 100**

ETUDE NO. 101

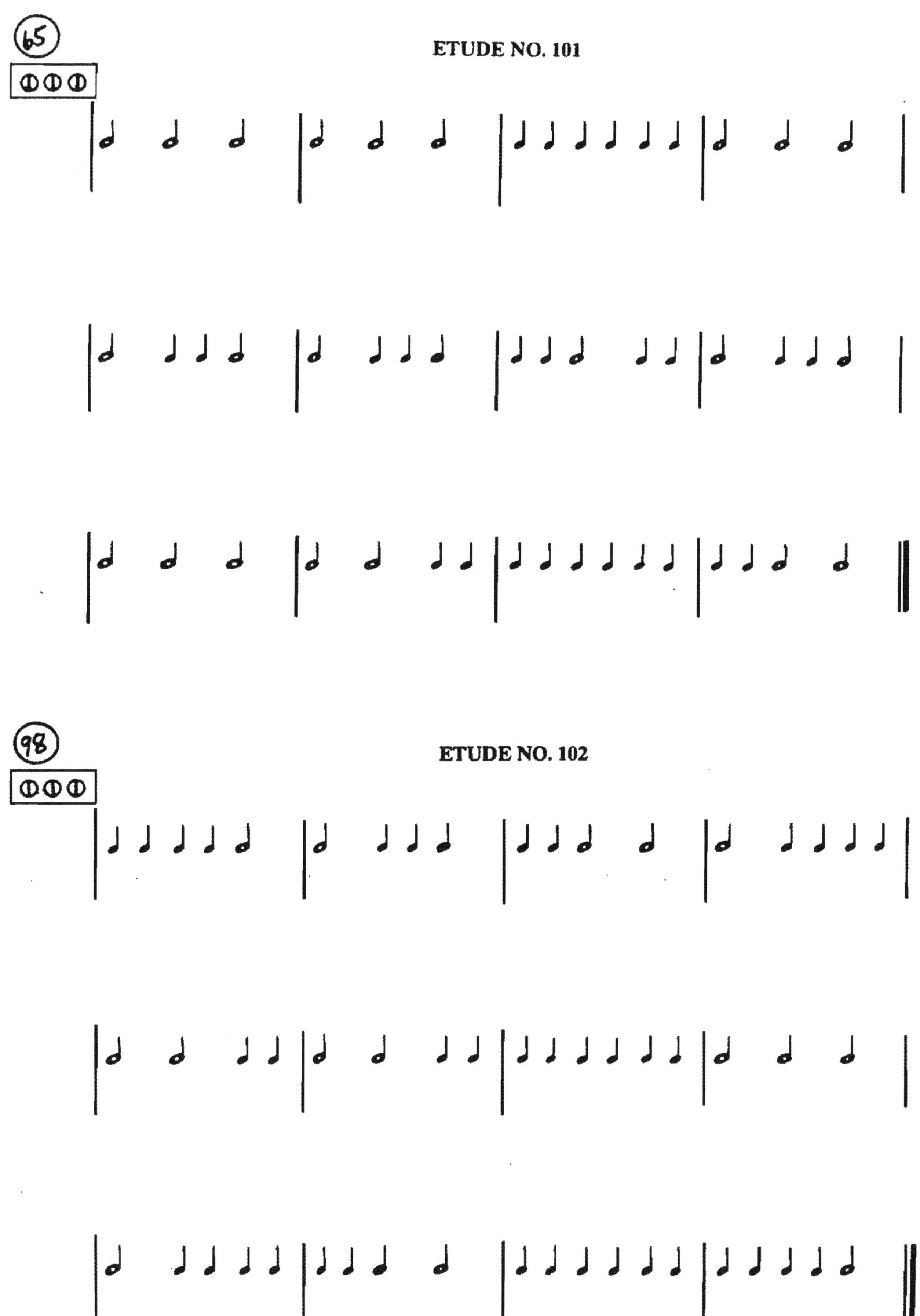

ETUDE NO. 102

**ETUDE NO. 103**

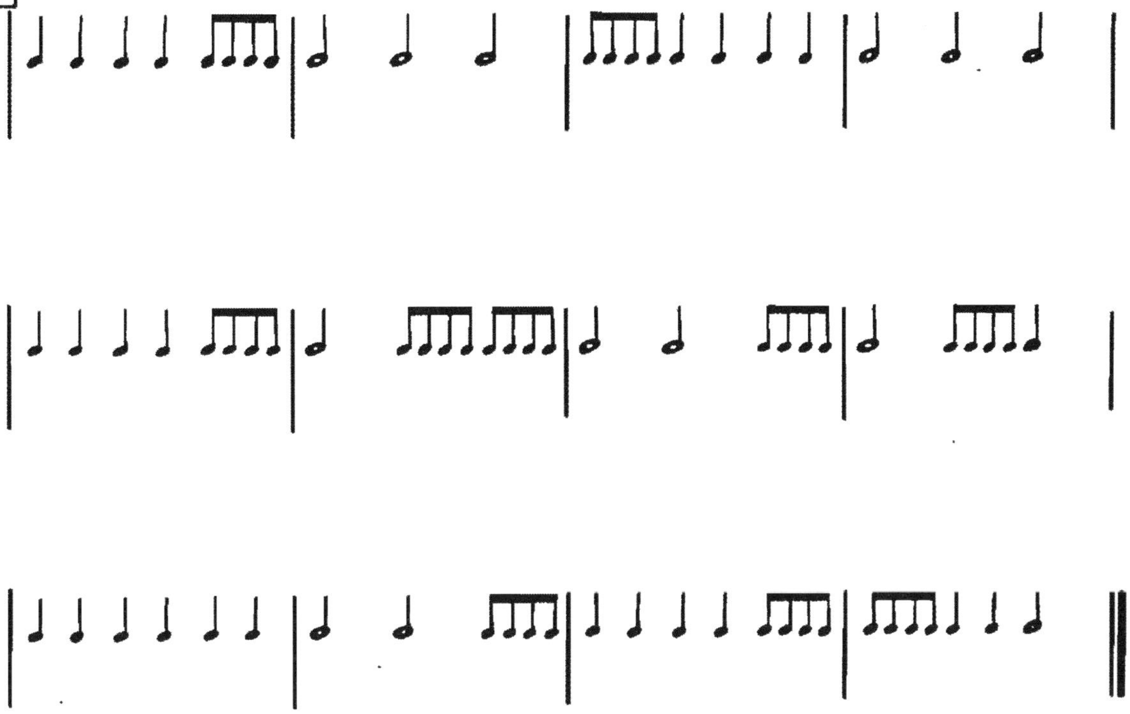

**ETUDE NO. 104**

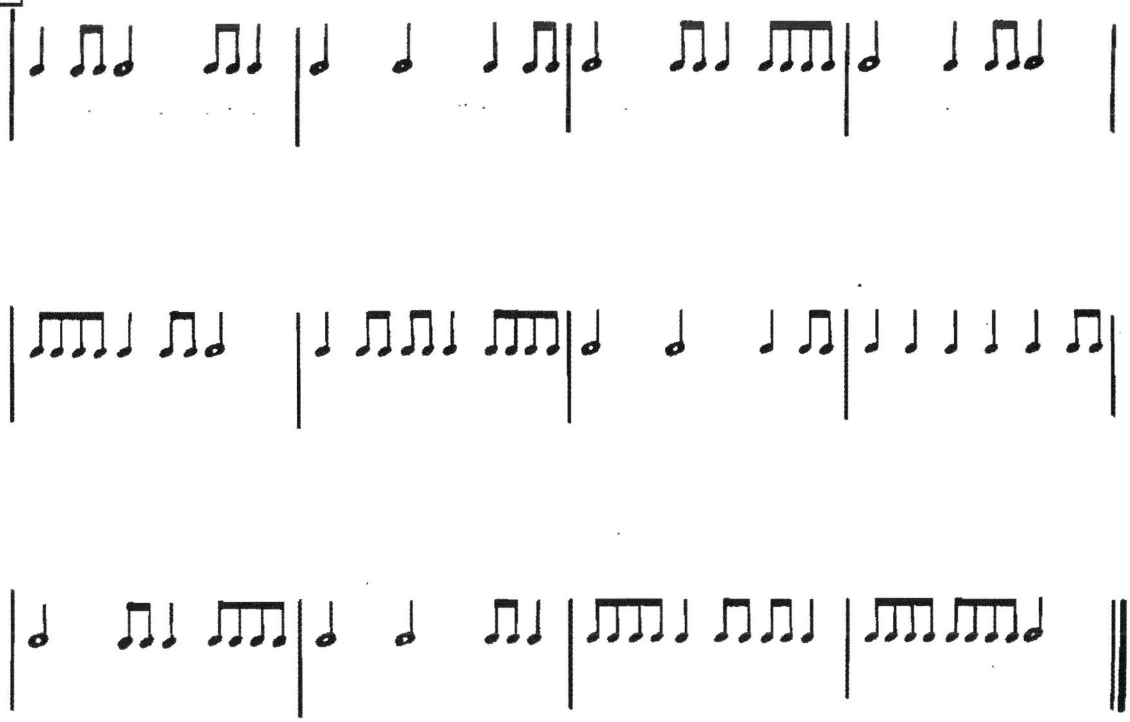

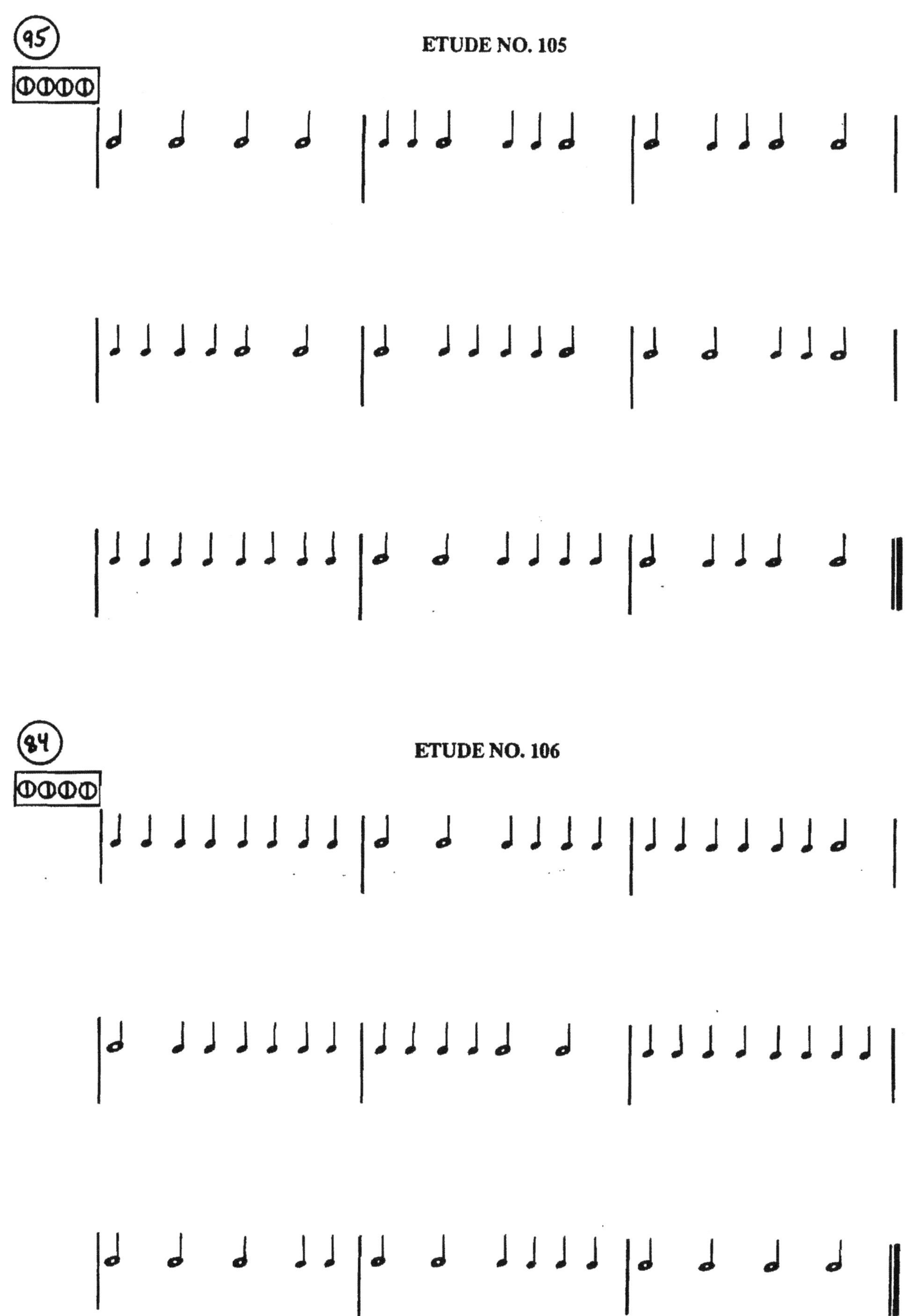
95
ETUDE NO. 105
84
ETUDE NO. 106

**ETUDE NO. 107**

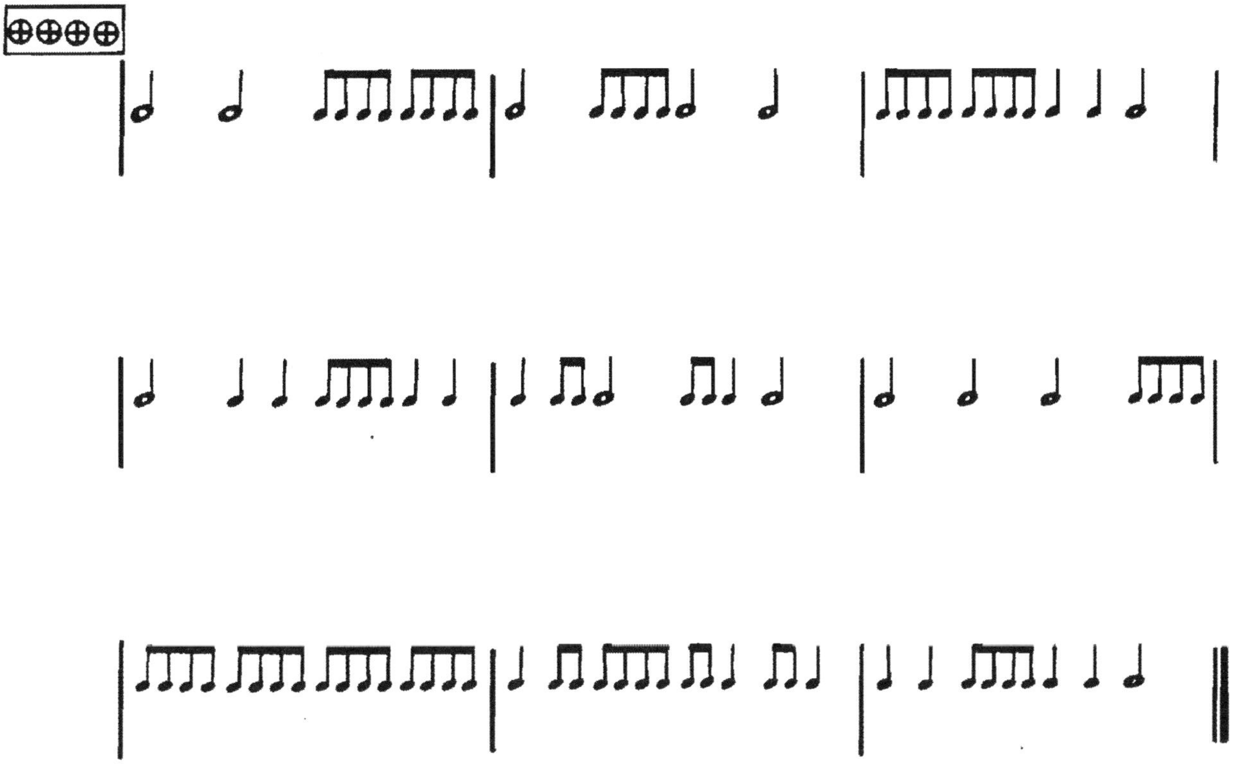

**ETUDE NO. 108**

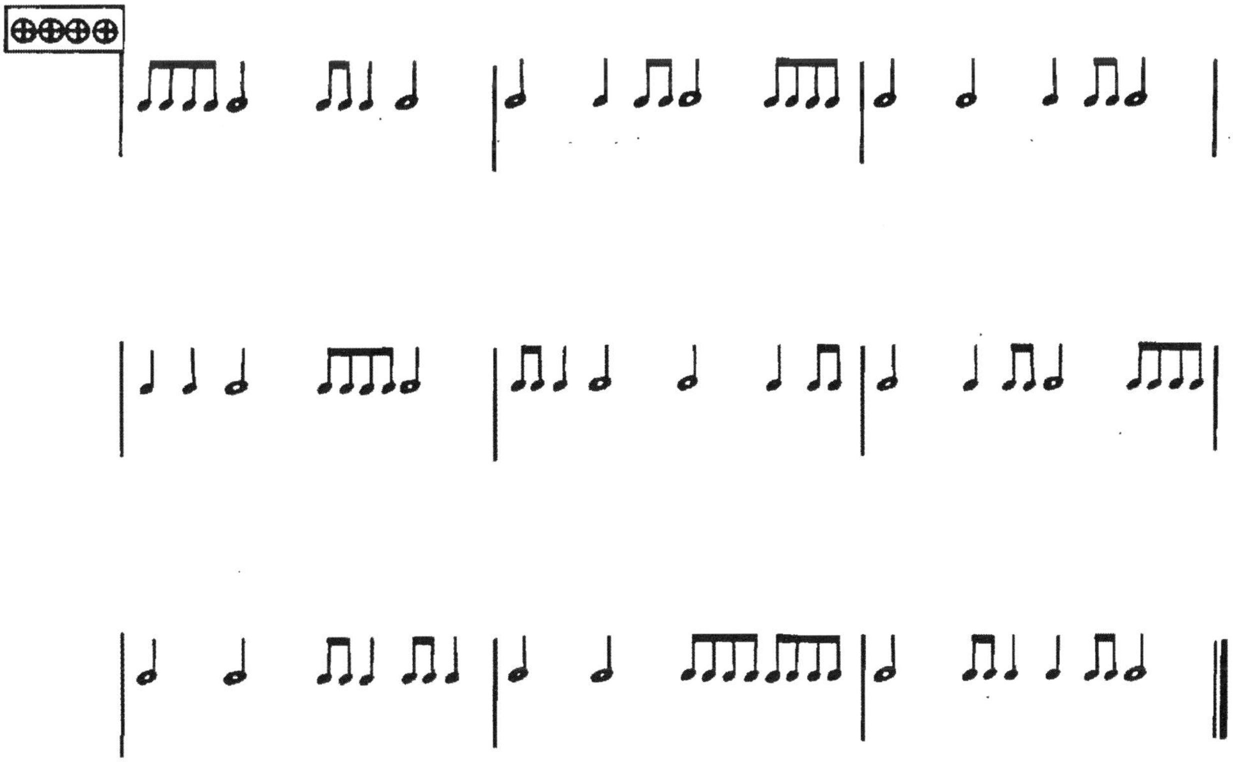

190
ETUDE NO. 109
135
ETUDE NO. 110

ETUDE NO. 111
ETUDE NO. 112

ETUDE NO. 113

ETUDE NO. 114

**ETUDE NO. 115**

**ETUDE NO. 116**

165

**ETUDE NO. 117**

145

**ETUDE NO. 118**

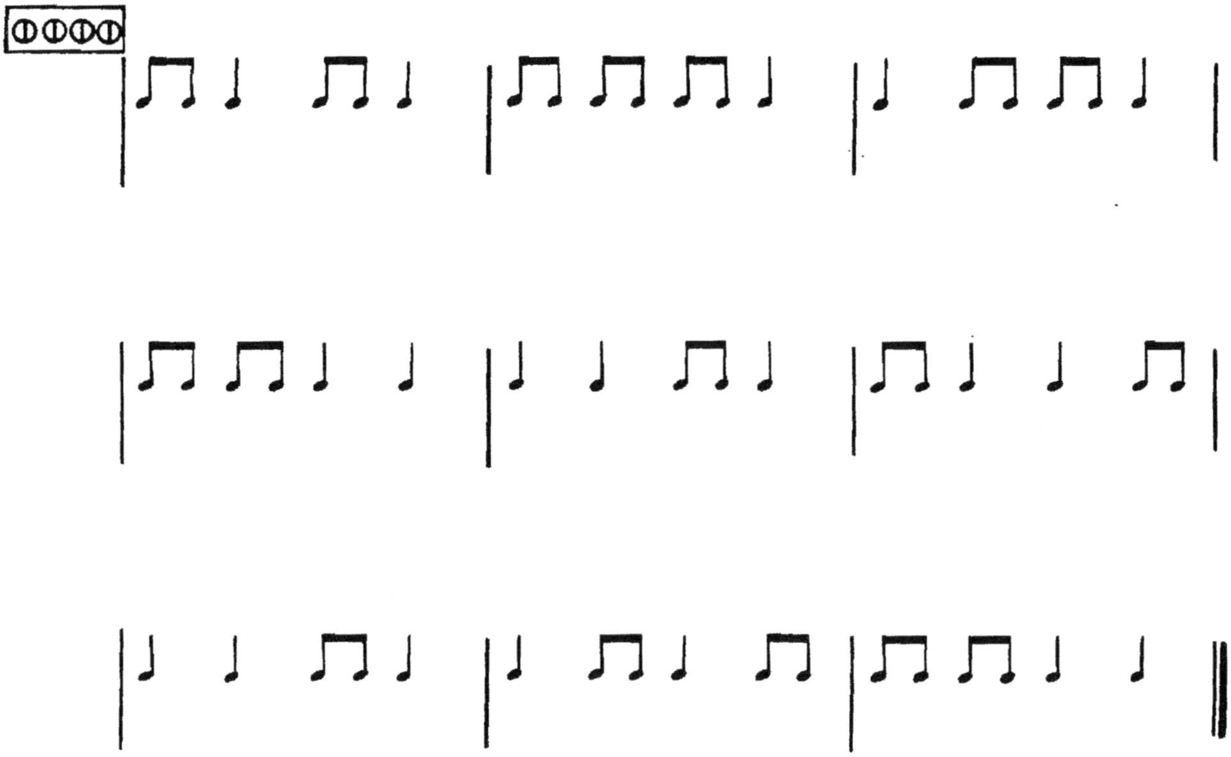

**ETUDE NO. 119**

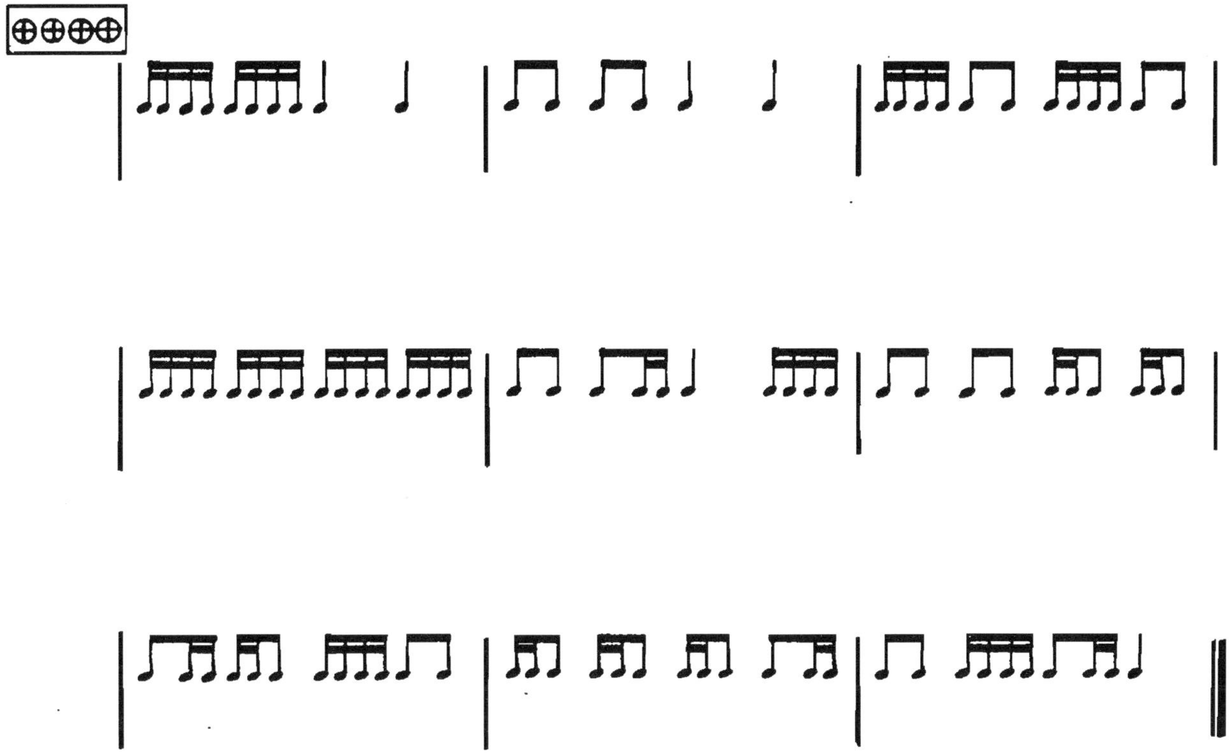

**ETUDE NO. 120

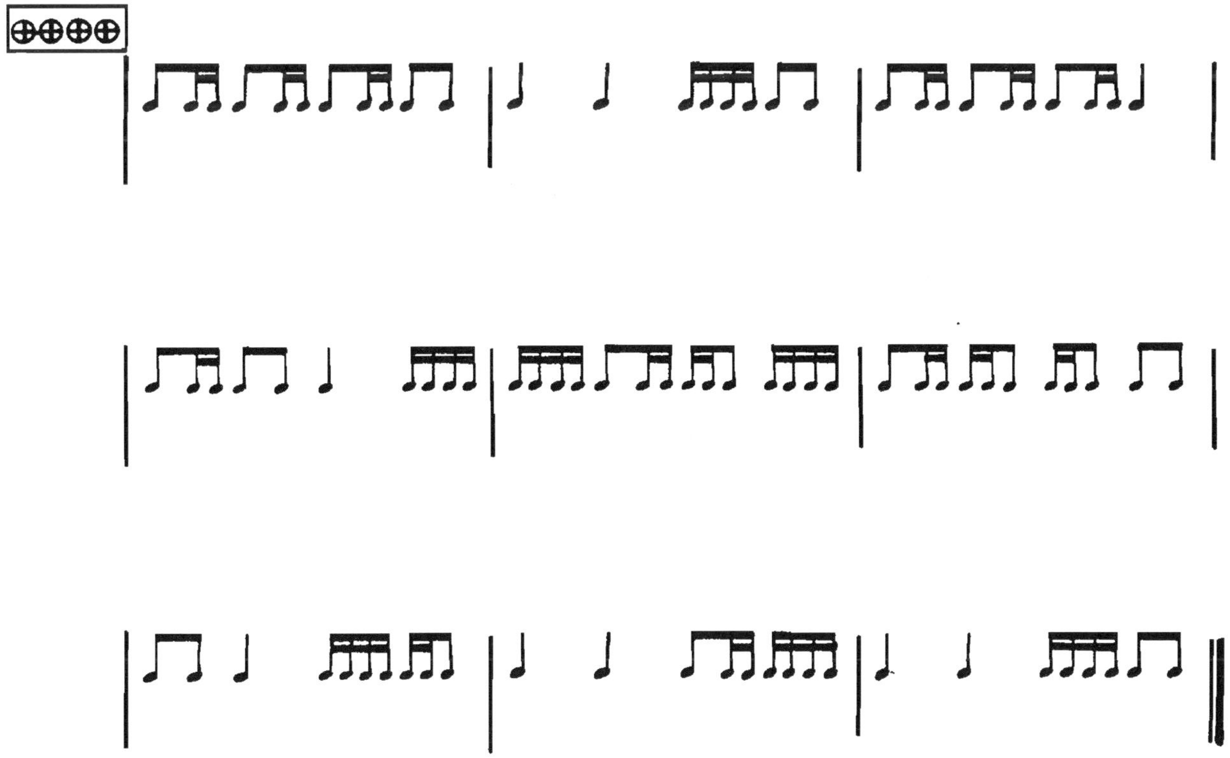

## "MEASURED MUSIC"  ASTERISK NOTATION

SINGLE BEAT (SINGLE METER):

METER BOX:



RHYTHM RULERS:



ASTERISK NOTATION:



## "MEASURED MUSIC"  BEAM-AND-STEM NOTATION

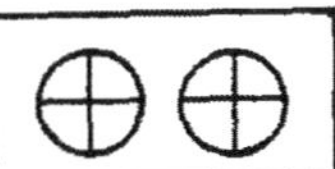

15 

16 

17 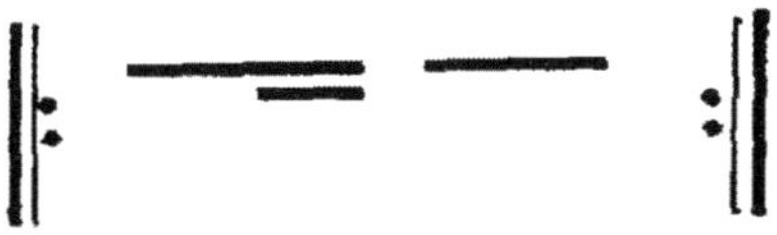

18 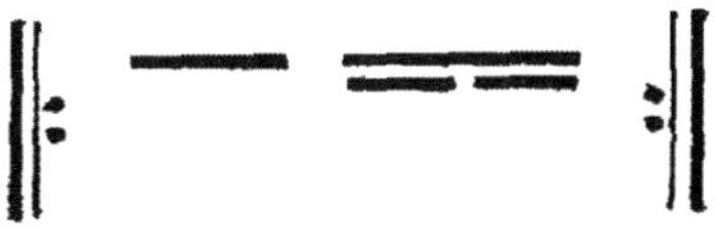

19 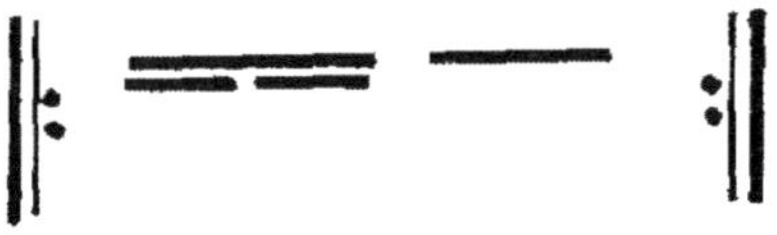

20 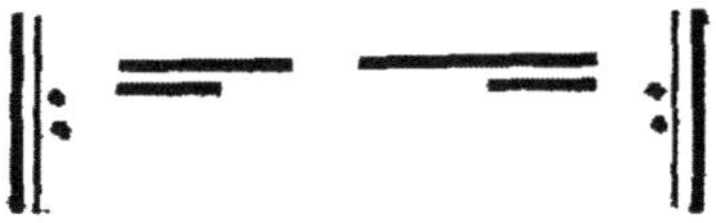

21 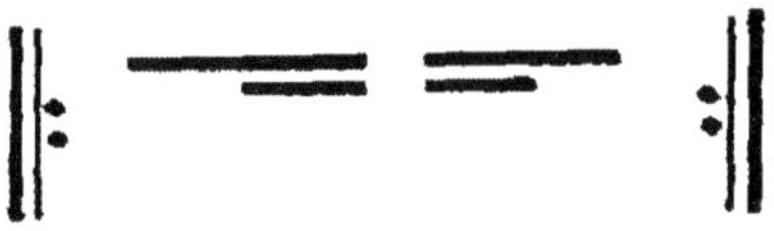

22 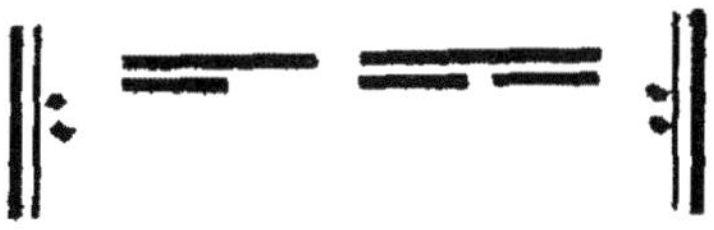

23 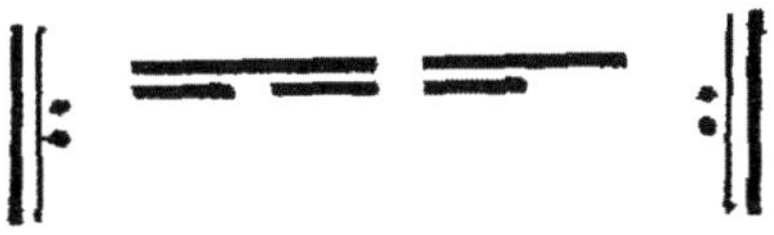

24 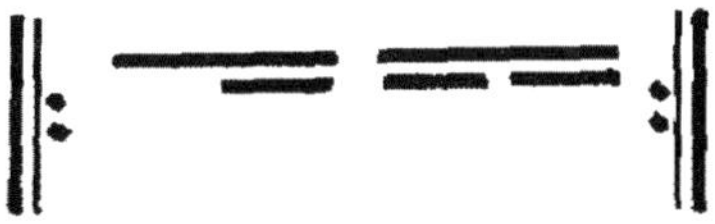

25 

# BEAM-AND-STEM ETUDE IN DUPLE METER

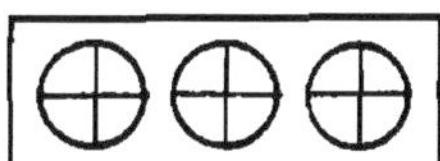

1 2
3 4
5 6
7 8
9 10
11 12
13 14

15     16

17     18

19     20

21     22

23     24

25     26

27     28

29   30

31   32

33   34

35   36

37   38

39   40

41   42

# BEAM-AND-STEM ETUDE IN TRIPLE METER

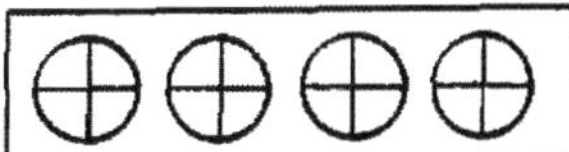

8

9

10

11

12

13

14

15

16

17

18

19

20

21

22

23

24

25

26

27

28

# Beam-and-Stem Etude in Quadruple Meter

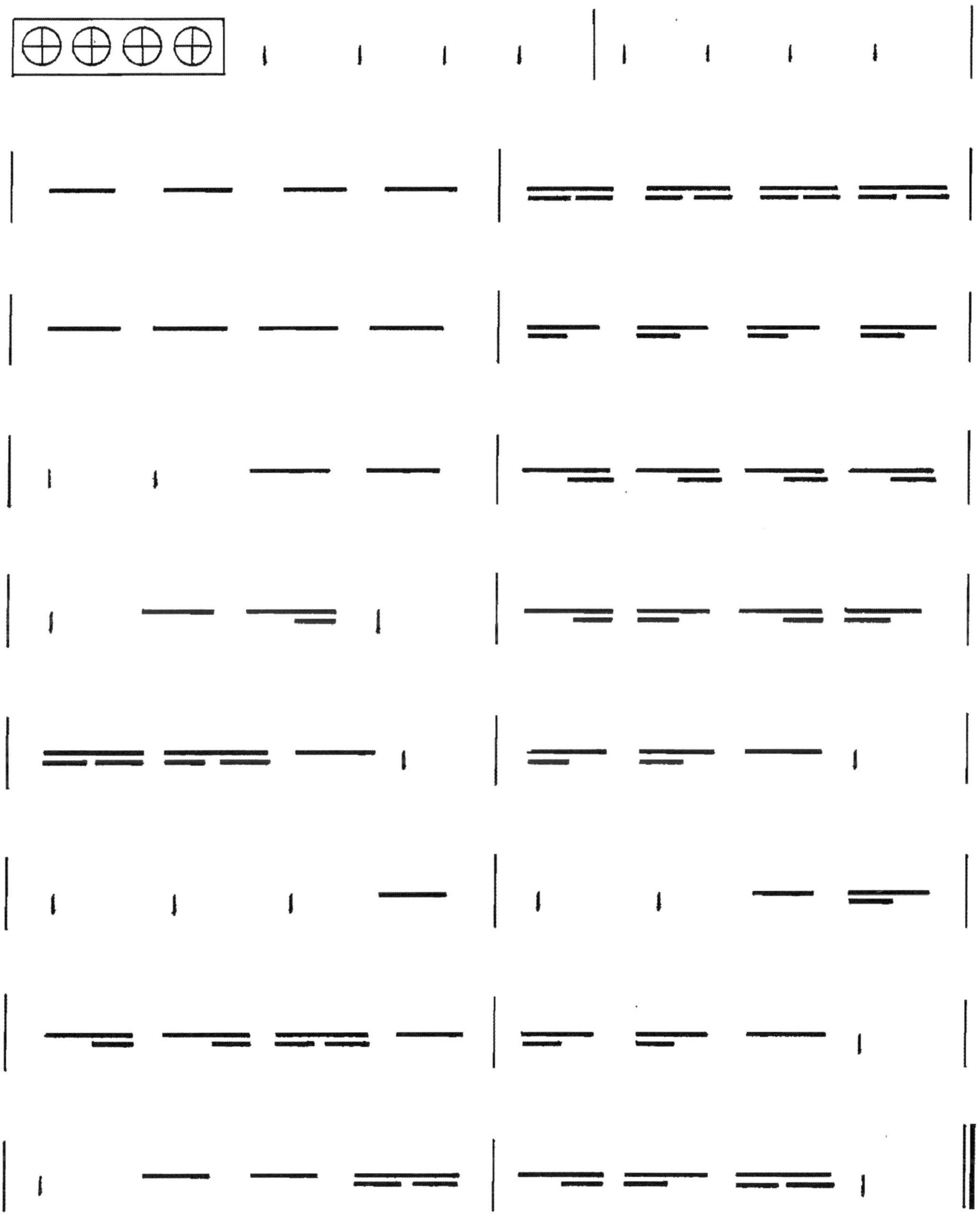

# SOUND-AND-SILENCE [STEM-AND-SPACE] COMBINATIONS

## — SIMPLE DIVISION —

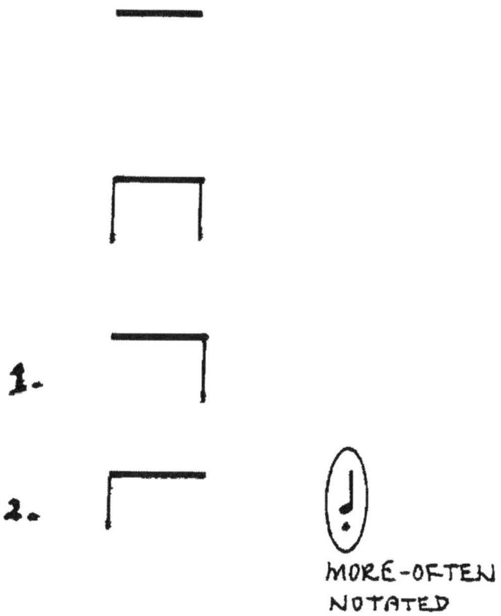

1.

2.

MORE-OFTEN
NOTATED

## — INCOMPLETE SUBDIVISION A —

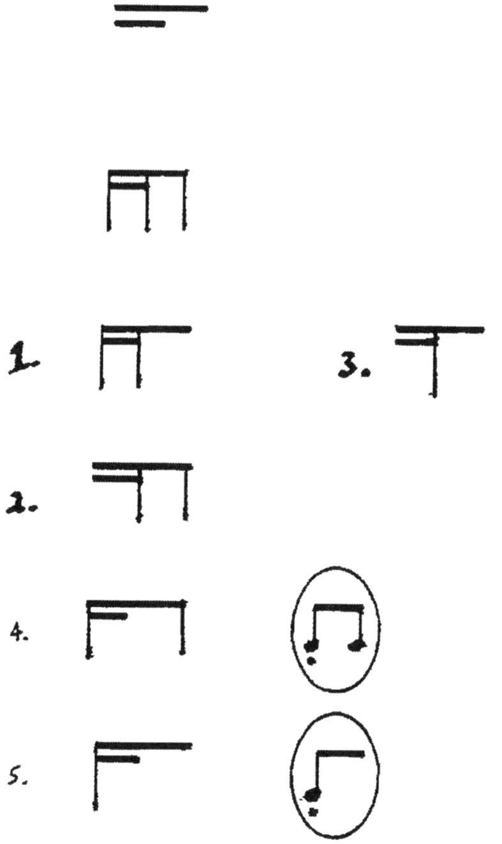

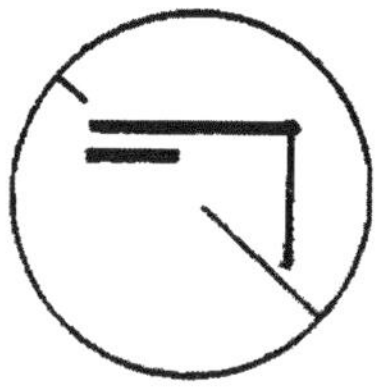

1.

2.

3.

4.

5.

BEAMS MUST BE SUPPORTED BY
A STEM ON AT LEAST ONE END.
BEAMS CANNOT BE "FREE-FLOATING".

— INCOMPLETE SUBDIVISION B —

— COMPLETE SUBDIVISION —

**1.**

**2.**

**3.**

4.

5.

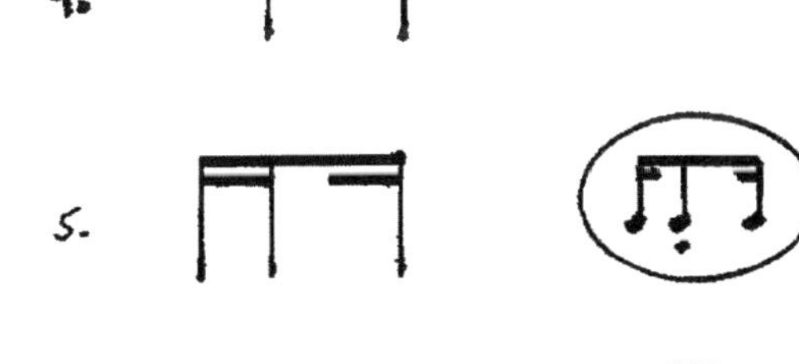

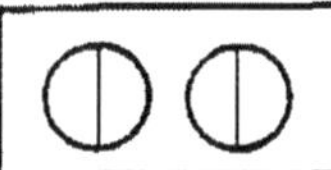

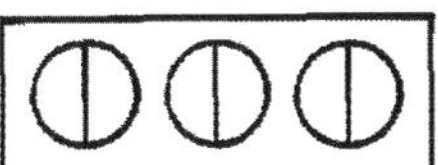

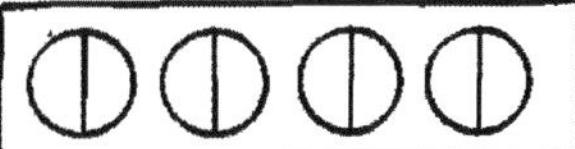

1

2

3

4

5

6

7

8

9

10

11

12

13

14

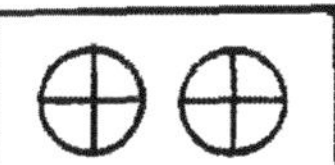

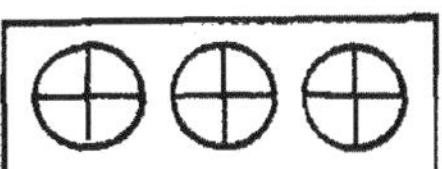

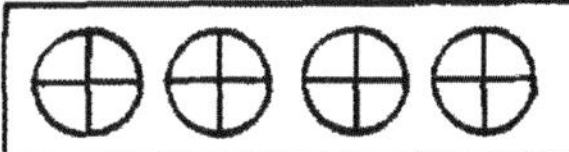

1
2
3
4
5
6
7

8
9
10
11
12
13
14

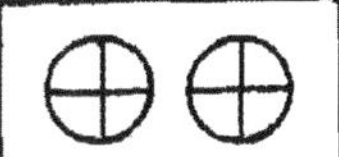

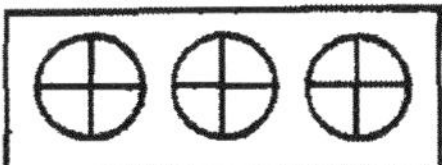

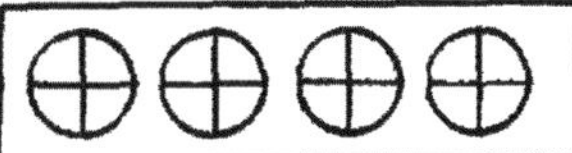

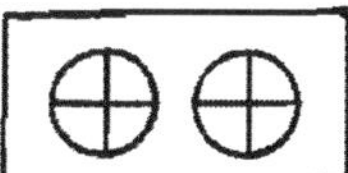

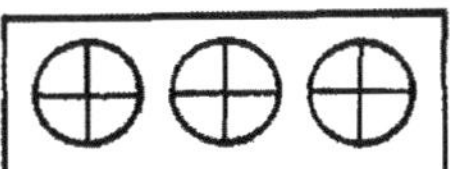

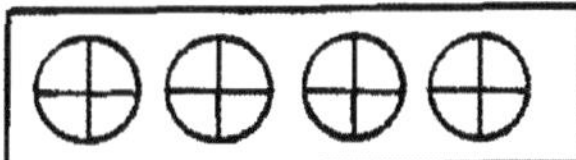

8 ‖: :‖

9 ‖: :‖

10 ‖: :‖

11 ‖: :‖

12 ‖: :‖

13 ‖: :‖

14 ‖: :‖

| Meter Box | Correct Name | Possible Time Signature(s) |
| --- | --- | --- |
| | Duple meter, simple division, beat only | $\frac{2}{4}$ $\frac{2}{2}$ (¢) |
| | Duple , simple division | $\frac{2}{4}$ $\frac{2}{2}$ (¢) |
| | Duple , simple subdivision | $\frac{2}{4}$ $\frac{2}{2}$ (¢) |
| | Duple , compound division | $\frac{6}{8}$ |
| | Duple , borrowed division | $\frac{2}{4}$ $\frac{2}{2}$ (¢) |
| | Duple , compound subdivision | $\frac{6}{8}$ |
| | Duple , borrowed subdivision | $\frac{2}{4}$ $\frac{2}{2}$ (¢) |
| | Duple , combination division | $\frac{5}{8}$ |
| | Duple , combination division | $\frac{5}{8}$ |
| | Duple , compound division, beat only | $\frac{6}{8}$ |



| Meter Box | Correct Name | Possible Time Signature(s) |
| --- | --- | --- |
| | Duple meter, simple division, beat only | $\frac{2}{4}$ $\frac{2}{2}$ (¢) |
| | Duple , simple division | $\frac{2}{4}$ $\frac{2}{2}$ (¢) |
| | Duple , simple subdivision | $\frac{2}{4}$ $\frac{2}{2}$ (¢) |
| | Duple , compound division | $\frac{6}{8}$ |
| | Duple , borrowed division | $\frac{2}{4}$ $\frac{2}{2}$ (¢) |
| | Duple , compound subdivision | $\frac{6}{8}$ |
| | Duple , borrowed subdivision | $\frac{2}{4}$ $\frac{2}{2}$ (¢) |
| | Duple , combination division | $\frac{5}{8}$ |
| | Duple , combination division | $\frac{5}{8}$ |
| | Duple , compound division, beat only | $\frac{6}{8}$ |

# Counting and Conducting Warm-Up

( MM= 50 → 90 )

Count and Conduct each "Meter Box" four times __ no pause between __ perform as one continuous exercise:

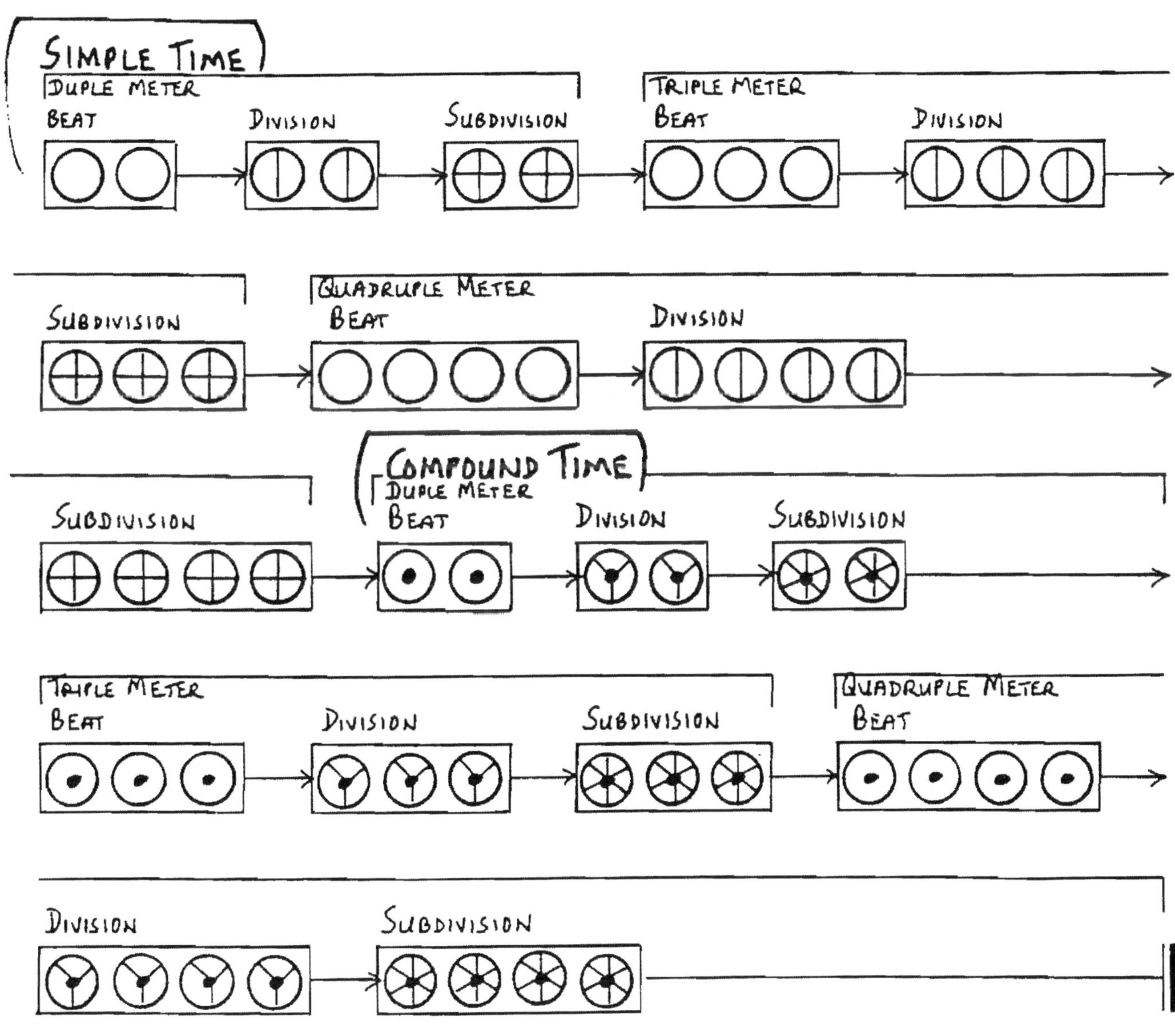

# Symbols-for-Sound Notation with Simple Division and Subdivision

STEMS UP: THEORETICALLY CORRECT NOTATION — STEMS DOWN: COMMON NOTATION

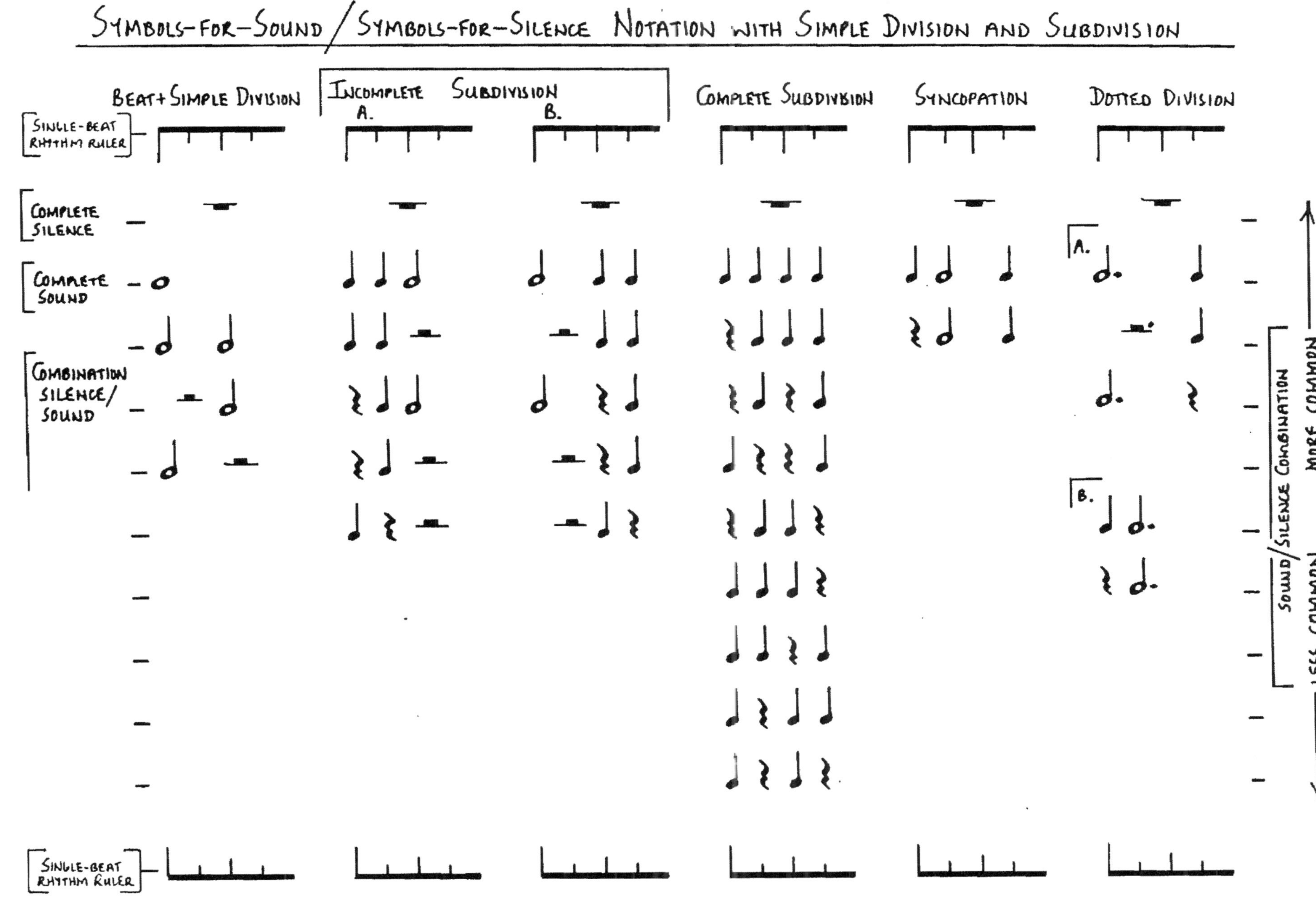

Symbols-for-Sound / Symbols-for-Silence Notation with Simple Division and Subdivision
Beat + Simple Division
Incomplete Subdivision
A.
B.
Complete Subdivision
Syncopation
Dotted Division
Single-beat Rhythm Ruler
Complete Silence
Complete Sound
Combination Silence / Sound
A.
B.
Single-beat Rhythm Ruler
Sound / Silence Combination
More Common
Less Common

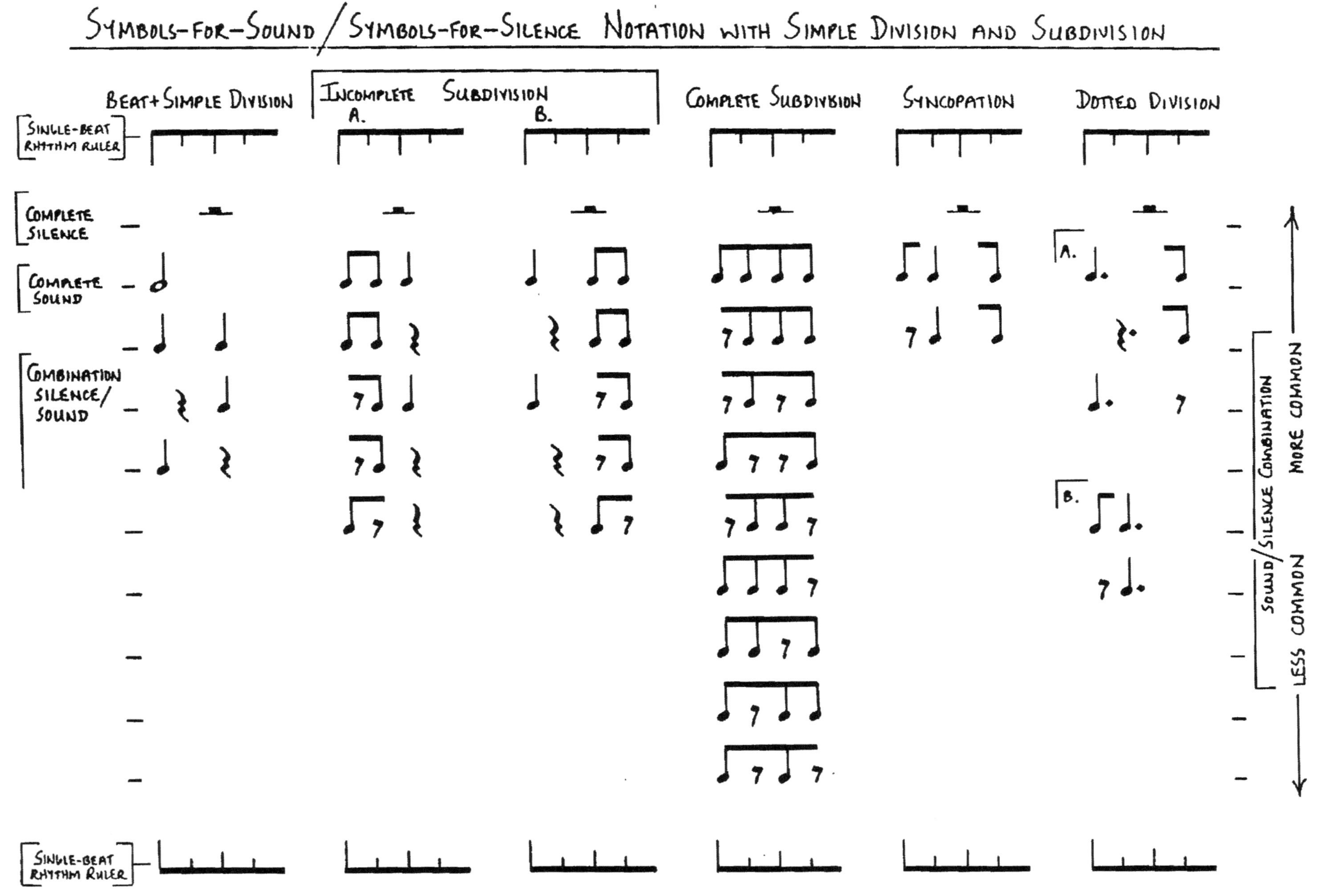

SYMBOLS-FOR-SOUND / SYMBOLS-FOR-SILENCE NOTATION WITH SIMPLE DIVISION AND SUBDIVISION
BEAT+SIMPLE DIVISION
INCOMPLETE SUBDIVISION
A.
B.
COMPLETE SUBDIVISION
SYNCOPATION
DOTTED DIVISION
SINGLE-BEAT RHYTHM RULER
COMPLETE SILENCE
COMPLETE SOUND
COMBINATION SILENCE/ SOUND
A.
B.
MORE COMMON
LESS COMMON
SOUND/SILENCE COMBINATION
SINGLE-BEAT RHYTHM RULER
138

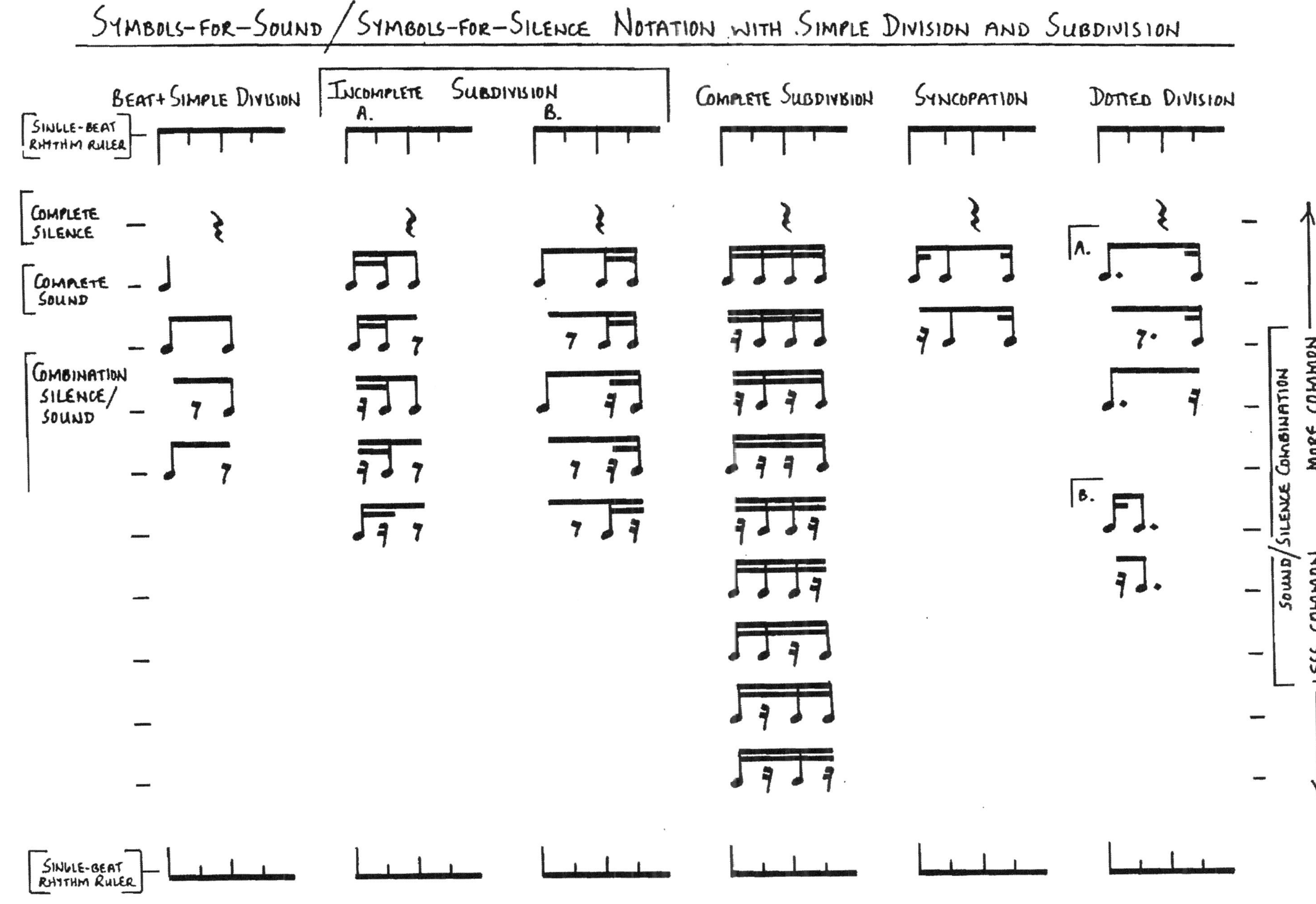

SYMBOLS-FOR-SOUND / SYMBOLS-FOR-SILENCE NOTATION WITH SIMPLE DIVISION AND SUBDIVISION
BEAT + SIMPLE DIVISION
INCOMPLETE SUBDIVISION
A.
B.
COMPLETE SUBDIVISION
SYNCOPATION
DOTTED DIVISION
SINGLE-BEAT RHYTHM RULER
COMPLETE SILENCE
COMPLETE SOUND
COMBINATION SILENCE/ SOUND
A.
B.
SINGLE-BEAT RHYTHM RULER
SOUND/SILENCE COMBINATION
MORE COMMON
LESS COMMON

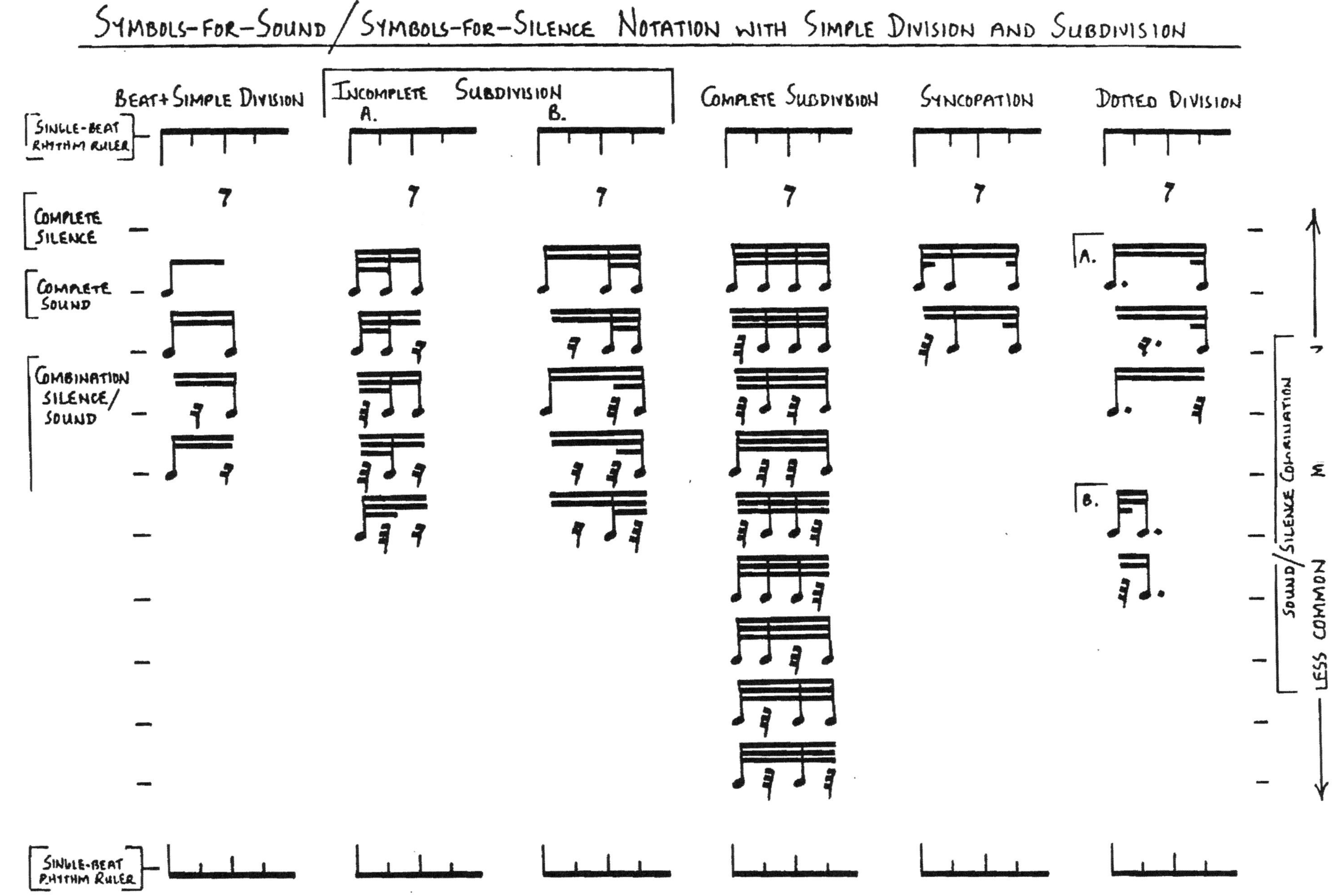

SYMBOLS-FOR-SOUND / SYMBOLS-FOR-SILENCE NOTATION WITH SIMPLE DIVISION AND SUBDIVISION
BEAT + SIMPLE DIVISION
INCOMPLETE SUBDIVISION
A.
B.
COMPLETE SUBDIVISION
SYNCOPATION
DOTTED DIVISION
SINGLE-BEAT RHYTHM RULER
COMPLETE SILENCE
COMPLETE SOUND
COMBINATION SILENCE/ SOUND
A.
B.
SINGLE-BEAT RHYTHM RULER
SOUND/SILENCE COMBINATION
MORE COMMON
LESS COMMON

# Symbols-for-Sound Notation with Compound Division and Subdivision

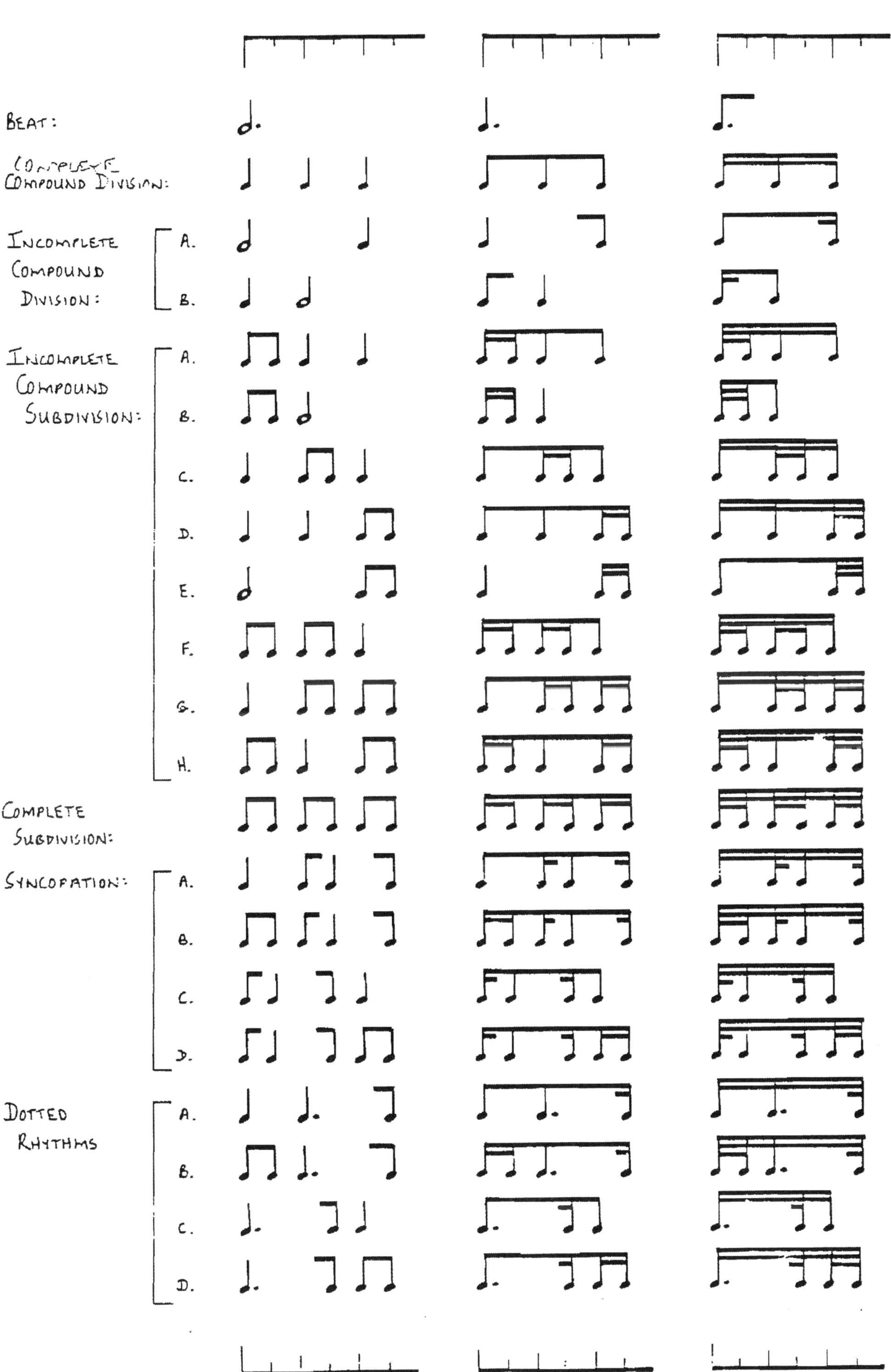

## Symbols- for- Sound/ Silence Notation
## with Compound Division and Subdivision

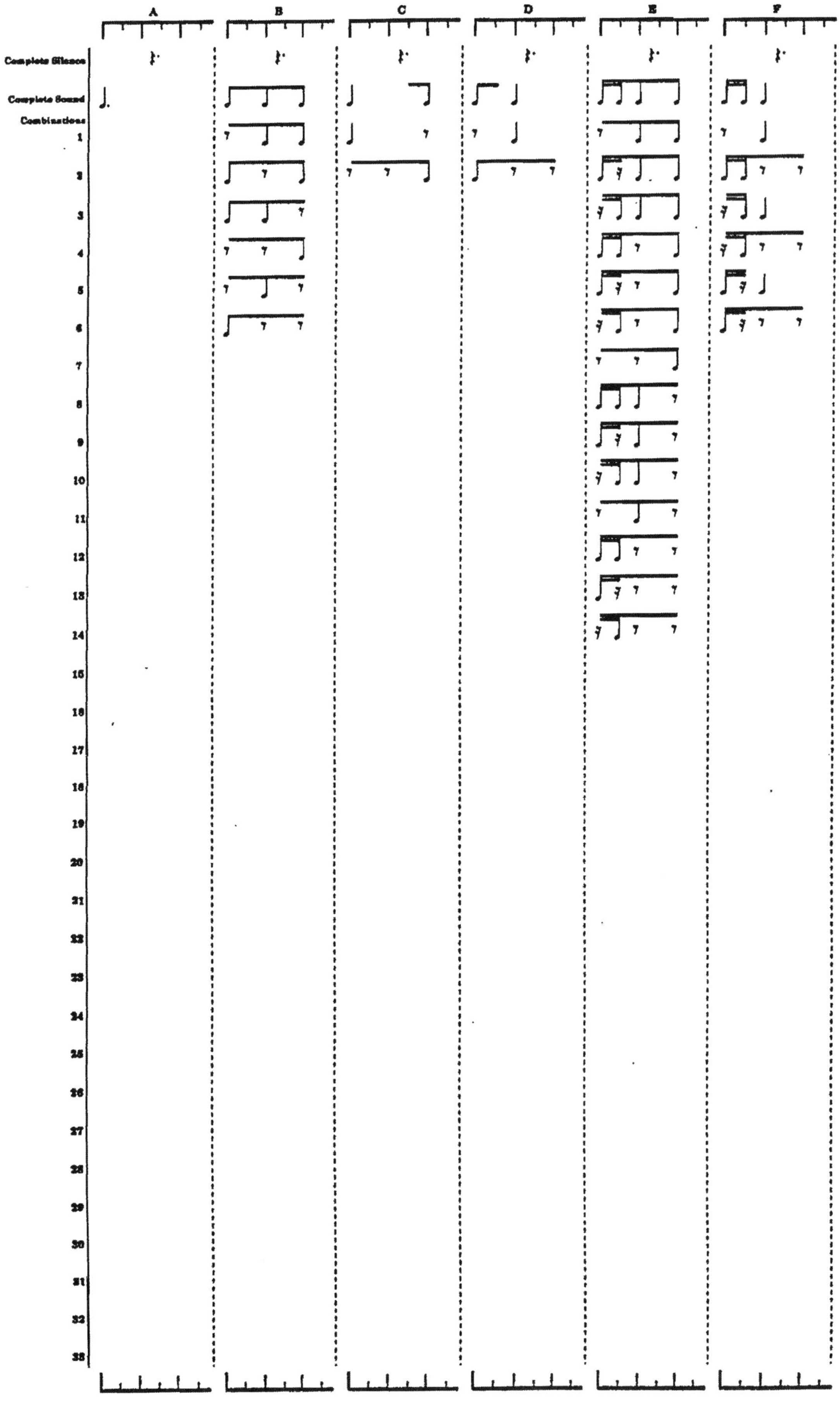

| | A | B | C | D | E | F |
|---|---|---|---|---|---|---|

Complete Silence

Complete Sound

Combinations

1
2
3
4
5
6
7
8
9
10
11
12
13
14
15
16
17
18
19
20
21
22
23
24
25
26
27
28
29
30
31
32
33

-2-

|  | G | H | I | J | K | L |
|---|---|---|---|---|---|---|
| Silence |  |  |  |  |  |  |
| Sound |  |  |  |  |  |  |
| 1 |  |  |  |  |  |  |
| 2 |  |  |  |  |  |  |
| 3 |  |  |  |  |  |  |
| 4 |  |  |  |  |  |  |
| 5 |  |  |  |  |  |  |
| 6 |  |  |  |  |  |  |
| 7 |  |  |  |  |  |  |
| 8 |  |  |  |  |  |  |
| 9 |  |  |  |  |  |  |
| 10 |  |  |  |  |  |  |
| 11 |  |  |  |  |  |  |
| 12 |  |  |  |  |  |  |
| 13 |  |  |  |  |  |  |
| 14 |  |  |  |  |  |  |
| 15 |  |  |  |  |  |  |
| 16 |  |  |  |  |  |  |
| 17 |  |  |  |  |  |  |
| 18 |  |  |  |  |  |  |
| 19 |  |  |  |  |  |  |
| 20 |  |  |  |  |  |  |
| 21 |  |  |  |  |  |  |
| 22 |  |  |  |  |  |  |
| 23 |  |  |  |  |  |  |
| 24 |  |  |  |  |  |  |
| 25 |  |  |  |  |  |  |
| 26 |  |  |  |  |  |  |
| 27 |  |  |  |  |  |  |
| 28 |  |  |  |  |  |  |
| 29 |  |  |  |  |  |  |
| 30 |  |  |  |  |  |  |
| 31 |  |  |  |  |  |  |
| 32 |  |  |  |  |  |  |
| 33 |  |  |  |  |  |  |

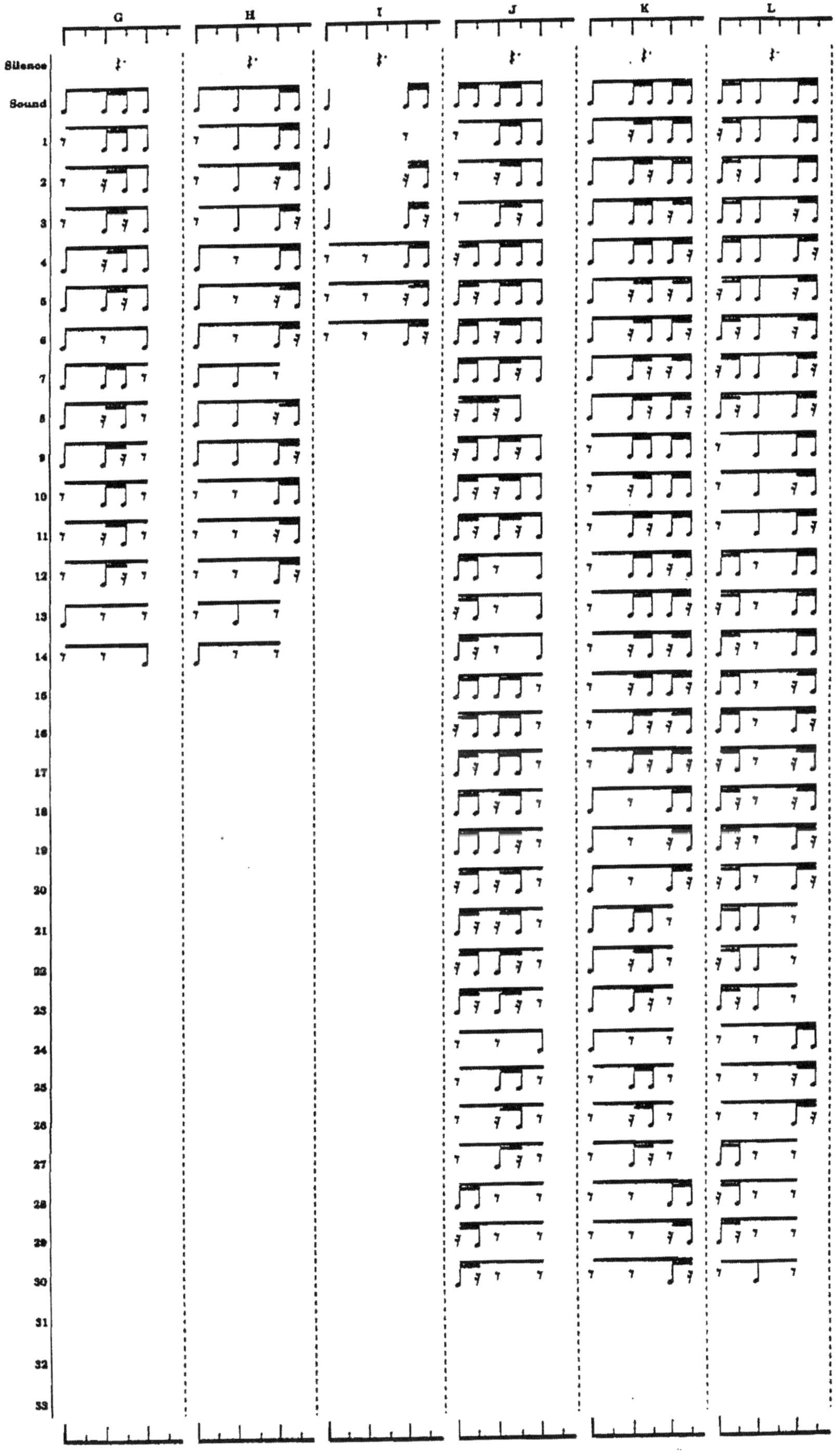

Symbols for Sound/Silence Notation

-3-

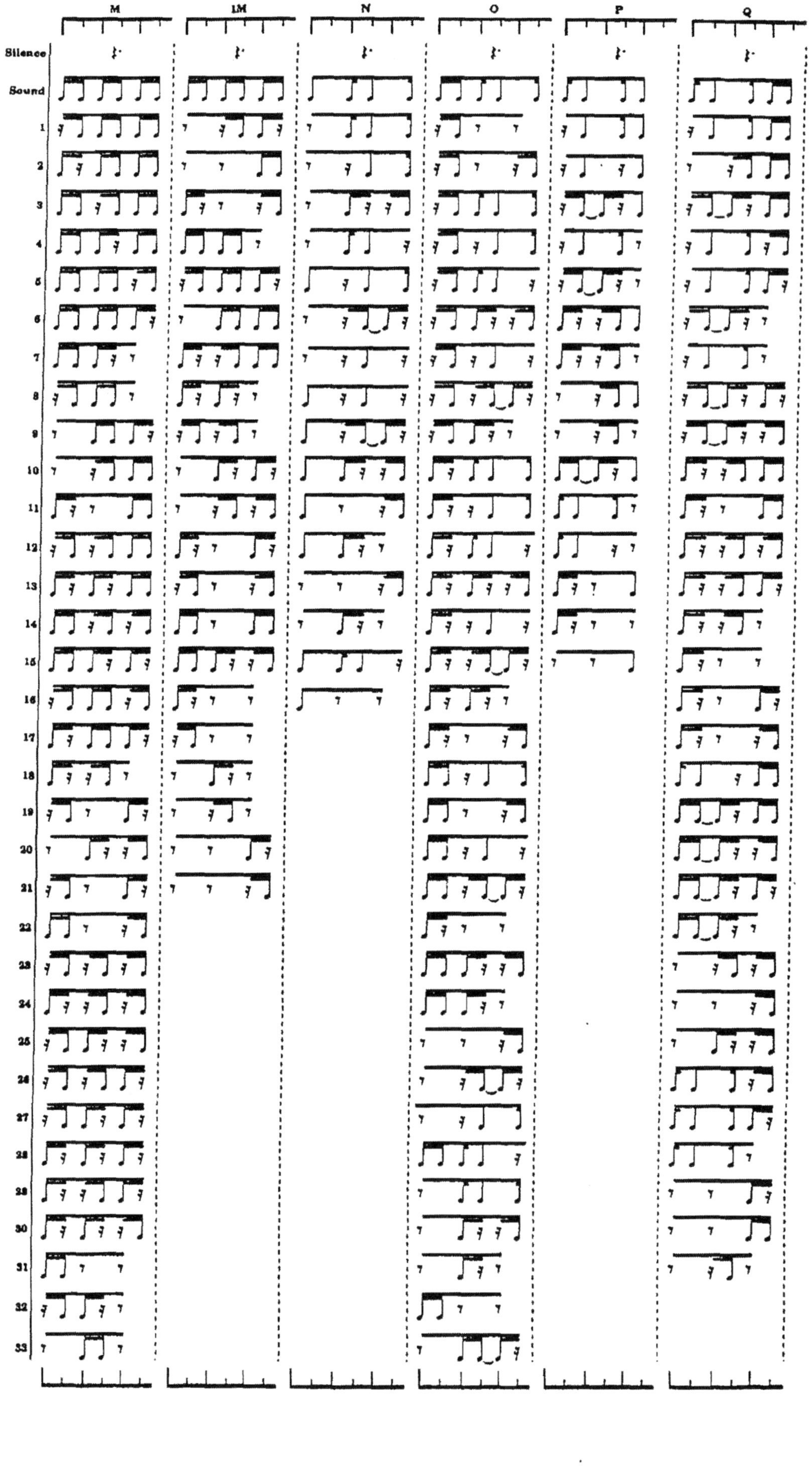

| | M | IM | N | O | P | Q |
|---|---|---|---|---|---|---|
| Silence | | | | | | |
| Sound | | | | | | |
| 1 | | | | | | |
| 2 | | | | | | |
| 3 | | | | | | |
| 4 | | | | | | |
| 5 | | | | | | |
| 6 | | | | | | |
| 7 | | | | | | |
| 8 | | | | | | |
| 9 | | | | | | |
| 10 | | | | | | |
| 11 | | | | | | |
| 12 | | | | | | |
| 13 | | | | | | |
| 14 | | | | | | |
| 15 | | | | | | |
| 16 | | | | | | |
| 17 | | | | | | |
| 18 | | | | | | |
| 19 | | | | | | |
| 20 | | | | | | |
| 21 | | | | | | |
| 22 | | | | | | |
| 23 | | | | | | |
| 24 | | | | | | |
| 25 | | | | | | |
| 26 | | | | | | |
| 27 | | | | | | |
| 28 | | | | | | |
| 29 | | | | | | |
| 30 | | | | | | |
| 31 | | | | | | |
| 32 | | | | | | |
| 33 | | | | | | |

## Symbols for Sound/Silence Notation

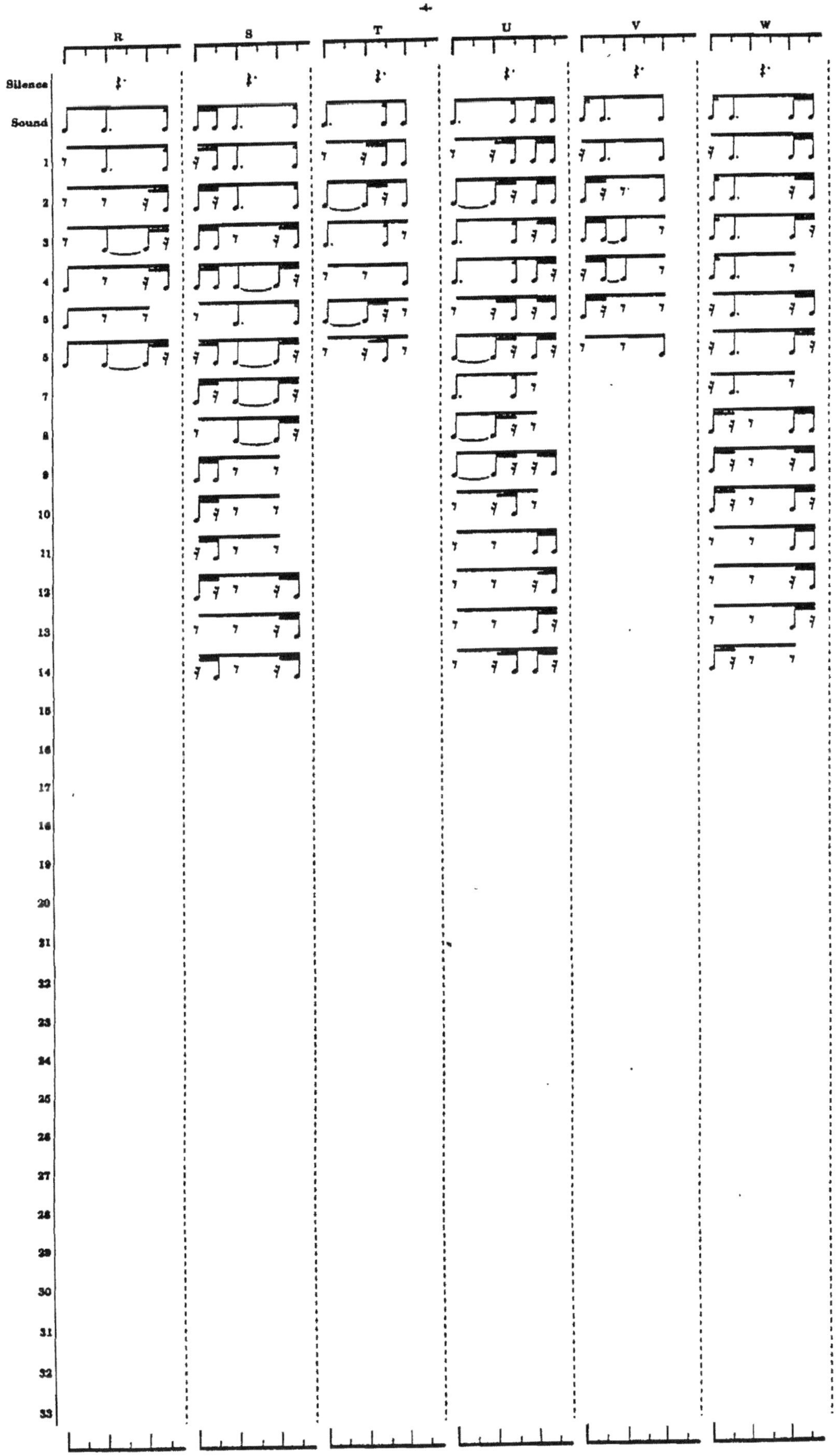

| | R | S | T | U | V | W |
|---|---|---|---|---|---|---|
| Silence | | | | | | |
| Sound | | | | | | |
| 1 | | | | | | |
| 2 | | | | | | |
| 3 | | | | | | |
| 4 | | | | | | |
| 5 | | | | | | |
| 6 | | | | | | |
| 7 | | | | | | |
| 8 | | | | | | |
| 9 | | | | | | |
| 10 | | | | | | |
| 11 | | | | | | |
| 12 | | | | | | |
| 13 | | | | | | |
| 14 | | | | | | |
| 15 | | | | | | |
| 16 | | | | | | |
| 17 | | | | | | |
| 18 | | | | | | |
| 19 | | | | | | |
| 20 | | | | | | |
| 21 | | | | | | |
| 22 | | | | | | |
| 23 | | | | | | |
| 24 | | | | | | |
| 25 | | | | | | |
| 26 | | | | | | |
| 27 | | | | | | |
| 28 | | | | | | |
| 29 | | | | | | |
| 30 | | | | | | |
| 31 | | | | | | |
| 32 | | | | | | |
| 33 | | | | | | |

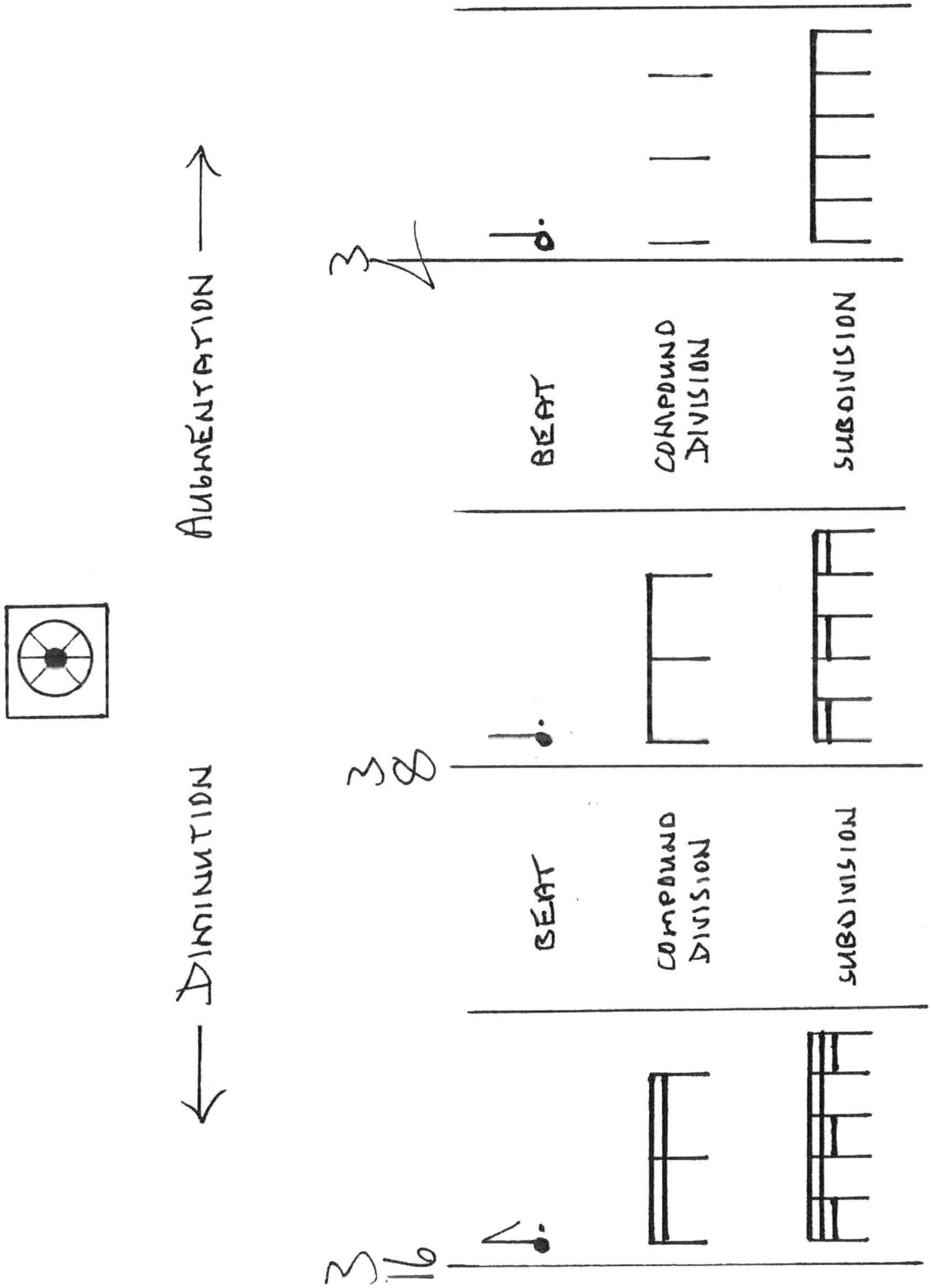

← DIMINUTION
AUGMENTATION →
3/16
3/8
3/4
BEAT
COMPOUND DIVISION
SUBDIVISION
BEAT
COMPOUND DIVISION
SUBDIVISION

DUET No. 3 RHYTHMIC RELATIONS 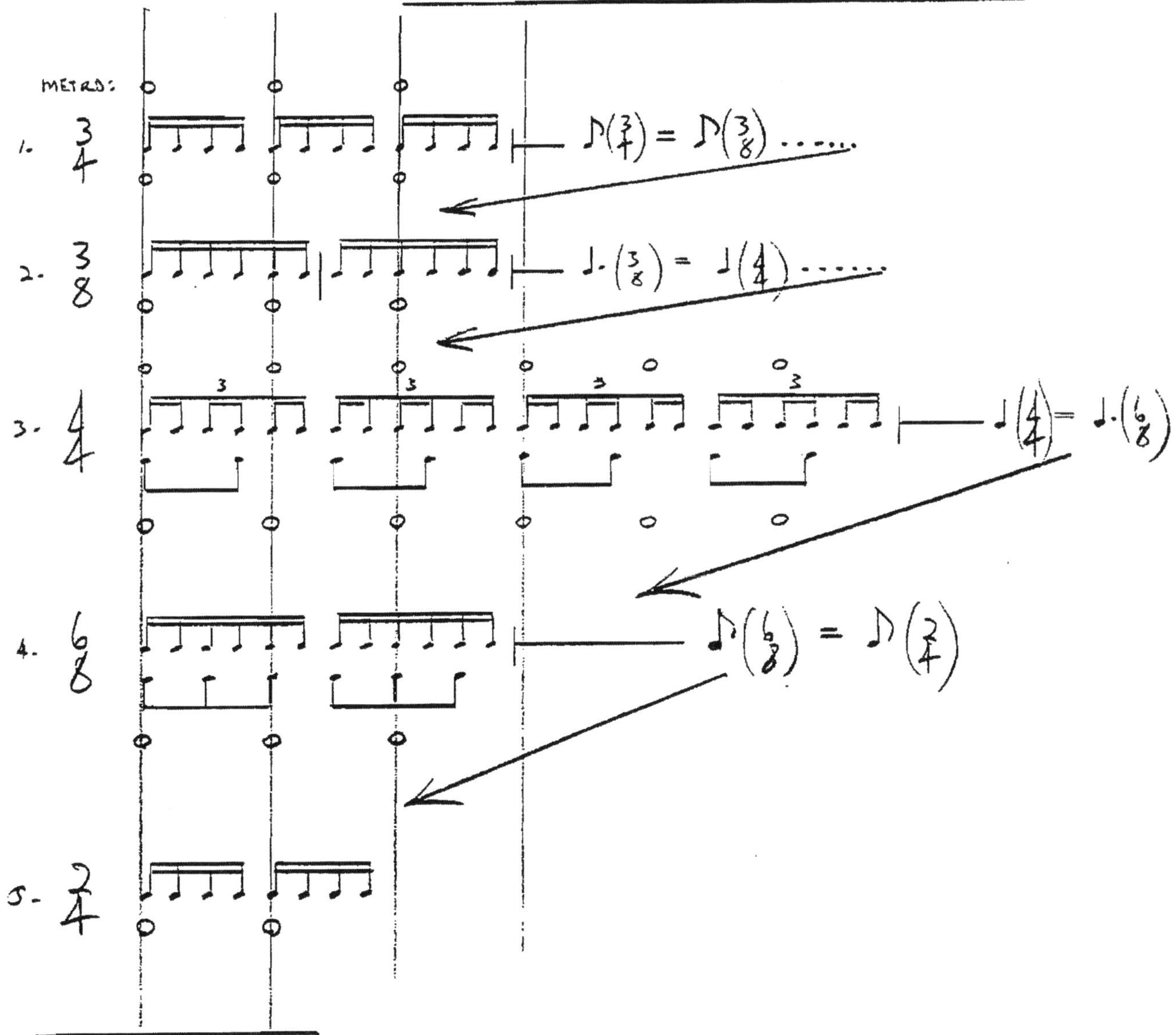
METROS:
1. 3/4
2. 3/8
3. 4/4
4. 6/8
5. 2/4
♪(3/4) = ♪(3/8) ......
♩.(3/8) = ♩(4/4) ......
♩(4/4) = ♩.(6/8)
♪(6/8) = ♪(2/4)
ACTUAL TEMPOS:
1. 3/4    ♩ = mm 80
2. 3/8    ♩. = mm 53.3
3. 4/4    ♩ = mm 53.3
4. 6/8    ♩. = mm 53.3
5. 2/4    ♩ = mm 80
1. 3/4 = 3 CLICKS PER MEASURE
2. 3/8 = 3 CLICKS EVERY 2 MEASURES
3. 4/4 = 6 CLICKS PER MEASURE
4. 6/8 = 3 CLICKS PER MEASURE
5. 2/4 = 2 CLICKS PER MEASURE

# COUNTING/PLAYING INDEPENDENCE ETUDE

60

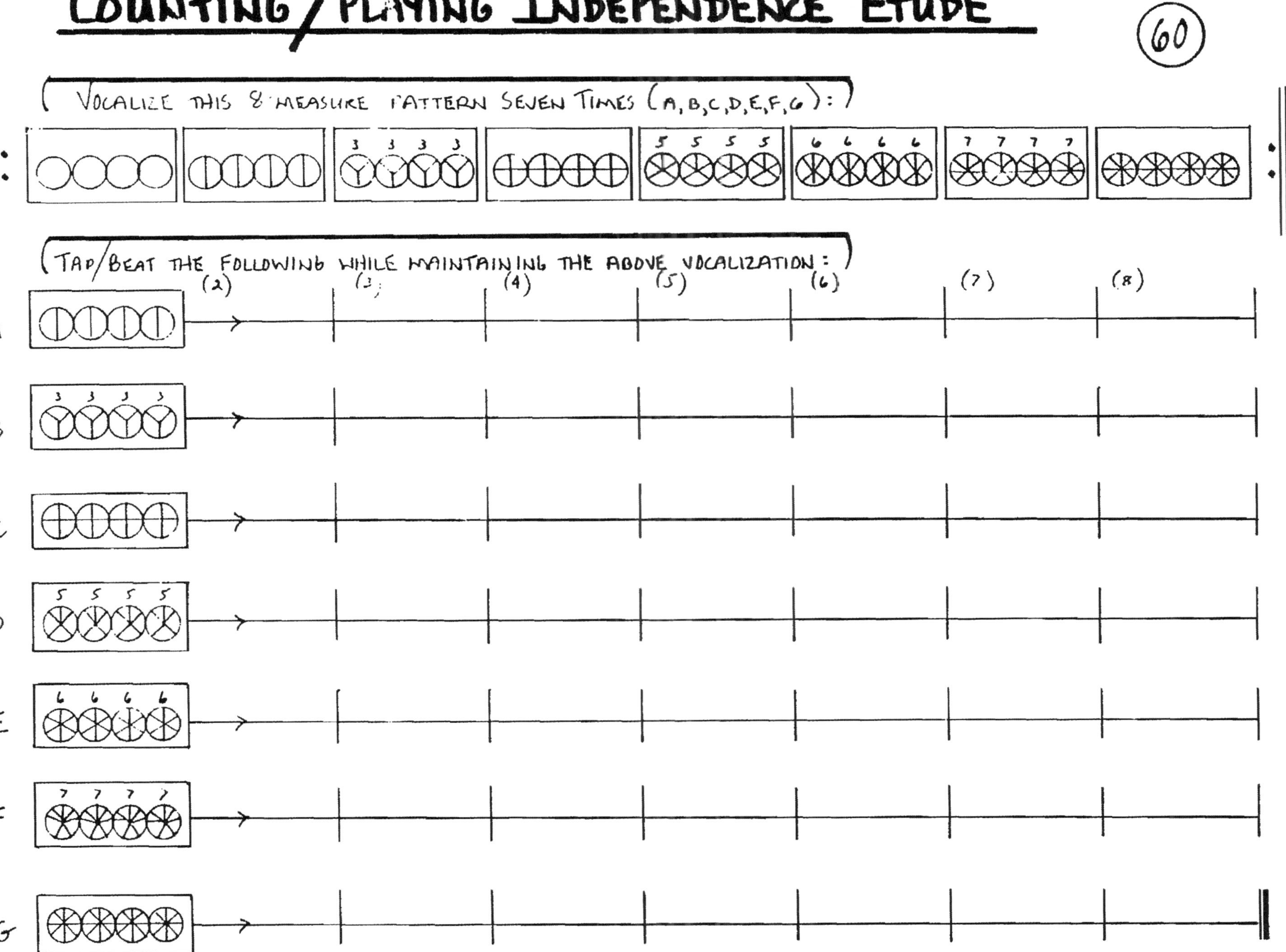

# Metronome Exercises



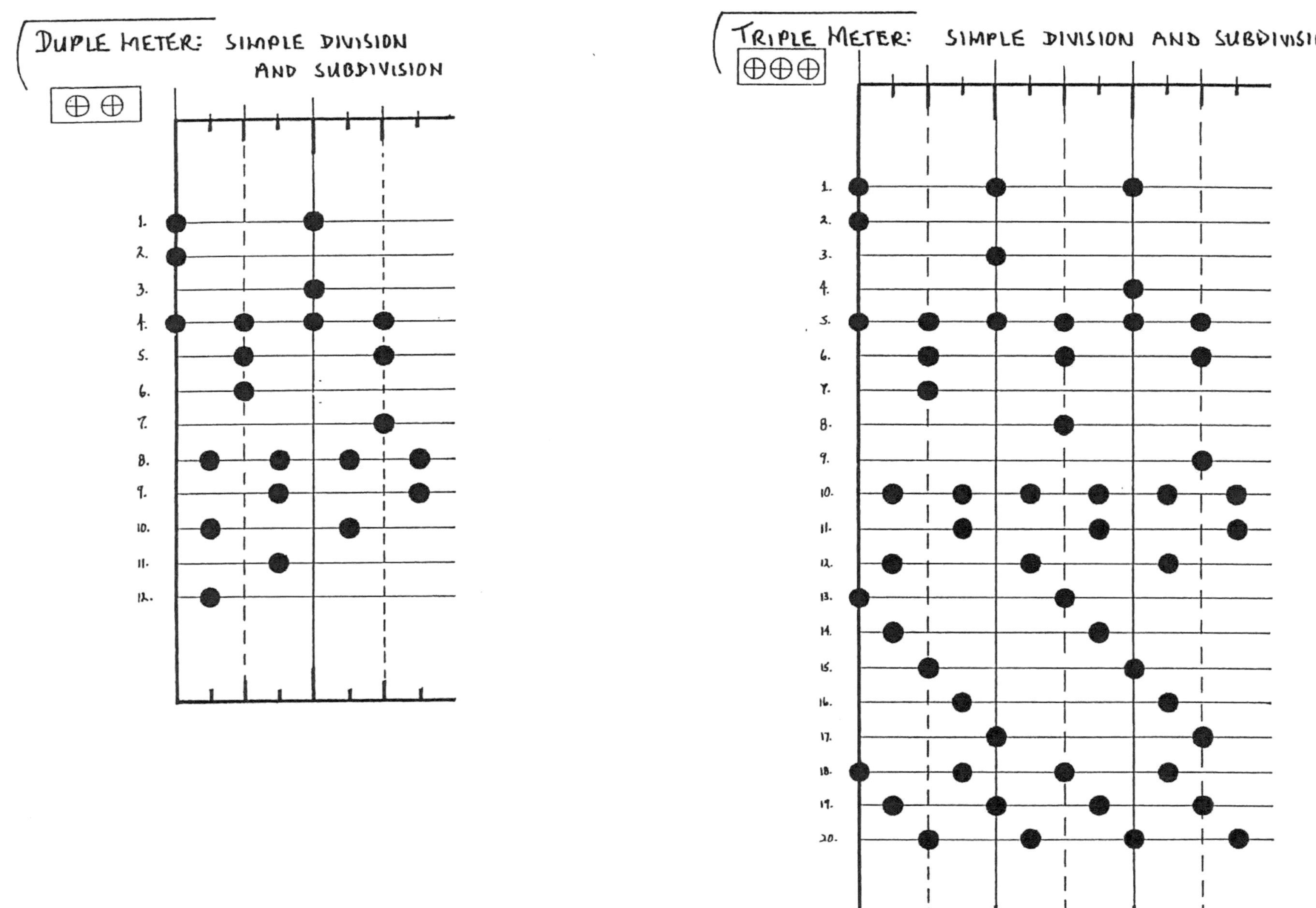

# METRONOME EXERCISES

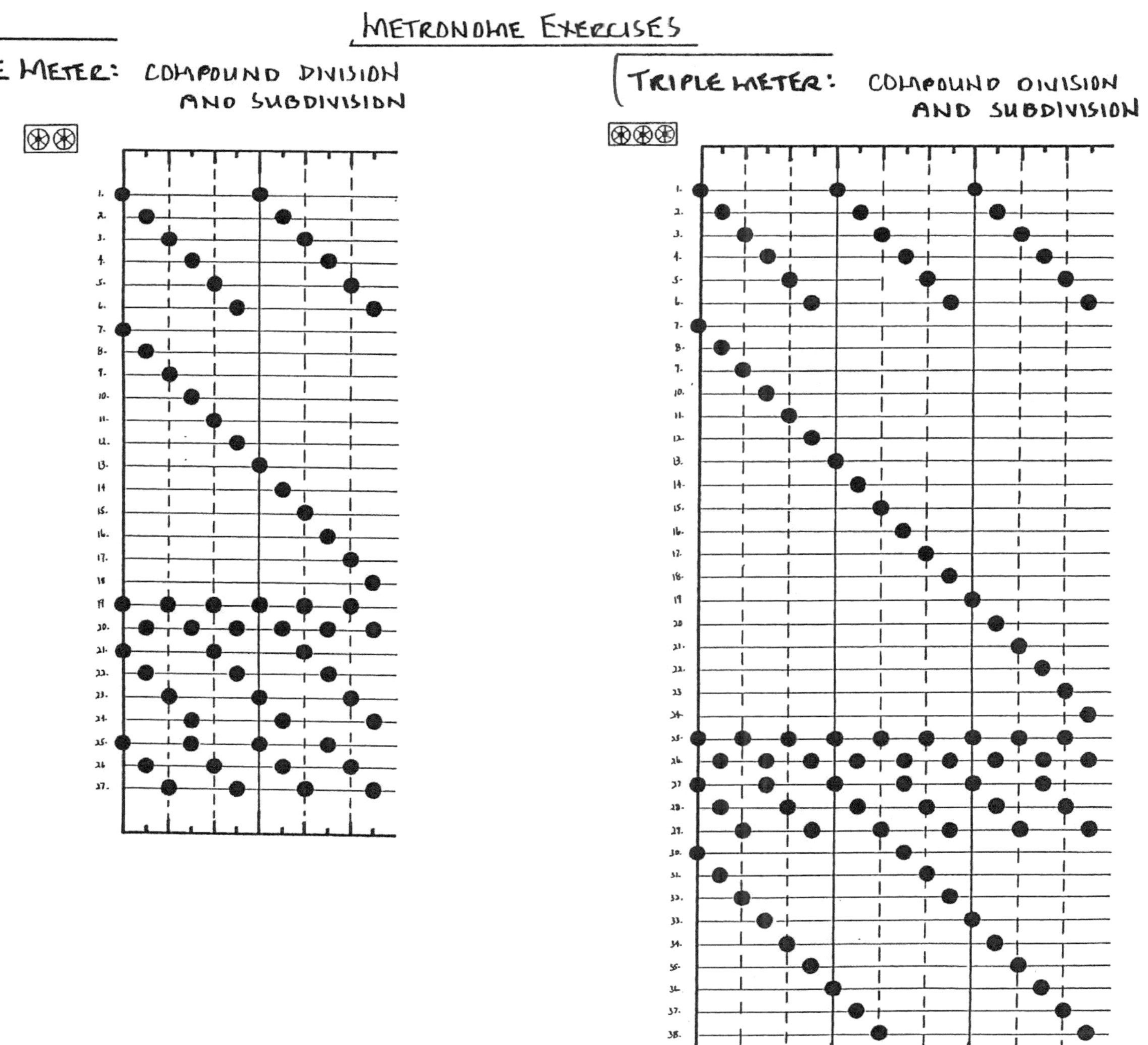

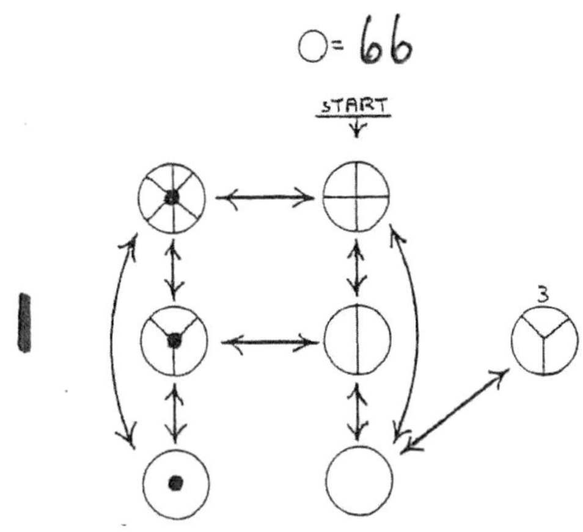
○ = 66
START
1
3

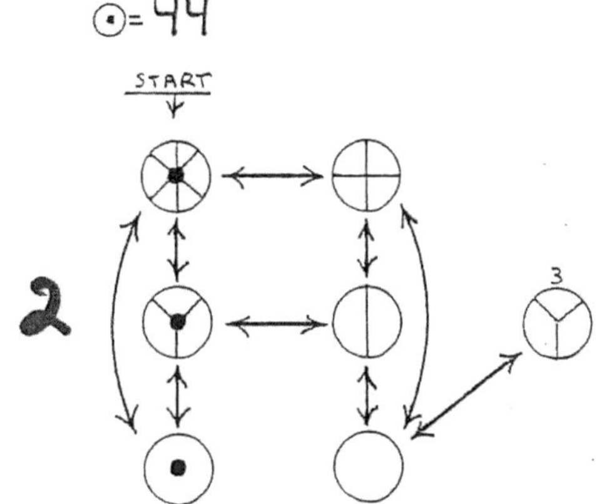
⊙ = 44
START
2
3

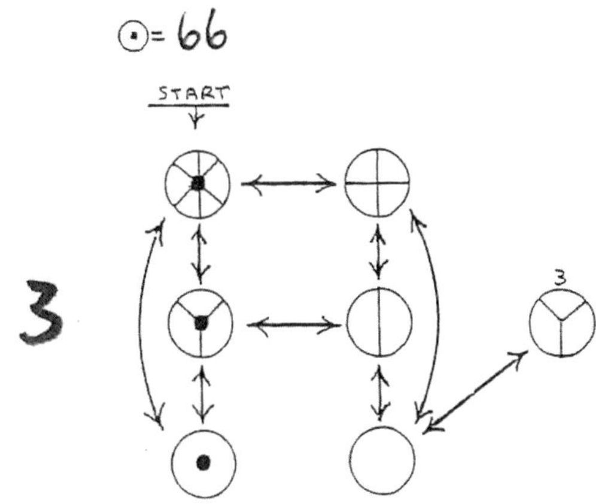
⊙ = 66
START
3
3

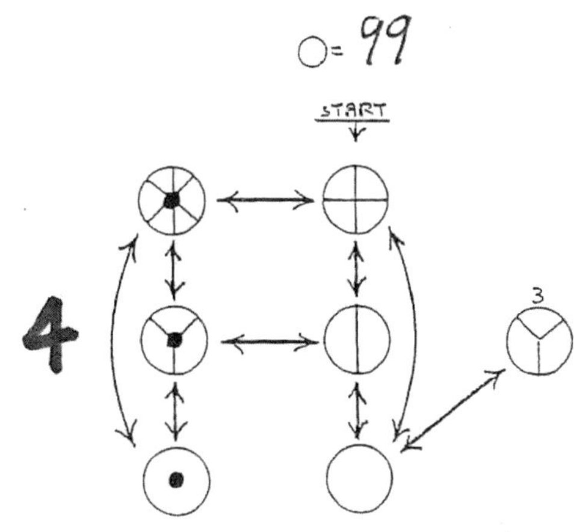
○ = 99
START
4
3

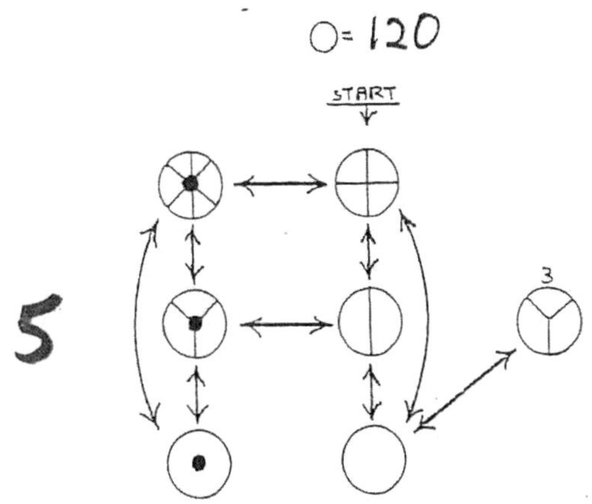
○ = 120
START
5
3

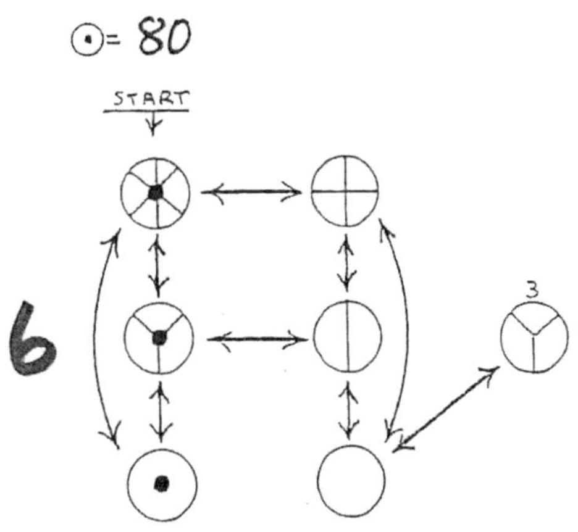
⊙ = 80
START
6
3

# DUPLE METER-BOX PATHWAYS

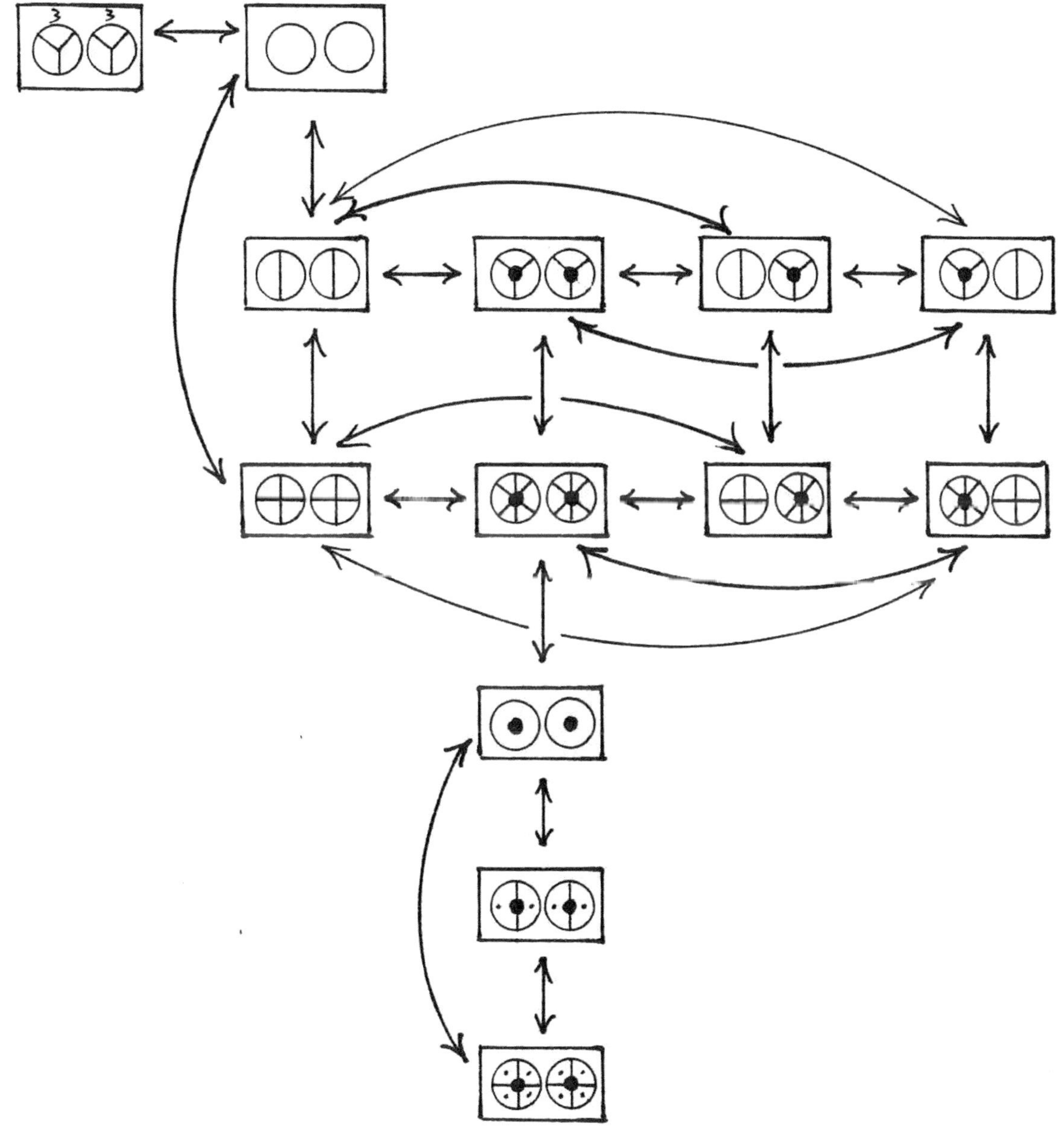